The Essentials of
NEGOTIATION

The Business Literacy for HR Professionals Series

The Business Literacy for HR Professionals Series educates human resource professionals in the principles, practices, and processes of business and management. Developed in conjunction with the Society for Human Resource Management, these books provide a comprehensive overview of the concepts, skills, and tools HR professionals need to be influential partners in developing and executing organizational strategy. Drawing on rich content from Harvard Business School Publishing and the Society for Human Resource Management, each volume is closely reviewed by a content expert as well as by senior HR professionals. Whether you are aspiring to the executive level in your organization or already in a leadership position, these authoritative books provide the basic business knowledge you need to play a strategic role.

Other books in the series:

The Essentials of Finance and Budgeting
The Essentials of Managing Change and Transition

BUSINESS LITERACY FOR HR PROFESSIONALS

The Essentials of
NEGOTIATION

Harvard Business School Press
Boston, Massachusetts
and
Society for Human Resource Management
Alexandria, Virginia

Library of Congress Cataloging-in-Publication Data

The essentials of negotiation.
p. cm. — (The business literacy for HR professionals series)
Includes bibliographical references and index.
ISBN 1-59139-574-7 (pbk. : alk. paper)
1. Negotiation in business. 2. Personnel management. I. Harvard Business School
Press. II. Society for Human Resource Management (U.S.) III. Series: Harvard
business literacy for HR professionals series.
HD58.6.E87 2005
658.3'001'4—dc22
2004019786

The paper used in this publication meets the minimum requirements
of the American National Standard for Information Sciences—Permanence
of Paper for Printed Library Materials, ANSI Z39.48—1992.

Contents

18 Making Negotiation a Core Capability   293
Building Organizational Competence

19 Sharpening Your Skills, Benefiting Your Company   307
HR Professionals as Seasoned Negotiators

Introduction

Negotiation is the means by which businesspeople create synergies and resolve differences. Whether a negotiation involves a labor contract dispute, the terms of a contract between an organization and a consultant, a complex alliance between two companies, or an informal discussion about whether a CEO will authorize funding for a new HR program, the parties involved generally seek mutually beneficial outcomes through dialogue.

Negotiation is an ever-present feature of the workplace. When HR managers strengthen their knowledge of their company's business with an eye toward strengthening their role in strategic planning, they are negotiating. So, too, are other managers and employees who are discussing possible changes to an employee's compensation, job description, or performance evaluation. And so are HR staff members who plan and lead integration programs after their company has merged with or acquired another organization. Indeed, the Latin root of the word (*negotiatus*) means "to carry on business." In modern Spanish, *negocios* means "business."

A business negotiation may be a formal affair that takes place across the proverbial bargaining table, in which you haggle over price and performance or the complex terms of a partnership venture. Alternatively, it may be much less formal, such as a meeting between you and several peer managers whose collaboration you need to initiate a new HR policy. If you are an HR executive, manager, or staff member, you probably spend a good part of your day negotiating with people inside and outside your organization—often without even realizing it. Whether you're putting the final touches on a contract with a vendor or getting a team leader or departmental manager to agree to a new performance-evaluation methodology, you are negotiating.

Given the role of negotiations in the workplace, it's important for all managers to improve their negotiating skills. Even a modest improvement in those skills can yield a sizable payoff, such as improvements to your company's bottom line or more effective working arrangements in the office. This book can help you improve your skills and become a more skillful negotiator, as well as encourage better negotiating by managers throughout your firm.

Drawing on the best available literature in the field, *The Essentials of Negotiation* explains the basic concepts followed by expert negotiators and creative problem solvers. A wealth of practical tips and examples will help you begin applying your negotiation skills immediately in the workplace.

What You'll Find in This Book

Chapter 1 sets the stage by laying out the benefits of effective negotiation. It then provides a glimpse into the world of HR negotiations—including the vital role that HR professionals can play in making negotiation a core competency in their organizations. Subsequent sections in the chapter provide an overview of the negotiation process and the characteristics of effective negotiators. The chapter concludes with two self-assessment tools: One enables you to evaluate your current negotiating skills; the other tests your current knowledge of negotiation.

Chapter 2 focuses on the subject of negotiating for others. In many negotiations, HR professionals serve as agents—that is, they represent their company (the "principal") in the bargaining process. For example, if you're negotiating the resolution of an employee dispute, selecting a vendor to provide an HR service, or participating in a negotiation with union representatives, you are seeking to arrive at the best possible outcomes for your organization. You even have legal and ethical obligations to fulfill your duties as an agent. As the chapter explains, conflicts can arise whenever someone serves as a negotiation agent. The chapter examines these conflicts and provides guidelines for avoiding or minimizing them.

Chapter 3 introduces the basic types of negotiations: distributive and integrative. In distributive negotiations, the value available to the parties is essentially fixed, and each side seeks to claim as much of the "pie" as possible. In this kind of negotiation, one party's gain comes at the expense of the others. This type is the so-called zero-sum game. In integrative negotiations, the parties apply creativity and information sharing to create greater value for eventual distribution— thus expanding the "pie." The chapter also provides information on handling negotiations that unfold over multiple phases and that involve more than two parties.

Chapter 4 focuses on the importance of relationships in the negotiating process. In a one-time transaction, one's future relationships with the other parties have little value. The goal is to claim as much value as possible. But many business deals involve multiple transactions over time among parties who seek to maintain productive relationships. These deals involve both tangible values and relationship values. This chapter shows you how to maneuver in this tricky terrain and how to separate deal values from relationship values.

Chapter 5 presents four concepts that every negotiator should understand and know how to apply: the BATNA, or best alternative to a negotiated agreement; the reservation price, the point at which you would decide to walk away from a negotiation; the ZOPA, or zone of possible agreement in which an agreement is feasible; and the notion of value created through trades. Each of these concepts is explained and supported with examples.

Chapter 6 turns your attention to the importance of preparing for a negotiation. You should never enter a negotiation cold; instead, lay the groundwork for success by learning as much as possible about your own interests and positions and those of the other side. This chapter outlines a nine-step process for preparing thoroughly for any negotiation.

Once you've learned the basics and know what's needed for preparation, you're ready for chapter 7, which emphasizes negotiation strategies. This chapter shows you how to get an unwilling party to negotiate with you, how to get negotiations off to a good start, and how to succeed no matter which type of negotiation you're involved in. Here you'll learn about techniques such as anchoring and framing, as well as altering the negotiation process in your favor. Chapter 8 continues the discussion with answers to frequently asked questions about negotiating tactics.

Chapter 9 shines the spotlight on manipulative negotiation ploys—and how to recognize and respond to them. As you'll discover in this chapter, the best way to respond to manipulation (such as attempts to intimidate you, lying, and other tactics) is not to respond in kind but to actively reshape the negotiation *process*.

Not every negotiation goes smoothly—even those that involve friendly, nonmanipulative parties. One or more barriers—such as structural impediments, lack of trust, and poor communication—can get in the way of a successful deal. Chapter 10 identifies these barriers and suggests how you can avoid them. Chapter 11 then discusses mental errors that negotiators sometimes bring to the process. These include overconfidence, irrational expectations, and the tendency to escalate offers in an ego-driven zeal to "win." Again, the chapter explains how to avoid making these errors.

In chapters 12–17, you'll jump into the rich, complex world of HR negotiations. Each of these chapters explores the unique trends, challenges, and techniques for success in a particular type of negotiation situation HR professionals commonly face. These situations comprise: negotiations with job seekers and employees; negotiations with your boss, peer managers, and senior executives; negotiations with vendors and consultants; negotiations with labor unions; negotiations involving legal disputes; and negotiations related to mergers and acquisitions.

Clearly, individuals need to develop their negotiating skills. But what about organizations? Chapter 18 advances the idea of developing negotiating skill as a companywide competence. Imagine what your firm could achieve if its salespeople, supervisors, managers, and executives became progressively better negotiators. This chapter brings together two powerful concepts, continuous improvement and core competencies, to demonstrate how HR professionals can use training, education, and the lessons learned from past negotiations to develop their company's negotiating prowess.

Finally, chapter 19 describes ways in which you can put into action the knowledge you've gained from reading this book. You'll find a summary of key principles and techniques, as well as recommendations for maintaining and enhancing your negotiation skills. The chapter ends with a recap of the benefits that your company, your HR department, and you can gain from knowing how to negotiate effectively.

The Essentials of Negotiation contains several supplements. The first is a glossary of terms. Every discipline has its special vocabulary, and negotiating is no exception. When you see a word italicized in the text, that's your cue that the word is defined in the glossary. Another supplement, "For Further Reading," identifies books and articles that can tell you more about the topics covered in this book. Many of these resources are available from Harvard Business School Publishing and from the Society for Human Resource Management's (SHRM) Web site. Listed resources include books published by Harvard Business School Press; articles from *Harvard Business Review*; online training materials developed by Harvard Business School Publishing; articles from *HR Magazine*, white papers and legal reports published by SHRM; and books published or copublished by SHRM. Readings from other sources are included as well. Each of these recommended resources will shed additional light on the topics covered in this book.

The Essentials of
NEGOTIATION

CHAPTER ONE

Negotiation and the HR Professional

A Crucial Activity

Key Topics Covered in This Chapter

- *The benefits of effective negotiation*

- *Negotiation as a critical HR activity*

- *An overview of common HR negotiations*

- *An overview of the negotiating process*

- *Characteristics of effective HR negotiators*

EVERY DAY, managers and employees in your organization engage in countless negotiations. An HR director persuades her CEO to support a new performance-management initiative she has developed. Purchasing agents negotiate contracts with suppliers. Marketing managers work out arrangements with domestic and foreign distributors. Salespeople decide on the contents of product and service bundles with customers. Product developers negotiate joint ventures with partnering companies. An IT manager negotiates the delivery and installation schedule for a new information system with peer managers who will be using the system. Shop-floor workers and their supervisors arrive at agreements about the volume and quality of work expected. An R&D director and her counterpart in sales resolve a conflict over whether sales can implement an idea generated by the research department. A CFO negotiates the terms of an acquisition with his counterpart in the target company. It's hard to think of any business initiative or daily workplace activity that doesn't require at least some form of negotiation at some time.[1]

Taken separately, any single negotiation—large or small, internal or external—won't likely make or break your company. But *in combination*, the thousands of negotiations that occur in the typical firm can exert an enormous impact on the bottom line. For this reason, the best companies make negotiation a core organizational competence—a process in which HR professionals are well positioned to play a crucial role. Equally important, HR directors and managers who master the art and science of negotiation themselves can provide critical value for their organizations.

The Benefits of Effective Negotiation

HR professionals who are skilled negotiators and who help strengthen negotiation skills throughout their firm generate numerous benefits for their companies:

- **Conflict resolution.** Some experts maintain that unmanaged employee conflict stands as the largest reducible cost in organizations today—and is the least recognized.[2] When managers and employees know how to negotiate workplace conflicts, general morale and productivity improve. People deal with problems early on, before they can escalate to unmanageable proportions. The organization thus gains a precious commodity—time—to do higher-potential things such as attract new business, create innovative products, and anticipate and satisfy customers' needs. Moreover, retention improves, as employees find the workplace a more positive place to be.

- **Cost reduction.** When companies develop competence in negotiation, they can reduce the costs associated with flawed contracts and the use of legal counsel to resolve conflicts that have escalated needlessly.

- **Better relationships.** When people negotiate effectively, they each exchange something of value to achieve mutually agreeable purposes. Successful negotiation thus strengthens relationships and builds a sense of trust that each party has the other's interests (as well as its own) at heart. Mutual benefits and trust in turn create a feeling of quality and satisfaction in the workplace.

- **Competitive advantage.** As people in an organization forge mutually beneficial agreements with others *inside* the company, they free up energy to identify and leverage new opportunities to improve processes and systems. As they negotiate successfully with others *outside* the company, they create valuable synergies. All of these advantages enable organizations to sharpen their competitive edge and boost their profitability.

A Critical HR Activity

As enticing as the benefits of effective negotiation may appear, systematically developing negotiating skills throughout an organization takes work. Companies stand a far better chance of building—and sustaining—this capability when HR professionals play a central role in the process. As an HR director, manager, or staff member, you can fulfill this role by viewing yourself as a "negotiation maven." Your goal? To improve the results of your company's many negotiations in ways that translate into better relationships and enhanced bottom-line performance throughout the organization.

As negotiation maven, you need to play not one but three roles:[3]

- **Advocate.** You maintain that negotiation is the preferred method of reaching agreement, changing behavior, and resolving conflict. You make the case that if employees can better manage their own interests and handle their own conflicts through skilled negotiation, they'll have more time to focus on more important business activities. By being an advocate, you persuade managers and employees throughout your firm to assume responsibility for their own problems. When they assume responsibility, they no longer need the involvement of third-party mediators or arbiters—and they avoid the costly escalation of disagreements. They also become problem solvers—generating opportunities for entrepreneurial (rather than bureaucratic) work to get done.

- **Builder.** You help identify and construct the skills needed to make negotiation a core competency in your organization. For example, effective negotiators have a vision of what they want to accomplish, are confident without being obnoxious or self-absorbed, and possess infinite patience and pragmatism. They view negotiation as a chance to test limits and are willing to move on when things aren't working out as they desired. They're also talented listeners, communicators, and persuaders—knowing how to explore possibilities with an open mind and persist in the face of adversity. They can tolerate criticism and disagreement, collaborate on teams, and take appropriate risks.

- **Practitioner.** You lead by example, honing your own negotiation skills as you hire employees, design executive-compensation packages, deal with transfers and dismissals, develop new personnel systems and practices, and negotiate labor-management contracts.

The World of HR Negotiations

As an HR professional, you'll likely find yourself in a wide array of negotiation situations, both informal and formal. Examples of *informal* negotiation situations might include:

- Arriving at agreements on starting salaries and benefits packages with job applicants

- Making a counteroffer to a valued employee who has received a job offer from another company

- Arriving at confidentiality agreements or noncompete contracts with new employees

- Persuading your boss to support a new HR initiative you've designed or to approve a professional-development opportunity you'd like to take advantage of

- Working out the details of HR policies with other managers in your company

   Examples of more *formal* negotiations might include:

- Negotiating contracts with consultants or vendors, such as compensation specialists or insurance providers

- Determining with your executive team how compensation and benefits programs will be integrated during a corporate merger or acquisition

- Participating in the collective bargaining process with union leaders and members

- Negotiating with employees and federal or state enforcement agencies (e.g., the Equal Employment Opportunity Commission) over discrimination or other claims or lawsuits brought by current or former employees

With most formal negotiations, the parties involved generally progress through a predictable series of steps:[4]

1. **Preparation.** You determine the following aspects of the negotiation:

   - *Who* are the individuals on both ends of the negotiation who will be critical to reaching an agreement?
   - *What* is the subject matter of the negotiation? (For example, what is the issue at hand, and what are the two parties' positions on the issue?)
   - *What* is your best alternative to a negotiated agreement (BATNA) and the least favorable point at which you will accept an agreement (your "walk-away" condition or reservation price)?
   - *What* do you estimate the other party's BATNA and walk-away to be?
   - *What* might the zone of possible agreement (ZOPA) be— the range in which a deal that satisfies both parties can take place? The ZOPA is the range between the two parties' walk-away condition.
   - *When* must the negotiations begin and end?
   - *Why* are the desired results of this negotiation important?

   See chapter 5 for more detailed information about BATNAs, reservation price or conditions, and ZOPAs. See chapter 6 for more detailed information about other aspects of the preparation phase.

2. **The initial meeting.** During this first gathering:

   - State your position on the issue at hand and explain your reasons for believing that your position is just. Your counterpart should do the same.

- Through dialogue, verify the information you developed during the preparation phase.
- Establish a civil working environment by checking your ego at the door. Understand that the best outcome of the transaction may not make everyone happy but will be fair to all participants.
- Determine where and when future meetings, if necessary, will happen. Often, a site that's neutral to both parties may give the proceedings a more level playing field.
- Identify items the other party seems to view as important and items you feel are less important to your position. This enables you to concede nonissues—which builds goodwill by communicating flexibility and fairness. The more goodwill you cultivate, the more likely you'll see comparable flexibility and fairness coming from the other party.

3. **Recess.** After the initial meeting, recess and evaluate the information you gleaned from the meeting. Assess your position relative to the other party's. Consider any give and take explored during the initial meeting, and decide its implications for the ZOPA between the parties.

4. **Follow-up meetings.** Decide whether to settle on the agreement that you and the other party are currently exploring— or to try for a higher position in the ZOPA. During follow-up meetings, the style of the negotiation will come into sharper focus, influenced by the relationship forged by the two parties and whether the parties have a history together or plan to continue the relationship beyond the current negotiation. If you expect the relationship with the other party to continue, cultivate a more collaborative approach. If the current negotiation is a one-time transaction, many negotiators adopt a firmer style by pushing the initiative and making few or no concessions.

Clearly, formal negotiations follow a highly structured process. But many negotiations have a far less formal framework. The majority of informal negotiations actually involve less preparation and fewer meetings than formal negotiations require. In fact, the parties involved may not even be aware that they're engaging in a negotiation!

In addition to the kinds of informal and formal negotiation situations described above, you may also find opportunities to play an important supporting role in other kinds of business negotiations. For example, you might assist in a valuation of your firm's worth for the purpose of making an initial public offering (IPO) of stock. In such cases, you can provide valuable information about human capital issues related to these transactions.

What Makes an Effective HR Negotiator?

Negotiation as a corporate competence is the sum of the competence of the company's individual members—including you. The best HR negotiators demonstrate specific behaviors, whether they're negotiating with employees, peers, supervisors, suppliers, or union leaders:

- **They align negotiating goals with organizational goals.**
  Effective negotiators operate within a framework that supports their organization's strategic goals. This is possible only when those goals are clear. As an HR professional, you have a responsibility to communicate goals to everyone in the company—including those who negotiate on the firm's behalf. That communication is the best assurance of alignment between goals and employee behaviors—and negotiated outcomes that serve your company.

- **They prepare thoroughly and use each negotiating stage to prepare further.** Effective negotiators come to meetings prepared with facts and proposals. They don't wing it, and they don't rush to reach a resolution to a negotiation. Before and during the bargaining, they spend time exploring each party's interests, identifying options, and learning about the other party's needs. They also understand that most negotiation is an ongoing process of maintaining relationships and developing win-win outcomes, not a one-time event that results in a winner and loser.

- **They use negotiating sessions to learn more about the issues at stake and the other party's BATNA and "walk-away" position.** Negotiators, like card players, must often operate in a fog of uncertainty. Advantage generally accrues to those who, through preparation and dialogue, gather the information that helps them penetrate that fog. You can relatively easily determine your own best alternative to a negotiated agreement and your walk-away point. And through effective dialogue and outside detective work, you can discern the same things about the other party.

- **They have the mental dexterity to identify both sides' interests and the creativity to think of value-creating options that produce win-win situations.** A really good negotiator confronted with what others perceive as a zero-sum game can change that game. He or she can help the other party see the value of sharing information and expanding the universe of value opportunities.

- **They can separate personal issues from negotiating issues.** Accomplished negotiators know that the negotiating process is not about them—or even about the individuals sitting across from them. They understand that the process is about producing the best possible outcome for all parties.

- **They recognize potential barriers to agreement.** Barriers aren't always obvious. A skillful negotiator ferrets them out and finds ways to neutralize them.

- **They know how to form coalitions.** Not every negotiator is dealt a winning hand. The other party often has greater power as the bargaining begins. However, good negotiators know that a coalition of several weak players can often counter that power. More important, they understand how to build such a coalition on a foundation of shared interests.

- **They develop a reputation for reliability and trustworthiness.** The most successful negotiations are built on trust. Trust formed through one phase of negotiation pays dividends in the next.

Good negotiators practice ethical behavior. They are as good as their word. And they always listen more than they talk. They know they can gather more information and create better outcomes by asking questions than by pushing their own agendas. Finally, they view negotiation as a positive aspect of their relationships with others, rather than as an adversarial interaction.

By following the strategies, techniques, and tips included in this book, you can hone these attributes in yourself and others. The payoff? You'll become a more effective negotiator not only in your role as an HR professional but in your personal life as well. Assessment tool 1-1 can help you gauge your current abilities as a negotiator and identify areas that need strengthening.

Equally vital, as you become more aware of the role negotiators can play in providing value for organizations, you'll help your company turn negotiation into a core corporate capability. Assessment tool 1-2 helps you take stock of your overall knowledge of negotiation and identify chapters in the book that you might decide to read most closely.

Assessment Tool 1-1
How Do You Rate as a Negotiator?

For each statement below, circle the number that best indicates how accurately that statement describes you. "1" indicates "not at all true"; "4" indicates "very true." Be honest with yourself; that way, you can better identify the areas where you need to strengthen your skills.

1. I see my negotiation activities overall as an ongoing process, not a one-time event.

   1   2   3   4

2. I view negotiation as an opportunity to establish positive relationships with others, not as an adversarial process.

   1   2   3   4

3. I always define my own BATNA and reservation price or condition—as well as estimate my counterpart's—before a negotiation. I then estimate the ZOPA for the negotiation.

    1   2   3   4

4. I focus more on interests than on positions while negotiating.

    1   2   3   4

5. I "check my ego at the door" before commencing a negotiation.

    1   2   3   4

6. I learn as much as I can about the other party before a negotiation begins.

    1   2   3   4

7. I adapt my negotiating style depending on whether I expect my relationship with the other party to continue in the future.

    1   2   3   4

8. I view negotiations as opportunities to achieve mutually beneficial outcomes, rather than as zero-sum games that must end with someone winning and someone losing.

    1   2   3   4

9. I try to communicate flexibility, trustworthiness, and fairness to the other party by conceding nonissues during a negotiation.

    1   2   3   4

10. I take steps to prevent tensions from escalating, avoid irrational expectations and overconfidence, and keep my emotions in check during negotiations.

    1   2   3   4

11. During a negotiation, I know how to identify and over-come barriers to agreement such as communication difficulties, gender and culture differences, and lack of trust.

    1   2   3   4

12. I know how to identify and counter manipulative negotiation ploys (i.e., "win-lose" tactics) used by the other party during a negotiation.

    1   2   3   4

13. I understand the different paths to agreement during a negotiation (i.e., distributive and integrative).

    1   2   3   4

14. I understand the legal duties and ethical responsibilities associated with negotiating for others.

    1   2   3   4

15. I know how to shape the negotiation process in my or my company's favor.

    1   2   3   4

16. I know how to interpret the other party's body language and other nonverbal cues during a negotiation.

    1   2   3   4

17. I understand the importance of helping to build negotiation as a core competence in my organization.

    1   2   3   4

18. I constantly look for opportunities to sharpen my negotiating skills.

    1   2   3   4

19. I know how to handle the common formal and informal negotiation situations that HR professionals engage in.

    1   2   3   4

20. In a negotiation involving multiple parties, if I sense that the other team has greater power, I know how to build a coalition of players for my side on a foundation of shared interests.

    1   2   3   4

Calculate Your Score

Add up all the numbers you circled. The higher your total, the more skilled a negotiator you are.

Score 20–40: Your negotiating skills need work overall if you are to sharpen your skills and help your organization build negotiation as a core competence.

Score 41–60: You have some abilities in the area of negotiation, but certain aspects would benefit from improvement.

Score 61–80: Your negotiation skills are strong overall. You're well positioned to negotiate effectively and help your company build negotiation as a core competence.

Assessment Tool 1-2
Gauge Your Overall Understanding of Negotiation

Answer the multiple-choice questions that follow. After you have answered the questions, check the accuracy of your answers, and see which chapters you need to focus on to strengthen your knowledge.

1. **What is a negotiation agent?**
   A. Someone who negotiates for another person or company.
   B. A person who searches for members to add to a negotiation team.

    C. A company that is represented by a specific individual during a negotiation.

    D. An issue or concern that triggers a negotiation.

2. **What is an integrative negotiation?**

    A. A negotiation in which the parties share their walk-away price with one another and thereby determine the zone of possible agreement.

    B. A negotiation in which the parties compete over the distribution of a fixed pool of value (often called win-lose).

    C. A negotiation in which the parties assemble teams that are as diverse as possible to participate in the bargaining.

    D. A negotiation in which the parties cooperate to achieve maximum mutual benefit in an agreement, creating new value in the process (often called win-win).

3. **Which of the following is *not* a reason that high-quality relationships are becoming more important in work-place negotiations?**

    A. With flatter organizations, more people are negotiating with others over whom they have no formal authority.

    B. Many companies are seeking long-term partnerships with vendors and other entities, rather than trying to "squeeze" them for the lowest-priced deals.

    C. Good working relationships based on respect, admiration, perceived need, obligation, and friendship provide a critical source of power in getting things done.

    D. New federal guidelines now require organizations to share information fully during a negotiation session.

4. **What is a reservation price in a negotiation?**

    A. A party's best option to forging an agreement during the negotiation.

    B. A negotiating technique by which one party withholds certain information requested by the other party.

    C. The least favorable point at which a party would accept a negotiated deal; the "walk-away" condition.

    D. A negotiating strategy by which one party presents the issues at the top of his or her priority list.

5. **What constitutes the first step to preparing for a negotiation?**

    A. Strengthening your BATNA, your best alternative to a negotiated agreement.

    B. Defining a good outcome for yourself and the other party.

    C. Gathering fairness standards and criteria.

    D. Addressing authority issues.

6. **Which of the following is *not* a good strategy for persuading a resistant person to negotiate with you?**

    A. Ask whether the person is committed to the best interests of your company or relationship.

    B. Offer incentives that speak to the other person's needs.

    C. Spell out the cost of not negotiating.

    D. Enlist support from others who have a reason to favor your goal.

7. **Which one of the following statements is true?**

    A. You should state a range of what you're willing to pay for a service or product if the other negotiator requests the information.

    B. When the other person in a negotiation shouts or acts threateningly, you should respond in kind, to avoid giving the impression that you can be intimidated.

    C. Negotiators who ask to change an agreed-upon term of a final negotiation probably have "winner's curse"—the relentless thought that they could have gotten more.

    D. It is illegal to bluff during a negotiation; that is, to emphasize the value you bring to the agreement over any risks you bring.

8. Which of the following is *not* a step you would use to handle a negotiation in which the other party uses a manipulative ploy?
   A. Raise the issue explicitly during the negotiation.
   B. Change the negotiation process.
   C. Know when the other side is using a tricky tactic.
   D. Present a direct, firm offer to refocus the other person's attention on the process.

9. You're negotiating with a die-hard bargainer—someone whom you sense is ready to battle for every scrap of value. What's your strongest strategy for bargaining with this person?
   A. Resist any urge to walk away; it's best to work slowly toward a mutually satisfying agreement.
   B. Describe one option to solving the problem, to gauge the other person's response.
   C. Anticipate low-ball offers, grudging concessions, and bluffing.
   D. Share information freely, to demonstrate that you're interested in building trust.

10. Which of the following defines the mental error known as partisan perceptions?
   A. Continuing a previously selected course of action beyond what rational analysis would recommend.
   B. Perceiving the world with a bias in one's own favor or toward one's own point of view.
   C. Setting expectations that cannot be fulfilled.
   D. Striving for unanimity so hard that one fails to realistically appraise alternative courses of action.

11. An employee has just announced that he is leaving for another company. How do you handle the situation?
   A. Begin preparing a counteroffer strategy promptly, before the employee becomes more committed to the idea of changing jobs.

B. Emphasize your company's needs, as well as those of the employee's manager, in your response to the person's announcement.

C. Carefully think through whether the person is part of your firm's "core competencies."

D. Ask the person to specify what is lacking in your company that has made him want to leave.

12. **You've introduced a new HR policy in your firm and want to lay the groundwork for negotiating with other managers over how the policy will be implemented. Which of the following is *not* a good strategy?**

A. Show how the policy you're advocating is sound.

B. Keep discussing the details of the policy with other managers.

C. Set a clear date for formal enforcement of the policy to begin.

D. Involve other managers early in the policy-development process.

13. **You're negotiating a contract with an HR services vendor. Which of the following bargaining techniques would you *avoid* using?**

A. Discuss price openly and honestly as soon as you begin speaking with candidates.

B. Include in the contract terms specifying how disputes will be resolved.

C. Don't take a candidate's references at face value; track down additional references of your own.

D. Ask for written proposals after you've narrowed your choices down to two or three candidates.

14. **Which of the following is *not* an important organized-labor trend that HR professionals should know about while participating in negotiations with labor unions?**

A. New, independent, and more specialized unions are cropping up.

B. Long-standing, international unions in large industries have begun attracting more members in the last two decades.

C. Union representation is decreasing in the private sector while growing in the public sector.

D. Unionized workers are putting more emphasis on the need for better benefits, particularly health care, and less emphasis on pay and work schedules.

15. Which of the following is *not* an important trend in workplace legal disputes that HR professionals should know about?

A. Companies are facing fewer restrictions on what may be defined as retaliatory actions against employees.

B. Sexual harassment and discrimination complaints are mounting, as are damages awarded to successful plaintiffs.

C. Some plaintiffs' attorneys are formulating more creative strategies for winning lawsuits, including fabricating claims.

D. There has been an increase in retaliation claims by current and former employees.

16. Your company is going to be merging with another organization. Which of the following would you consider the *least* important question for your HR department to answer before the merger takes place?

A. Which company's HR personnel will provide the most guidance in the newly formed entity once the merger takes place?

B. How will the newly formed company integrate rewards programs?

C. How should HR be restructured to best serve the new entity's needs?

D. Will the newly formed organization combine HR information systems, use one or the other company's existing system, or adopt an entirely new system?

17. **Which of the following is an effective way for HR professionals to help make negotiation a core competency in their organization?**
    A. Provide training and preparation resources for anyone in the company who engages in negotiations.
    B. Develop mechanisms enabling managers to capture and reuse any lessons from previous negotiations.
    C. Develop negotiating performance measures and link them to rewards.
    D. All of the above.

18. **Which of the following statements is false?**
    A. Knowing your company's competitive strategy is the best way to boost your chances of successfully negotiating new HR policies with peer managers.
    B. Networking and relationship building are vital techniques for improving your negotiation skills.
    C. Negotiation is best viewed as a process, rather than a series of one-time, disparate events.
    D. When HR professionals strengthen their negotiating skills, they enhance the HR function's reputation within and outside their company.

Answer Key
See the following chapters to learn more

1. A: Someone who negotiates for another person or company. *Chapter 2: The HR Professional as Negotiation Agent*

2. D: A negotiation in which the parties cooperate to achieve maximum mutual benefit in an agreement, creating new value in the process (often called "win–win"). *Chapter 3: Types of Negotiation*

3. D: New federal statutes now require organizations to emphasize relationship issues in negotiations; for example, by

sharing information fully and not "walking away" from a negotiation session.
Chapter 4: The Importance of Relationships

4. C: The least favorable point at which a party would accept a negotiated deal; the "walk-away" condition.
Chapter 5: Four Key Concepts

5. B: Defining a good outcome for yourself and the other party.
Chapter 6: Preparing for a Negotiation

6. A: Ask whether the person is committed to the best interests of your company or relationship.
Chapter 7: Negotiation Strategies

7. C: Negotiators who ask to change an agreed-upon term of a final negotiation probably have "winner's curse"—the relentless thought that they could have gotten more.
Chapter 8: Frequently Asked Tactical Questions

8. D: Present a direct, firm offer to refocus the other person's attention on the process.
Chapter 9: Manipulative Negotiation Ploys

9. C: Anticipate low-ball offers, grudging concessions, and bluffing.
Chapter 10: Barriers to Agreement

10. B: Perceiving the world with a bias in one's own favor or toward one's own point of view.
Chapter 11: Mental Errors

11. C: Carefully think through whether the person is part of your firm's "core competencies."
Chapter 12: Negotiations with Job Seekers and Employees

12. C: Set a clear date for formal enforcement of the policy to begin.
Chapter 13: Negotiations with Your Boss, Peer Managers, and Other Senior Executives

13. A: Discuss price openly and honestly as soon as you begin speaking with candidates.
    Chapter 14: Negotiations with Vendors and Consultants

14. B: Long-standing, international unions in large industries have begun attracting more members in the last two decades.
    Chapter 15: Negotiations with Labor Unions

15. A: Companies are facing fewer restrictions on what may be defined as retaliatory actions against employees.
    Chapter 16: Negotiations over Legal Disputes

16. A: Which company's HR personnel will provide the most guidance in the newly formed entity once the merger takes place?
    Chapter 17: Negotiations Related to Mergers and Acquisitions

17. D: All of the above.
    Chapter 18: Making Negotiation a Core Capability

18. A: Knowing your company's competitive strategy is the best way to boost your chances of successfully negotiating new HR policies with peer managers
    Chapter 19: Sharpening Your Skills, Benefiting Your Company

Summing Up

In this chapter, you learned about:

- The benefits of effective negotiation for individuals and their companies

- The important role HR can play in building negotiation as a core organizational competence

    You also read overviews of:

- The common negotiation situations—formal and informal

- HR professionals' experience as negotiators

- Basics of the negotiation process

- The characteristics of skilled negotiators

The chapter concluded by giving you an opportunity to assess your own negotiation skills and to take a multiple-choice test that can help you prioritize your learning as you work your way through this book.

Leveraging Chapter Insights: Critical Questions

- What aspects of negotiation are you strongest in? Weakest? How might you strengthen weak areas?

- How would you rate the overall quality of the negotiations in which your company engages? What steps might you take to improve their quality?

- What types of negotiation situations do you find yourself most often involved with? How might you deepen your knowledge of less familiar types of negotiation situations?

- Think about the people in your organization who have the strongest negotiation skills. How do they approach negotiations? What results do they usually get?

- Think about successful and not-so-successful negotiations you've been involved in previously. What distinguished the two experiences?

CHAPTER TWO

The HR Professional as Negotiation Agent

Whose Interests Come First?

Key Topics Covered in This Chapter

- *What agents are and why people engage them as representatives in negotiations*

- *The problems of informational asymmetries, divided interests, and conflicts of interest—and how to deal with them*

- *Agents' legal duties*

- *Agents' ethical responsibilities*

- *When not to be a negotiation agent*

I N S O M E N E G O T I A T I O N S, people and organizations represent their own interests. In many other negotiations, however, the negotiating sides' interests are represented by third parties. These third parties may be independent agents contracted by one of the negotiating parties. Or they may be non-independent agents—such as HR staff members—charged with representing their companies. Or they may be officials of an organization, such as a labor union, who have the responsibility of representing their members' interests. This chapter considers the role of these various agents and the potential problems that arise from their use, with an emphasis on the HR professional as negotiation agent.

Independent Agents

An *independent agent* is a person charged with representing the interests of another (a *principal*) in a negotiation. Many professionals—lawyers, accountants, brokers—enter into contracts to represent others. Consider an employment attorney's role in a dispute between an employee and employer. We might describe the attorney as an agent, because he or she represents a client in return for a fee. Think of a typical attorney in an employment case. She has no involvement with the client except insofar as she has been engaged to represent the client in a highly defined manner: drafting legal documents and negotiating a settlement with the other side—and possibly representing the client in court.

In theory, the attorney in such a case must put her personal interests on the shelf and represent only those of her client. By statute, case law, and custom, she has a fiduciary responsibility—an obligation to demonstrate trustworthy behavior—toward the client to do so. But in practice, no human being is capable of acting as the perfect agent of another. For example, the attorney will have concerns about time and reputation that will inevitably influence what she does.

Generally, people hire an independent agent to represent them for either or both of the following reasons:

- **The agent has greater expertise.** Engaging the services of an agent is usually a good idea when one party in a negotiation has more experience, more knowledge, or sharper bargaining skills than the other. For example, 49-year-old William is a talented engineer recently dismissed from a new company. He wonders whether he was dismissed unfairly because of his age, but has little knowledge about employment law. Recognizing his own shortcomings in this area, he hires an attorney who has the knowledge and experience to represent him.

- **To put some distance between parties who have a close relationship.** Negotiators who are planning on bargaining with a friend or valued business associate may feel reluctant to drive a hard bargain for fear of damaging that important relationship. By engaging an agent, such individuals can put some distance between themselves and the other party, thereby avoiding some (but not all) relationship complications. Consider the case of Veronica, an HR manager who is considering buying a new home closer to her office to reduce the length of her commute. The home is being sold by Tony, a colleague. To avoid straining her relationship with Tony, Veronica engages a real-estate agent to represent her in the upcoming negotiations. Because the agent is not a friend of Tony's, he'll be eager to press for the best possible deal for Veronica and will handle all the details of the negotiation with Tony's agent. By using agents, Veronica and Tony won't have to deal directly with one another on the many details of the sale.

Non-Independent Agents

Some individuals act as *non-independent agents* in negotiations. For example, a purchasing manager negotiates regularly with suppliers on behalf of his employer. He acts as the employer's agent but, unlike the attorney described earlier, is part of the organization on whose behalf he is negotiating. The same can be said of the union representative involved in a collective bargaining process, and of the corporate advertising manager whose job is to select an ad agency and negotiate terms of payment and the timing of delivery.

And the same can be said of the HR professional who is seeking to:

- Negotiate a resolution to a dispute between a manager and employee at his or her company

- Resolve a grievance filed by an employee

- Come up with a performance-improvement plan for a worker

- Change policies regarding pay raises, promotions, training, and other terms of employment in the company

- Work out pricing and other terms with a consultant hired to provide training at the firm

As non-independent agents, HR professionals often face unique challenges in negotiations. For example, internal HR staff members are the legal agents of their organization and have a duty to act on behalf of the organization during negotiations with employees. However, HR's responsibility to the firm includes helping the organization manage its employees in ways that will benefit the company the most—for example, by treating employees fairly. To strike this delicate balance, HR professionals must actively solicit employees' concerns, positions on the issues at hand, and interests in the negotiation in question. They must then convey these objectively to management. *And* they must encourage the same flow of information from management to employees.

In this sense, an HR professional—more than any other type of manager—is a kind of dual agent. In your role as a human resources director or manager, you may well have felt a sense of divided loyalties at times. You're legally responsible for your company's welfare, yet you may have chosen your profession based on a desire to help individuals. This can be a difficult position. But it's vital that you keep your top priority—your company's welfare—in mind.

The Challenges Agents Face

Whether the position is independent or as a member of the represented organization, the decision to serve as an agent—or use one—poses some big challenges. These challenges stem from information asymmetries, divided interests among the principals, and conflicts of interest.

Asymmetric Information

Information asymmetry describes a situation in which one person has more information than another. This condition can present a problem during negotiations. If the person the agent is representing—the principal—has more information than the agent, then the agent may not know how best to represent the principal. More often, however, the agent—whether independent or non-independent—possesses the greater share of information. Some of this information flows from the agent's superior expertise; other critical information is often picked up during the negotiating itself. An agent's greater information can erode trust between the principal and the agent. For example:

> *Fred, an HR manager at engineering firm XyCorp, is negotiating a consulting engagement with ProCorp Partners, a company that specializes in change-management consulting. XyCorp and ProCorp Partners have not done business before. In the past, XyCorp's strategy in dealing with external consulting firms has been to extract the lowest price and the best conditions, often by pitting one supplier against another. The company's senior management team has grown up on that approach. Fred, however, is beginning to question that low-price practice. ProCorp*

*has demonstrated its ability to provide high-quality consulting services
that get measurable results.*

*Fred likes what he's heard from ProCorp's references, and he be-
lieves that the company can deliver on its promises. "A deal with Pro-
Corp would help us implement that companywide process-improvement
initiative we've got in the pipeline," Fred tells a colleague in HR, "and
give us a real opportunity to move ahead of the competition." He adds,
"We'll pay more to do business with ProCorp, but we'll be gaining real
advantages in return."*

In this example, Fred has gathered vital information in the negotiating sessions with ProCorp's representatives. That information has
opened his mind to opportunities to improve XyCorp's approach to
change management. The company's decision makers, however, are
not privy to this information and its nuances. All they know is that
doing business with this new supplier will cost them more money.
"I'm starting to wonder if Fred knows what he's doing," says the
CEO. The information asymmetry has separated the principals from
their agent, creating a gap of distrust.

How can principals and their agents avoid the problems caused
by information asymmetries? Here are some suggestions:

- To the greatest extent possible, principals should give agents
  information about their interests—what they care about.

- Agents should regularly communicate to principals the information they've gathered at the negotiating table. Agents and their
  principals should discuss that information, and the agent should
  ask, "In light of this new information, how should I proceed?"

Divided Interests

Many agents face the challenge of serving divided internal interests.
Not every organization—be it a union, a company, or an operating
unit—is of one mind as to its core interests. This fact puts those who
represent the principal in a difficult position. How should the agent

prioritize the issues? If the other party drives a tough bargain, where should trade-offs be made? Are the interests of other constituencies at stake in a particular deal?

> *While Fred is negotiating a consulting engagement with ProCorp, other managers at XyCorp ask him whether he can also arrange for ProCorp to provide services specifically for their departments. For instance, Sally, the head of marketing, needs help addressing high turnover in her department. And Thomas, the customer service director, wants to explore the possibility of installing new customer relationship management software. If Fred agrees to negotiate these additional services with ProCorp, he may harm his own chances of forging the best possible agreement with the consulting company. Why? ProCorp, sensing that XyCorp may be desperate for help, may bargain for higher fees. In addition, if ProCorp specializes in process improvement, XyCorp might not get the highest-quality assistance on the additional services ProCorp is asked to supply.*

There's no easy answer to the question of how to handle a situation of divided interests. Politicians face the same problem every day and usually try to solve it by promising to give at least something to everyone. But this is rarely possible in the business sphere, where constraints cannot be legislated away.

As is often the case, the best solution is for agents to communicate with the various constituents—in ways that aim for consensus on what constitutes the top priorities. In these instances, an agent has to act as an educator, helping constituents understand external realities. And sometimes the agent must be a coalition builder, assisting constituents in arriving at agreement on their common priorities.

Conflicts of Interest

The third major issue in the principal/agent relationship is the fact that every agent is bound to have a personal agenda. And that agenda may conflict with the principal's agenda. Michael Watkins and Joel

Cutcher-Gershenfeld have used the example of sports and entertainment agents to indicate how an agent's personal interest may
eclipse his or her clients' interests. "These agents may even court
controversy or engage in other behaviors designed to attract future
clients—with neutral or negative implications for the present clients
they ostensibly represent."[1] Ambitious sports and entertainment
agents are not the only representatives who may be tempted to
direct negotiations in ways that benefit themselves. Consider a business executive charged with negotiating an important deal. If several
constituencies within his company have stakes in the outcome, this
executive may be tempted to produce a good result for whichever
constituency can best advance his career.

This type of problem crops up repeatedly, and at the very highest levels. CEOs, for example, are, by definition, agents of their company's shareholders. They are hired to maximize shareholder wealth
and are bound by fiduciary duty to do so. However, that duty has not
prevented many CEOs from treating themselves to lavish perks or
cutting sweetheart retirement deals with corporate boards. Conflicts
of interests in which business leaders put their own interests above
those of their organizations, shareholders, and employees can destroy
entire companies—as the fates of once-mighty firms such as Enron,
Arthur Andersen, WorldCom, and Tyco have revealed. Even high-
level executives in not-for-profit organizations can fall victim to the
temptation to plunder their organizations out of self-interest. Giving
in to self-interest can also destroy careers and even put a manager or
executive in jail. Witness the lurid footage of "perp walks" in recent
years, as corporate criminals in handcuffs have been convicted of
felonies, thrown into prison, or heavily fined.

Generally, companies (and shareholders) use incentives to align
the interests of agents with their own interests. The concept is simple:
The agents only do well if the organizations they represent do well.
Bonuses, profit sharing, and stock options are the primary tools of
alignment. However, in practice this simple idea is difficult to implement. Watkins and Cutcher-Gershenfeld note that "it is not possible
for a principal to design an incentive system that perfectly aligns an

agent's interests with her own."[2] Create a pay-for-performance system, and employee-agents will immediately channel their ingenuity into tactics for playing the game in their favor.

Though imperfect as a tool for controlling agents' behavior, incentives are better than nothing. When combined with careful oversight and close communication, they help ensure that agents adequately represent their principals' interests in negotiations.

Agents' Legal Duties

In addition to the inherent challenges faced by agents, attention to agents' legal duties is essential. As agents who negotiate with various parties on behalf of their organization, HR professionals have the same legal duties toward their principal that any agent has. And like other agents, HR professionals may be personally liable for breach of these duties. Such breaches may arise when an HR professional breaks a contract, fails to perform his or her duties through negligence or intentional misperformance, tries to profit secretly from a negotiation, or behaves in ways that violate specific laws. (Of course, these duties apply to all HR activities—not just negotiations.) Table 2-1 shows how an agent's legal duty manifests itself and provides examples of breaches.

As an HR professional, *you* must take responsibility for learning about these duties, any laws that apply, and the areas in which you may be personally liable for breach of duties. See "Tips for Avoiding Personal Liability" for some basics to consider. You also need to ensure that managers throughout your company understand all laws regarding treatment of their employees—to help *them* avoid personal liability for breaking the law while they're engaged in negotiations with direct reports. In cases where your own judgment on such matters differs from that of other executives in your firm, provide articles, legal documents, and other sources of information supporting your view and reinforcing the importance of fulfilling these legal responsibilities. Examples of the possible consequences of breaching these duties are also helpful reminders.

TABLE 2-1

An Agent's Fiduciary Duties

Duty	Definition	Example of Breach
Loyalty	Acting exclusively for the interests of the principal	An HR professional recommends more attractive hiring terms to a friend or family member who has applied for a position at the company, even though the HR professional knows the individual is only on par with the other applicants for the job.
Obedience	Doing what the principal asks	An HR professional conducting a negotiation over outsourcing payroll services substitutes his or her own terms for those specifically required by the company controller without consulting with the controller.
Reasonable care	Applying sufficient attention and energy to the job	An HR professional lets a valuable job candidate slip away by failing to send an offer letter to the applicant within a reasonable period of time after management decided to extend an offer.
Confidentiality	Not disclosing information that, in the best interests of the principal, should remain confidential	An HR professional reveals to employees the fact that a plant is about to close before management chooses to share that information, resulting in more complex negotiations with union representatives.

Source: Gene Thornton, e-mail to author, 15 January 2004.

Tips for Avoiding Personal Liability

To protect yourself further from personal liability—and help other managers in your firm protect themselves—practice the following principles yourself and encourage other managers to do the same.

- **Know the law.** Familiarize yourself with applicable federal, state, and local statutes and obtain ongoing training in how to uphold and implement the laws' requirements.

- **Be consistent in treatment of employees.** Whenever a company departs from its normal course of treatment of employees, it risks creating discrimination—an employee may claim that he or she was treated differently from other employees for discriminatory reasons. For example, if you've negotiated different severance packages for two groups of laid-off employees, the members of one group may decide that they've been discriminated against.

- **Be truthful in dealing with employees.** Some managers avoid the drudgery of documenting an employee's poor performance, providing counseling, and taking other disciplinary steps by instead negotiating a demotion or other action based on a fictional reason (such as "We're eliminating this position"). Resist this urge. Many employees can easily discover the real reason behind such actions. When they find out they haven't been treated truthfully, many feel highly motivated to sue.

- **Don't act in anger.** During difficult negotiations, such as the terms of a laid-off employee's departure, anger on your part can increase the likelihood that you'll make physical contact with the employee—e.g., snatching documents from the person's hand, holding onto his or her coat or chair, or physically removing the employee from the room. All of these actions can lead to assault and battery charges—so keep any angry emotions firmly in check.

- **Let employees respond.** If you're negotiating a painful dismissal of an employee, give the person the opportunity to tell his or her side of the story, in writing or orally. When people feel their side *hasn't* been heard, emotions can escalate—turning a relatively harmless situation into an explosive one that leads to a lawsuit.

Liability for breach of agency duties can take several forms. For example, suppose an HR manager negotiates to have a particular employee selected for layoff because of a personal grudge rather than objective and impartial reasons. In this case, the affected employee might have a cause of action against both the HR professional and the employer for tortious interference with the employment relationship. The employer might in turn have a cause of action against the HR manager for such a breach of the duty of loyalty. The company might also be liable for the HR manager's torts. Meanwhile, the HR professional might be required to indemnify the company for any damages the firm suffered as a result of the tortious conduct toward the employee.

But laws are complex and change frequently. Like many HR professionals, you may not know all there is to know about a particular point of law. You can improve your knowledge by referencing your company's legal department, doing independent reading, and attending courses and workshop on these subjects. It's beyond the scope of this chapter to include a comprehensive discussion of employment and other law, but the following sections can shed light on at least several situations relevant to many HR professionals and the negotiation situations in which they may find themselves.

Fiduciary Duties Under ERISA

Do you negotiate contracts with benefits providers and consulting companies that run your company's benefit plan? If so, you're what's known in legal terms as a *fiduciary*. Laws regarding fiduciaries' responsibilities can differ depending on the country in question. In the United States, as Carolyn Hirschman points out, "fiduciaries are held to strict standards of performance under the same federal law (the *Employment Retirement Income Security Act of 1974*, or ERISA) that protects employees from abuse, fraud, and negligence in the operation of their retirement and health plans."[3] To avoid mismanaging benefits plans—and incurring personal liability for doing so—fiduciaries (at least in the United States) must educate themselves on the complexities of ERISA.

Despite all the media focus on lawsuits filed against firms alleging breaches of fiduciary responsibility, most such breaches stem from ignorance of the law, poor judgment, or negligence. For example, a benefits-management firm hired by a fiduciary fails to deposit employee contributions promptly, neglects to balance a portfolio with sufficient asset classes, or fails to remove underperforming retirement funds or monitor fund managers closely enough. In such a case, the fiduciary who negotiated a contract with this benefits-management firm and then failed to monitor the firm's performance may be blamed for such breaches. And despite the lack of malice behind most breaches, fiduciaries who are accused of neglecting their duties can become defendants in federal civil suits filed by the U.S. Department of Labor or by benefit-plan participants and their beneficiaries. Judges can also remove and replace fiduciaries. Finally, in the United States, the government can force fiduciaries to restore losses or profits to their plans and to pay "excise taxes" of up to 20 percent of amounts recovered. The government also has the power to take fiduciaries' homes, cars, and other personal assets to cover losses.

As you probably know, ERISA compliance is complex and requires ongoing, close attention and often the expertise of specialists. Yet you can strengthen your knowledge of the law and protect yourself and your company from liability through the following guidelines:[4]

- **Document everything.** Record the reasons behind every decision you've made regarding why you negotiated a contract with a particular provider and how you monitored the provider's performance and addressed problems. Though this is time-consuming, it'll be well worth the effort if you ever find yourself in court defending your actions against an employee's lawsuit. To prove that you've followed all procedures in accordance with ERISA, keep reports, letters, minutes, investment scoring sheets—anything relevant to your benefits-plan decisions.

- **Form a pension committee.** Many large companies have internal pension committees comprising HR and other executives who oversee benefits-plan selection and management. Often, these committees hire consultants to help. They also meet regularly (usually quarterly) to review plan designs, examine investment results, and make necessary changes in investment options. If you work for a small firm, you may need to rely on your company's accountants or attorneys to select the best benefits providers for your organization.

- **Select plan providers carefully.** Outline the kind of benefits plan you're seeking, set objective criteria for the plan, and gather at least three proposals from potential providers. Examine each candidate's qualifications and services, obtain and contact references, and check for proper licensing. Find out if anyone has filed lawsuits against the providers, and check their financial stability. Select a provider whose core clients resemble your company in size and issues. The more informed you are, the more effectively you'll be able to negotiate contracts with providers.

- **Don't assume that the lowest bidder is best.** Making an "apples-to-apples" comparison of plan providers' fees is difficult because no standard format has been established for proposals. However, don't feel obligated to pick the lowest bidder. Instead, determine how much providers charge for comparable services and whether fees get charged to plan assets or the plan sponsor. Though there's no one right fee, you need to justify the proposed fees as appropriate.

- **Review plan performance regularly.** Once you've selected and implemented a plan, review its expenses every year or so to ensure they're reasonable. Monitor vendors' performance at least yearly—evaluating investment decisions, each investment's performance against benchmarks and plan goals, and the quality of the vendor's customer service. Check retirement accounts for "churning"—unnecessary buying and selling for the sole purpose of generating commissions. If you're unsure of how to conduct these reviews, negotiate an agreement with a knowledgeable consultant who can help you. Also consider arranging a fiduciary audit, in which a lawyer or consultant examines your company's fiduciary activities to safeguard against breaches and potential lawsuits. If insolvable problems arise, replace a vendor.

HR Professionals and Employee Litigation

More and more employees in the United States are filing lawsuits to address workplace grievances.[5] And courts increasingly face the question of whether individual managers—including HR professionals—can be held personally liable for violations of various employment-related laws. As an HR executive, manager, or staff member, you need to know as much as possible about employment law and the criteria by which you *or* other managers in your firm may have personal liability for violation of such laws. By making other managers throughout your firm aware of the laws, you can help protect them and your company from litigation. How does understanding employment-related law relate to your skills as a negotiator? When you know the law, you can negotiate employee complaints from a more informed position. You'll have a clearer sense of whether an employee's complaint is legitimate, and may be able to resolve conflicts so that the employee doesn't feel the need to file a lawsuit.

There are a number of federal employment statutes that you and other managers need to understand in order to avoid personal liability for violating the law. Let's take a closer look at two of these below.

- **The Fair Labor Standards Act (FLSA).** This law establishes minimum wage, overtime pay, equal pay, record keeping, and child-labor standards for employees covered by the *FLSA*. Whenever a manager has the power to hire, fire, or discipline employees, or to negotiate pay rates or working schedules, he or she may be defined by the courts as an employer—and thus be personally liable for violating this law. By overseeing payroll or compensation issues, HR professionals may be liable if an employee argues successfully in court that such responsibilities provide the imprimatur of an employer. To protect yourself against such an outcome, take steps to ensure FLSA compliance throughout your company. And remind executives and managers that the courts define *employer* broadly.

- **The Family and Medical Leave Act (FMLA).** This law requires companies with at least fifty employees to provide eligible employees with up to twelve weeks of leave for the birth or adoption of a child, to care for a seriously ill family member, or to cope with a serious health condition of their own. As with the FLSA, the potential exposure of an HR professional for personal liability under the *FMLA* can be unclear. However, in some cases, HR professionals have been held personally liable under the Act. Additionally, individual supervisors of the eligible employees may be held personally liable under this law. For this reason, you need to actively ensure that you and other managers throughout your firm understand and comply with the details of the FLSA while negotiating leave terms with employees.

Agents' Ethical Responsibilities

In every negotiation in which you participate, as well as throughout the full range of your on-the-job activities as an HR professional, you have a broad range of ethical responsibilities. As the SHRM Code of Ethical and Professional Standards in Human Resource Management indicates, you have the duty to apply the following principles while carrying out negotiations:[6]

- **Professional responsibility:** adding value to the organization you serve and contributing to its ethical success

- **Professional development:** striving to meet the highest standards of competence and committing to strengthening your competencies continually

- **Ethical leadership:** serving as a role model for maintaining the highest standards of ethical conduct

- **Fairness and justice:** promoting and fostering fairness and justice for your organization and its stakeholders

- **Conflicts of integrity:** maintaining a high level of trust with your organization's stakeholders by protecting their interests as well as your professional integrity, and by avoiding negotiation situations that create actual, apparent, or potential conflicts of interest

- **Responsible use of information:** protecting the rights of individuals while ensuring truthful communications and facilitating informed decision making during negotiations

Whenever you serve as an agent for your company in a negotiation, these ethical duties become all the more crucial. But what *are* ethics, exactly, and why have they garnered so much attention lately? Moreover, how do they play out in typical negotiation situations?

As Howard M. Pardue explains, "Ethics primarily concerns the interrelationships that exist between individuals. Most often, ethics is defined as honesty, integrity, or fairness. Proper ethical conduct involves the application of these values."[7] In the United States, at least, business trends such as unprecedented acquisitions, divestitures, downsizing, and deregulation of industries have raised the question of what constitutes ethical business behavior. In addition, companies have come under increasing pressure to show impressive, short-term profits—again raising the question of which profit-making behaviors are ethical and which are not. Finally, with the globalization of business, the "rules of the game" have become a lot more complicated than just "Don't lie, cheat, or steal." Every time a national border is crossed, and whenever legislation is vague, businesspeople need that much more guidance on how to "make the numbers" ethically.

How do questions about ethics manifest themselves in everyday business negotiations? Here are just a few examples:[8]

- When you're negotiating job offers with candidates, are you following the principles of equal employment opportunity fairly and honestly?

- While working out bonus incentives with various department heads, are you applying the incentives fairly—that is, is it ethical to allot a bonus to one group but not others?

- Are the salary increases you and other managers negotiate with employees based on honest evaluations of performance? Are managers held accountable for fair appraisal through a checks-and-balances system of management review?

- If your firm must downsize and you and other managers must negotiate severance packages with affected employees, what is the most ethical way to do so? Will your company grant exorbitant severance pay to certain employees based solely on their title or tenure? Again, what actions seem most ethical?

You can play a critical role in ensuring that ethical behavior is woven throughout the fabric of your firm. How? Take part in creating a code of ethics for your company. Then model the code yourself and encourage others to do the same by establishing and maintaining the right systems. See "Elements of an Effective Code of Ethics" for more information.

Elements of an Effective Code of Ethics

A good code of ethics defines the following:

- **Personal integrity.** The organization values and insists on integrity in all its dealings with employees, customers, suppliers, investors, and other stakeholders.

- **Compliance and laws.** The company doesn't tolerate discrimination against or harassment of employees or other stakeholders, or the violation of antitrust, labor, and other laws.

- **Political contributions and activities.** The firm sets forth a clear policy about whether or how it will provide personal and financial support to political parties.

- **Confidential information.** The code defines how sensitive information (such as customer contact information, financial performance, or other data) will be treated and what the company considers confidential. It also defines limits on employees' privacy (for example, use of e-mail).

- **Conflicts of interest.** The organization prohibits behavior that gives even the appearance of a conflict of interest (for instance, an HR manager who recommends the hiring of a personal friend).

- **Records.** The code mandates accurate, truthful reflection of business transactions (such as the recording of revenues) in the company's books and records.

- **Employment policies.** The code clearly states how the organization treats its employees, including issues of fairness of pay, discrimination, career development, and safety.

- **Securities transactions.** The code describes securities trading restrictions that exist in the organization, such as no insider trading.

- **Use of company assets.** The organization's assets will be used only for its purposes, not for the personal gain of officers or others employed by the company.

- **Gifts, gratuities, and entertainment.** The code spells out policies regarding the giving and receiving of these items; for instance, whether salespeople can take potential customers to dinner while negotiating a possible sale, and, if so, how much is considered appropriate to spend on such entertainment.

- **The environment.** The code specifies the organization's responsibility toward the environment; for example, during negotiations with vendors over waste removal or disposal.

- **Compliance.** The code describes how compliance with the code's provisions is communicated and certified, and how breaches or suspected breaches of provisions are handled.

SOURCE: Frank Z. Ashen, "Corporate Ethics—Who Is Minding the Store?" SHRM white paper, July 2002.

Are you facing an ethical dilemma during a current negotiation, or has another manager who's involved in a negotiation come to you for advice on how to handle such a dilemma? For example, perhaps the other party is asking for something in order to forge an agreement, but if you or the manager agree to provide it, one or more of your company's code of ethics might be violated. See assessment tool 2-1 if you need help determining how to respond in such a situation.

Once your company has developed a code of ethics, *everyone* is responsible for following it. You can do your part by:[9]

- Communicating the code to prospective employees, new employees, and long-standing employees

- Encouraging senior managers to lead by example by ensuring that their own behavior is at the highest level of integrity during all negotiations—and reminding them that employees will know if their behavior is *not* ethical

- Providing regular, formal training that includes realistic case studies and open, honest discussion of ethical questions that arise during negotiations

- Making it obvious in job descriptions and performance reviews that unethical behavior during a negotiation has consequences, including discharge

- Enabling employees to get clarification about an ethics issue that arises during a negotiation or to report a possible breach of ethics without fear of punishment—for example, by accessing an ethics hotline, speaking with an ombudsman, or contacting a designated individual in HR

Whether you're negotiating with an employee, a potential supplier, a job candidate, or some other party in your role as agent for your organization, it's crucial that you embody the highest standards of honesty, integrity, and fairness. By doing so, you represent your *company* as ethical—thereby strengthening its reputation among employees, shareholders, and the public.

Assessment Tool 2-1
The Ethical Dilemma Checklist

How to determine whether an agreement you or another manager is considering would violate your company's code of ethics? Use this tool to analyze the agreement's possible relevance to the code. For each statement, circle "Yes," "No," or "Unsure." When you're finished, review your responses. If you've answered "Yes" for any statement, the solution to your dilemma is clear: Don't commit this violation of your company's code. If you've answered "Unsure" to any statements, conduct further research or consult your firm's legal counsel to gain clarity.

The agreement the other party is asking me to make could . . .

1. Bring my personal integrity into doubt with an employee, customer, supplier, investor, or other stakeholder.

   Yes   No   Unsure

2. Result in discrimination against or harassment of employees or other stakeholders, or would violate antitrust, labor, and other laws.

   Yes   No   Unsure

3. Violate my company's policy about providing personal or financial support to political parties.

   Yes   No   Unsure

4. Make information my firm has defined as confidential available to the public or violate employees' privacy.

   Yes   No   Unsure

5. Create a conflict of interest.

Yes   No   Unsure

6. Result in inaccurate or deceptive recording of a business transaction.

Yes   No   Unsure

7. Violate my company's employment policies.

Yes   No   Unsure

8. Violate my firm's rules about securities transactions.

Yes   No   Unsure

9. Result in my organization's assets being used for something other than its own purposes.

Yes   No   Unsure

10. Violate stipulations about what kinds of gifts, gratuities, and entertainment are considered appropriate.

Yes   No   Unsure

11. Violate the company's stated responsibility to the environment.

Yes   No   Unsure

When *Not* to Be an Agent

In order to act with the utmost integrity, it's sometimes better *not* to be an agent. Though anyone can develop and improve his or her negotiation skills through learning and practice, there are certain situations in which you may not be the best person to represent your company during a negotiation. These situations include the following:

- You have insufficient negotiation experience, and the outcome of a particular negotiation can make or break your organization.

- You're considerably junior in rank and experience to the negotiators for the other party.

- You have a possible conflict of interest related to the parties or to the potential outcome of the negotiation.

- You have a close personal relationship with or strong feeling of animosity toward the negotiator for the other party

If you find yourself in any of these situations, it may be best to find someone else—another HR staff member, an outside consultant—to serve as your company's agent during a negotiation.

Summing Up

In this chapter, you learned:

- The difference between independent and non–independent agents

- How HR professionals play a unique role as agents representing their companies during negotiations

- The ways that serving in the role of agent can pose unique challenges for HR executives, managers, and staff members— including:
  - Asymmetric information
  - Divided interests
  - Conflicts of interest

The chapter also examined:

- Agents' legal duties, particularly responsibilities regarding the Fair Labor Standards Act (FLSA) and the Family and Medical Leave Act (FMLA)

- Agents' ethical responsibilities, including the principles laid out in the SHRM Code of Ethical and Professional Standards for Human Resource Management

- Guidelines for establishing and enforcing a code of ethics for your company.

Leveraging Chapter Insights: Critical Questions

- Have you ever experienced a conflict of interest while representing your company during a negotiation? If so, how did you resolve the conflict? What, if anything, would you do differently the next time you encounter a similar situation?

- Think about some upcoming negotiations in which you'll be participating. How comfortable do you feel about representing your firm during these negotiations? After reading this chapter, do you think you should excuse yourself from serving as agent in any of these negotiations? If so, which ones? And why?

- Does your firm have a code of ethics? If so, how does it compare with the guidelines you read about in this chapter? What, if any, changes might you recommend for the code?

- If your firm has a code of ethics, what actions do you take to model it yourself and to ensure that others throughout the company follow the principles laid out in the code? How might you design better systems to encourage compliance with the code?

CHAPTER THREE

Types of Negotiation

Many Paths to Agreement

Key Topics Covered in This Chapter

- *Distributive negotiation: claiming value*

- *Integrative negotiation: creating and claiming value*

- *The negotiator's dilemma: determining which approach to take*

- *Multiphase and multiparty negotiations*

T HERE ARE two primary kinds of negotiation. Chances are, you have been involved in both at one time or another in your work as an HR professional:

- **Distributive:** In a distributive negotiation, the parties compete over the distribution of a fixed sum of value. The key question in a distributed negotiation is "Who will *claim* the most value?" In distributive negotiations, a gain by one side is made at the expense of the other.

- **Integrative:** In an integrative negotiation, the parties cooperate to achieve maximum benefits by integrating their interests into an agreement. These negotiations center on *creating* value, in addition to claiming it.

Few of the negotiations you participate in are likely to be purely distributive. Although direct competition between the interests and goals of negotiating parties is commonplace, opportunities to integrate the parties' interests and preferences usually exist. But for the purposes of learning, this chapter examines each type in its pure form. These forms are complicated by two other facts of life—negotiations often take place in phases and may involve multiple parties—which are addressed at the end of the chapter.

Distributive Negotiation

In a *distributive negotiation*, the bargaining centers on who will claim the most value. Some people refer to this type of negotiation as *zero-sum* or constant-sum negotiation. The term *win-lose* is probably more representative of what's involved. Classic examples include the following:

- **The sale of an automobile when the buyer and the seller do not know one another.** There is no relationship; all that matters is the price, and each side haggles for the best deal. Every gain by one party represents a loss to the other.

- **Wage negotiations between business owners and their union employees.** The owners know that any amount conceded to the union will come out of their own pockets—and vice versa.

In a purely distributive negotiation, the value at stake is fixed, and each side's goal is to get as much of the transaction as possible. Consider the example of two people negotiating over shares of a freshly baked apple pie. Each aims to negotiate for as large a portion of that pie as possible, knowing that any concession made to the other party will reduce his or her share by an equal amount. Or consider this typical business example:

LaNita, an HR manager at WildWear Outdoor Apparel, is evaluating several potential providers of a new performance-management methodology. The company she ultimately selects will provide training in the new methodology to specific units within WildWear. LaNita is currently negotiating with EvalPro, a new consulting firm that specializes in the methodology. EvalPro is a small start-up, and wants to charge as high a fee as possible to fuel cash flow. But WildWear, a more established, esteemed company, wants to keep costs under control in order to free up funds for investing in a major new product line.

LaNita and Jorge, one of EvalPro's founders, focus on price during the negotiating process. Neither seems willing or able to expand the discussion to include talk of other interests besides price. In the end, LaNita holds firm to the price she believes WildWear can tolerate. She tells Jorge that she's planning to interview several other potential providers. Worried about losing this opportunity to gain a new client and knowing that EvalPro currently has no other prospects in the pipeline, Jorge agrees to LaNita's price. LaNita is satisfied with the outcome of the negotiations. But Jorge, though relieved to have the WildWear business, knows that it's going to be very difficult to do a high-quality training job on the revenues that will come from the WildWear engagement. As he's leaving the meeting with LaNita, he's already feeling resentment over being "backed into a corner."

In any purely distributive negotiation, the "seller's" goal is to negotiate as high a price as possible; the "buyer's" goal is to negotiate as low a price as possible. A dollar more to one side is a dollar less to the other. Thus, the seller and the buyer compete to claim the greatest possible value for themselves. This competition results in a tug of war. Each negotiator aims to "pull" the final outcome as close to his or her side's desired goal as possible (or even beyond it).

Relationship and reputation mean little in this kind of exchange: The negotiators are not willing to trade value in the *deal* for value in their *relationship*. For example, a business executive being transferred to another metropolitan area is shopping for a house. She is not concerned with her long-term relationship with a home seller when she begins negotiating to purchase the seller's house. Chances are that the seller is a total stranger—and will remain so after the transaction takes place.

Information plays an important role in distributive negotiations. The less the other party knows about your weaknesses and real preferences, and the more they know about your bargaining strength, the better your position becomes. For example, Jorge would not want LaNita to know that his company was struggling for cash. LaNita, of course, would be eager to let Jorge know that other consulting firms were currently knocking on her door, each eager to get WildWear's business.

To achieve success in a distributive negotiation, remember the following:

- **Control the "anchor point."** The first offer made by either party can become a strong psychological anchor point, one that sets the bargaining range. Studies show that negotiation outcomes often correlate with the first offer. So start at the right place.

- **Share information shrewdly.** Do not disclose any significant information about your circumstances—including why you want to make a deal, your real interests or business constraints, your preferences among issues or options, or the point at which you'd walk away from the bargaining. However, do let the other side know that you have good options if this deal falls through.

- **Learn about the other party.** Information about the other party can benefit you. Learn as much as possible about their circumstances and preferences—including the reasons they want to make a deal, their real interests and business constraints, and their preferences among issues or options. Then leverage what you've learned in setting your first offer or request.

- **Don't overshoot.** If you claim value too aggressively or greedily, the other side may walk away—possibly depriving you of an opportunity to fashion a valuable agreement.

Integrative Negotiation

In an *integrative negotiation*, the parties cooperate to achieve maximum benefits by integrating their interests into an agreement while also competing to divide the value. In integrative negotiations, you have to be skilled at both creating value and claiming it. Consider how the negotiation between LaNita and Jorge may have turned out if both had taken an integrative, rather than distributive, approach:

Through increasingly frank discussion, LaNita and Jorge discover that they both have interests beyond just price. Though LaNita does want to control costs for WildWear, she also tells Jorge that WildWear is interested in expanding its community-outreach efforts. Jorge responds by explaining that in addition to wanting to boost cash flow as much as possible in EvalPro's early years, he also wants to build a base of high-profile clients for EvalPro and offer educational opportunities for young people who'd like to intern at companies like EvalPro.

By learning about one another's full range of interests, LaNita and Jorge arrive at an agreement that integrates these interests while also enabling both companies to divide the monetary value of the agreement.

The results of their bargaining? Jorge and LaNita agree to a price that's somewhat higher than what LaNita originally demanded but quite a bit lower than what Jorge originally wanted. LaNita sweetens the deal by agreeing to let EvalPro list WildWear as a client in its marketing materials—if WildWear is fully satisfied with EvalPro's service. In addition, LaNita and Jorge make arrangements for EvalPro interns to come to WildWear on a specified number of days in order to "shadow" several managers and employees for the purpose of learning about the performance-management consulting business. This part of the agreement satisfies WildWear's interest in expanding its community outreach and enables EvalPro to provide more educational opportunities for its interns.

Both LaNita and Jorge leave the meeting feeling excited about the agreement and more positive about their two companies' relationship. Moreover, rather than haggling over a limited "pie," they've managed to expand the pie beyond just price, so that it provides a lot more value to each of them.

Examples like this one have become more and more commonplace in business as big companies shift their tactics from squeezing vendors—and dealing with many of them through short-term transactions—to developing long-term relationships with a few select, loyal suppliers. In many of these cases, both parties may end up collaborating in unexpected, highly positive ways—such as WildWear and EvalPro's collaboration on intern education. The growing use of joint ventures and outsourcing has likewise motivated organizations to think more about relationships and less about winning what often appears to be a zero-sum game.

In an integrative negotiation, your task is twofold: (1) to create as much value as possible for yourself and for the other party, and (2) to claim value for yourself. Many use the term *win-win* in referring to this type of arrangement. Unfortunately, that term implies that all parties get everything they want, which is rarely the case. More likely, each makes trade-offs to get the things they value most, while giving up other, less critical forms of value. For example, in the WildWear and EvalPro case, WildWear paid a bit more than it wanted to for EvalPro's services, while EvalPro accepted a substantially lower fee than it wanted. However, both companies won other forms of value in the exchange.

Sometimes—as in the WildWear and EvalPro case—the interests of the two parties in an integrative negotiation do not compete at all. In these situations, the negotiators can relatively easily fashion an agreement that integrates their interests as efficiently as possible. Agreeing to yield more of what one negotiator values does not necessarily require the other negotiator to take less of anything he or she values. Thus, the ability of one side to claim or win what it wants or needs in the negotiation does not necessarily detract from the other's ability to claim or win just as much. Bear in mind, it's more likely that interests in a negotiation will compete in some way. (In fact, some think that in such a case, there may not be a win-win possibility. See "Is Win-Win for Real?") Nevertheless, as you saw in the negotiation between LaNita and Jorge, there are often many items or issues to be negotiated in an integrated negotiation—not simply price, delivery date, or any other single term. Indeed, opportunities for creativity abound.

Negotiation specialist Mark Gordon, who coined the term "collaborative bargaining" for this type of negotiation, says that the parties should look for creative options, and not focus on which concessions to make. "You have to believe that it's in your interest to look for ways to benefit your negotiating counterpart. Your goal is not to hurt them, but to help them at little cost to yourself—and have them help you at little cost to them. The more creative you are at coming up with things that are good for both of you the happier both of you will be."[1] See "The Negotiator's Dilemma: A Preview" for a further dimension of this complex relationship. This creativity is possible only if both parties understand their own key interests *and* the key interests of the other side.

As Gordon told readers of the *Harvard Management Communication Letter*, "If you read the classic texts, they talk about extreme opening positions, getting the other side to make a concession first, offering to split the difference only after both sides have gone a few rounds, and so on." In Gordon's view, concessions are not necessary. "Instead, you look for creative options. . . . If there is a range of possible acceptable

Is Win-Win for Real?

Most books and training courses on negotiations use the term "win-win" to describe integrative deals. In fact, both the term and the concept have become so popular that they have become clichés: "We're looking for a win-win deal with our customers." "Here at GenCo, management and employees share a win-win attitude."

It all sounds very high-minded. Win-win resonates with our cultural belief that relationships should be mutually beneficial, not exploitive, one-sided, or coercive.

But not everyone is happy with the term. Author and negotiating consultant Jim Camp is an outspoken critic. To him, win-win is a sucker's game, and more likely to be a losing game for the unwary:[a] "[S]hrewd negotiators in every field understand that a gung ho, win-win negotiator on the other side of the table is a sitting duck. . . . Those smooth-talking negotiators don't compromise, but they demand that you do. (In the case of corporate purchasing departments, I guess their compromise is that they're buying from you instead of from someone else.) And all the while, they put the happy face on their negotiations."[b]

[a] "Win-win" in this sense follows the old Soviet approach to "getting to yes" in its negotiations with the West during the Cold War era: "What's ours is ours; what's yours is negotiable."

[b] Jim Camp, *Start with No* (New York: Crown, 2002), 4–6.

outcomes, then there is always a set of outcomes that will make both of us happier than the minimum acceptable outcome would."[2]

Fisher, Ury, and Patton's popular book *Getting to Yes* supports this view. It shifted people's focus from "I-win-you-lose" situations to integrative negotiations, in which each party can claim satisfaction. Some have mistaken this to mean that everybody can get everything they want (win-win), which is *not* what the authors mean. Instead, these negotiation experts provide approaches both for creating value

The Negotiator's Dilemma: A Preview

Few business negotiations are purely distributive or purely integrative. Most are integrative to some degree, containing opportunities for both competition and collaboration. Indeed, the playing field of negotiations is better described as a continuum that includes those two extremes and mixtures of the two in between. Knowing where to play in that continuum involves a tension known as the *negotiator's dilemma*. "Should I compete for as big a share of this small pie as possible," one participant asks, "but risk having the other side claim the value? Or should I collaborate in hopes of doing well?" These questions involve difficult strategic choices, which means balancing competitive strategies with cooperative strategies. Knowing whether to compete where interests conflict—claiming more instead of less—or to create value by exchanging the information that leads to mutually advantageous options lies at the core of the negotiator's art.

(focus on interests, not position; separate the people from the problem) and for "principled" value claiming (identify objective standards). Likewise, other authors, notably David Lax and James Sebenius in *The Manager as Negotiator*, tell readers to focus on enlarging the pie through trades (creating value) while seeking to get a reasonable piece of the expanded pie for themselves (claiming value).

Finding opportunities for mutual benefit naturally requires information sharing. Unlike the distributive situation, in which you deliberately "play your cards close to the vest," an integrative negotiation encourages participants to do the following:

- Provide significant information about their circumstances

- Explain why they want to make a deal

- Talk about their real interests or business constraints

- Reveal and explain in general terms their preferences among issues or options

- Consider and reveal any additional capabilities or resources they have that might meet the other side's interests and could be added to the deal

- Use what they learn to find creative options that will meet the interests of both parties to the greatest extent possible

Use assessment tool 3-1 to determine whether an upcoming negotiation you'll be participating in is better suited to an integrative or a distributive approach.

Assessment Tool 3-1
An Integrative or Distributive Negotiation?

Think of an upcoming negotiation that you're going to participate in. For each statement below, circle "Agree" or "Disagree."

In this upcoming negotiation . . .

1. The most important thing is for me to negotiate as favorable a price as possible.

   Agree   Disagree

2. Price is the one most important issue on the table.

   Agree   Disagree

3. My reputation or the other party's reputation mean little to me.

   Agree   Disagree

4. I don't intend to cultivate a long-term business relationship with the other party.

   Agree   Disagree

5. I feel that I can't concede anything to the other party.

Agree   Disagree

6. There are more issues on the table for discussion than price.

Agree   Disagree

7. I see opportunities to create new forms of value that both parties will find important.

Agree   Disagree

8. I hope to establish a positive, long-term working relationship with the other party.

Agree   Disagree

9. I'm willing to make trade-offs to get the things I value most, while conceding other, less critical forms of value.

Agree   Disagree

10. I don't need to get the most favorable price.

Agree   Disagree

Calculate Your Results

If you circled "Agree" for statements 1–5 or "Disagree" for statements 6–10, you most likely would want to approach your upcoming negotiation using a distributive process and techniques. For example, you might want to share information shrewdly and make a first offer to set a psychological anchor point that favors your position as much as possible.

If you circled "Disagree" for statements 1–5 or "Agree" for statements 6–10, you would likely want to approach the negotiation using an integrative process and techniques. For instance, you may want to share information more freely, learn more about the other party's full range of interests, and reveal your preferences among options discussed during the negotiation.

Multiple Phases and Multiple Parties

When thinking about negotiating, most people envision one person or one team of people facing another.[3] The individual parties eventually hammer out their differences or walk away. This characterization is often accurate. It describes how some bosses and their direct reports deal with performance and pay issues, how an individual negotiates for the purchase of a new car, and so forth. Such negotiations are one-on-one and focus on a clear issue, and they are usually handled in a single meeting.

In reality, many negotiations are not so simple. They involve more than two parties, and they sometimes take place in phases, each devoted to one of several important issues. For example, as an HR executive or manager, you might find yourself participating in ongoing HR department budget negotiations or large, long-term projects with HR consultants (multiphase negotiations). In addition, you may be involved in class-action employment litigation or simultaneous contract negotiations with two or more company unions (multiparty negotiations). Though a detailed examination of these more complex situations lies beyond the scope of this book, you need to be aware of them. The following sections lay out the foundations upon which these situations are built.

Multiphase Negotiations

Multiphase negotiations and the prospect of future dealings offer important advantages for parties who are trustworthy and who would like to foster cooperative behavior. In these situations, early phases allow the parties to build trust by performing their agreements as promised. A failure to perform on the part of one party warns the other side to tread carefully in the future and to create enforcement mechanisms for agreements. Early phases also provide opportunities for the parties to get to know each other's communication and negotiation styles. That familiarity often makes subsequent phases more productive.

To get a sense of what a multiphase negotiation might look like for HR professionals, consider this situation: You want to hire a consulting company to perform a complex set of HR services for your firm. You anticipate that the term of the engagement would last for several years and require significant investment on the part of your firm. In this case, you would want to structure the negotiation so that it unfolds over several phases. In the earlier phases, you might discuss your needs in detail and take plenty of time to evaluate the consulting company's expertise and track record. You might also agree to have the company perform one of the specified services that requires a shorter time period, so that your firm and the vendor could assess how things were going for everyone concerned. You might then add details to your contracts with the vendor based on what you both learned during the early phases; for example, adjusting time estimates for completion of certain kinds of work, or fine-tuning fees if that seems appropriate. In the later phases of the negotiation, if things have gone well so far, you might consider committing to longer-term stretches of service from the vendor.

Multiparty Negotiations

Business and professional negotiations commonly involve more than two parties, and certainly more than two people. Such *multiparty negotiations* can differ significantly from two-party negotiations in one important respect: Coalitions can form among the parties. Coalitions make it possible for weaker parties to gather the strength to push through their preferred proposals, or at least to block those they find unacceptable.

There are at least two types of coalitions: a *natural coalition* of allies who share a broad range of common interests, and a *single-issue coalition*, in which parties that differ on other issues unite to support or block a single issue (often for different reasons). The challenge of multiparty negotiation is managing coalitions—breaking them apart or keeping them together depending on your own interests. Just as in a two-party negotiation, you must understand the goals, interests, and relationships of the many parties, and work from there.

A natural coalition of allies is hard to break. For example, an environmental agency and a citizen's nature-conservation group share basic agendas and will often act in concert to block development initiatives, even without explicit agreement to do so.

A single-issue coalition of otherwise disassociated parties, in contrast, is generally more vulnerable. For example, a group of managers and a group of employees within a company may object to a proposed new method of evaluating performance. Each has different reasons for resisting the suggested method. (Perhaps the managers feel that the new method would take up too much of their time, while the employees believe that the method will subject them to more scrutiny than they're comfortable with.) But the fact that the two groups have different concerns makes it easier for those advocating the method to break up the coalition. To illustrate, if you supported the new performance-evaluation method, you might gather information demonstrating to the managers that the method requires no more of their time than the current evaluation approach requires. If the managers felt that you had addressed their concerns, they might withdraw their opposition, leaving the employee group as the sole resisters.

Summing Up

This chapter introduced the basic types of negotiation you're likely to encounter, and what's at stake in each.

- A distributive negotiation pits two or more parties in competition for a fixed amount of value. Here, each side's goal is to claim as much value as possible, as bargainers do at an automobile dealership. Value gained by one party becomes unavailable to others.

- Integrative negotiation is about both creating *and* claiming value. Through collaboration and information sharing, the parties look for opportunities to satisfy one another's key objectives, recognizing that they will probably have to give ground on other objectives.

- The negotiator's dilemma describes the situation faced by people who enter any type of bargaining situation. They must determine whether to aggressively claim the value currently on the table (and possibly come out the loser), or work with the other side to create even better opportunities that both parties can share.

- No matter which type of negotiation you're faced with, it's bound to become more complex if it is multiphased or involves multiple parties. If your negotiation is multiphased, use the early phases to build trust and to familiarize yourself with the other party or parties. If many parties are involved, consider the benefits of forming a coalition to improve your bargaining power— or breaking up a coalition that's opposed to your proposal.

Leveraging Chapter Insights: Critical Questions

- Think of a negotiation that you'll be participating in soon. In what ways might you transform the transaction from a distributive to an integrative negotiation, if that seems most appropriate? If you're aiming for an integrative negotiation, how might you go about learning more about the other party's full range of interests, so that you can brainstorm ideas for expanding the "pie" rather than haggling over a smaller "pie"?

- Consider the various types of negotiations you normally participate in. Which of these would you approach from a distributive angle? Which would you approach from an integrative angle? Why?

- Think of a multiparty negotiation you're currently involved in. Have coalitions formed among the parties? If so, are they natural coalitions or single-issue coalitions? How might you best manage those coalitions?

• Think of multiphase negotiation you're facing in the near future. In what ways might you cultivate trust with the other party during the early stages of the negotiation? In what ways might you get to know the other party's interests, concerns, and negotiating style as the bargaining starts to unfold?

CHAPTER FOUR

The Importance of Relationships

Different Notions of Value

Key Topics Covered in This Chapter

- *Why relationships matter*
- *How perceptions of relationship value affect negotiations*
- *Separating the deal from the broader relationship*

I N Y O U R N E G O T I A T I O N S as an HR professional, you deal with a wide range of people—from employees and your own direct reports to peer managers, suppliers, and executives. In all of these exchanges, the quality of the relationships among the parties is just as important—if not more so—as the quality of any financial or other non-relationship outcomes of the bargaining. This is particularly true because you have longstanding relationships with negotiation counterparts within your organization, and you may well want to cultivate enduring relationships with suppliers and other parties *outside* your company. In negotiations, "winning" often means more than simply claiming the most value. It means forging and maintaining positive, mutually beneficial relationships during *and* after a negotiation.

Why Relationships Matter

People tend to think of negotiating as something that takes place between arm's-length, impersonal entities trying to cut the best possible deal for themselves without regard to the future: an automobile salesperson and potential customer, a plaintiff and defendant in a product liability case, and so forth. Although this impression is valid in many cases, many other negotiations take place between individuals and entities that are not dealing with one another at arm's length or in solely transactional ways. These parties have important, valuable relationships and for one reason or another hope to maintain them. Such parties include managers and their direct reports, peer managers, companies and their key suppliers and customers, and individual employees who are trying to get things done by collaborating with others.

Relationships are mattering more and more in most companies, thanks to several business trends. One of these trends involves the flattening of organizations. Flatter organizations and wider spans of management control have dispersed power, giving lower-level managers and employees greater autonomy to take action and make decisions. With power dispersed, few individuals can order others around so as to focus resources and get work done. Instead, people need to negotiate solutions to problems with others over whom they have little or no formal authority. Under these conditions, successful negotiations hinge on the cultivation of strong relationships.

Another trend involves changes *between* companies. Many organizations have become less inclined to pit one supplier against another to extract the best deal. Instead of squeezing their suppliers, numerous leading companies now seek to establish long-term partnerships with a few selected suppliers. At the same time, companies have entered into many more joint ventures and strategic alliances—deals in which executives, managers, and employees must manage relationships with care.

Harvard professor John Kotter underscores the importance of relationships and their features:

> *Good working relationships based on some combination of respect, admiration, perceived need, obligation, and friendship are a critical source of power in helping to get things done. Without these relationships, even the best possible idea could be rejected or resisted in an environment where diversity breeds suspicion and interdependence precludes giving orders to most of the relevant players.*[1]

The increasing importance of good relationships has changed how people deal with each other when they negotiate. In particular, it has prompted many bargainers to avoid extreme value-claiming behavior. Why? Three reasons:

1. **You anticipate future transactions of value:** By being too greedy today, you risk losing future valuable transactions with the other party.

2. **You except reciprocity by the other party:** You assume that if you give a little in this transaction, the other party will help you later.

3. **You know that a good relationship engenders trust:** Trust reduces the cost of monitoring compliance and nitpicking adherence to the terms of an agreement.

How Perceptions of Relationship Value Affect Negotiations

Negotiations between parties who value their relationship will differ markedly from those between parties who place no value on the relationship. Consider these examples:

After six months of constant disagreement with his boss, the CEO, over how much to spend on a new training program and several other human resource initiatives, Mica decides that he stands little chance of getting the resources he needs to launch the HR programs he sees as essential for Pichon Industries. Embittered by what he perceives as a "brick wall" erected by "higher-ups," he resolves to start looking for another job elsewhere.

Lydia, who manages benefits programs at Marvex Inc., is negotiating a dispute with Nate, a representative from a plan provider with whom Marvex had done business for several years. Lydia tells Nate, "Those errors your investment manager made last quarter really worried our 401(k) employees. And we had to spend a lot of time away from other projects in order to fix the mistakes. That's expensive, and I think Marvex should be compensated for the problem."

Nate replies, "I can see how that must have been very frustrating. I've looked into the situation, and I don't see where our investment manager did anything wrong. But I'd like to get at the root of what happened. And certainly, if we're at fault, some sort of restructuring of our fees might be appropriate."

Lydia says, "Why don't we walk through the documentation and see what went wrong? I think that if we work together, we can make sure it doesn't happen again."

Nate nods. "I agree," he says, "We've always had a good working relationship, and I want to do whatever I can to keep it that way."

The negotiators in each of these examples are participating in relationships, but they treat them in dramatically different manners. Mica and the CEO are negotiating as if their relationship has no future value—which appears to be the case. All Mica can see is the need to invest in the HR programs he supports, and all the CEO can see are the costs of those programs. Each is focused only on the question of money, rather than the importance of their relationship.

Lydia and Nate likewise have a relationship, but each of them values that bond. Lydia knows from experience that a plan provider's performance can exert a significant impact on her company's operations. In her view, finding reliable providers and learning to work with them over the long term is the best way to stabilize Marvex's management of its benefits plan. Nate has a similar view of the situation. As a result, both he and Lydia are willing to temper any desire to be "right," to assign blame for mistakes, or to focus only on the financial implications of the situation in their dispute. Instead, they take a collaborative approach to looking into the source of the errors, and a long-term view toward ensuring that similar mistakes don't occur in the future. They each know that they need to balance their bottom-line business needs against the value they gain from a trusting, committed relationship.

The value to be claimed in both examples can be envisioned as a fixed pie, as shown in figure 4-1. Mica and his CEO see that pie as 100 percent monetary value and, in a sense, each is trying to claim as large a piece as possible—Mica by lobbying for more funding, and the CEO by resisting his requests. As far as the two are concerned, there is no relationship value. By contract, Lydia and Nate recognize that both monetary and relationship values are at stake in their dispute over the investment errors. And each knows that being too aggressive in claiming monetary value will reduce the relationship value.

Now, here's one important complication: Although both Lydia and Nate recognize relationship value as part of the negotiation dynamics, neither of them likely sees that value to quite the same degree. In such situations, one party will most certainly value the relationship more highly than the other. It's also very likely that the following are true:

1. **Neither side can quantify its view of relationship value.** In fact, the assessment of value is likely to vary among individuals within the same company. For example, Lydia may have very different perspectives on the relationship with Nate's company than Marvex's CFO might have. The CFO will be more interested in monetary measures. Lydia may also be concerned with dollars and cents, but she will probably also place a value on the plan provider's accuracy rate, quality and speed of customer service, and flexible array of services.

FIGURE 4-1

Monetary and Relationship Values

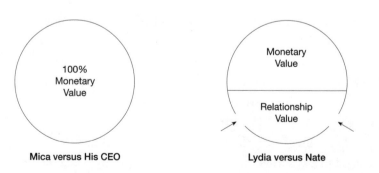

Mica versus His CEO   Lydia versus Nate

Source: Adapted from *Harvard Business Essentials: Negotiation* (Boston: Harvard Business School Press, 2003), 113.

2. **Neither side can know how the other assesses the relationship value.** For example, Lydia may have her own thoughts about the relationship value, but she cannot know with any certainty how Nate's company values its relationship with Marvex. "Do they value our relationship so highly that they'll agree to our demand for monetary compensation?" she wonders.

These two sources of uncertainty will affect the way each party interacts with the other as the negotiation unfolds.

Now consider the negotiations in which you are presently engaged. Try to answer these questions:

- **How strongly should relationship value influence my negotiating goals and tactics?** Your answer should be framed by two considerations: (1) the extent to which you will deal with the other party in the future, and (2) a rough calculation of the present value of benefits you anticipate receiving through future dealings with this party. Obviously, if you are unlikely to deal with this party again, there will be no relationship value to worry about. In this case, value claiming would be your goal. But if the opposite is the case, you need to make a mental tally of the future benefits and develop a strategy for creating and sharing value with the other party.

- **To what extent does relationship value matter to the party with whom I'm dealing?** If you can answer this, you'll know how far you can push in claiming value for yourself. To determine the answer, put yourself in the shoes of the other party and apply the two framing considerations discussed earlier: the likelihood of future dealings with the other side and an estimate of anticipated future benefits from those dealings.

Doing It Right

Negotiation expert Danny Ertel underscores the problems associated with negotiations in which elements of the deal and the relationship are intertwined:

[Negotiators] fear that if they push too hard to get the best deal possible today, they may jeopardize their company's ability to do business with the other party in the future. Or they fear that if they pay too much attention to the relationship, they'll end up giving away too much and make a lousy deal. Though natural, such confusion is dangerous. It leaves the negotiator open to manipulation by the other party.[2]

The danger of manipulation is obviously greatest when one party values the relationship and the other does not. Ertel gives the example of an accounting firm that must annually renew its auditing contract with a major client company. The client is interested in cutting a lower-priced deal, while the accounting firm is interested in a long-term relationship. So when the client demands a lower price, the accounting firm capitulates for the sake of the relationship. Several years of this, however, make the relationship profitless for the accounting firm.

Is this scenario reminiscent of your negotiations? If it is, you might consider the actual value of your relationships with those particular "customers." How mutually beneficial are they? "Over the years," writes Ertel, "I have asked hundreds of executives to reflect on their business relationships and to ask themselves what kind of customer they make more concessions to, do more costly favors for, and generally give away more value to."[3] Their usual response, he reports, is that many companies make concessions to their most difficult and least valuable customers—and always in the vain hope that the relationship will improve!

As an HR professional, you engage in many negotiations that don't necessarily hinge on profitability. But you still need to take stock of the value of those relationships. And you need to ask yourself, "Am I making more concessions with my more difficult negotiation counterparts? If so, what is happening to the quality of those relationships over time?" In any relationship in which one party "holds the other hostage" because it values the relationship less than the other party, the quality of that relationship is bound to decline over time.

How can you avoid falling into this trap? Ertel's advice is to distinguish between the deal and the relationship. That is, draw a clear distinction between the components of the deal and the components of the relationship. It may help to create a list like the one in table 4-1, in which one column itemizes all the deal issues and the other does the same for relationship issues. See also "Tips on Managing Relationship Value." Then decide how to avoid making concessions on items in one column to save items in the other column.

Tips on Managing Relationship Value

If you want to keep a relationship on an even keel, manage it as you would any other activity that matters to you.

- **Create trust.** You create trust when you demonstrate that your words and actions are in harmony. So avoid making commitments you may be unable to honor, and always do what you have committed to do and when you've committed to do it. You also create trust when you acknowledge and demonstrate respect for the other party's most important interests.

- **Communicate.** The different parties should communicate their interests, their capabilities, and their concerns to each other. For example, if you agreed to complete an employee-satisfaction survey for the HR director within thirty days but have hit a logjam, communicate that information to him or her.

- **Never sweep mistakes under the rug.** Mistakes are bound to happen. Acknowledging and addressing them—quickly— is always your best course of action.

- **Ask for feedback.** If everything appears to be going as planned, never assume that the other party sees it the same way. Proactively work to uncover problems. The other person will respect you for it. Ask questions such as these: "Is everything happening as you expected?" "Did those survey results reach you on schedule?" "Did my report cover all the important points?"

TABLE 4-1

Categorizing the Issues in a Negotiation

Deal Issues	Relationship Issues
Price at different volume break points	Recognition of mutual long-term goals
Service agreements	Recognition of individual goals and interests
Replacement of obsolete equipment	Future opportunities for collaboration
Disputed resolutions	Continued trust and respect
Termination terms	
Assignment of the vendor's respon-sibilities under the contract	

Source: Adapted with permission from Danny Ertel, "Turning Negotiation into a Corporate Capability," *Harvard Business Review*, May–June 1999, 62.

Don't look at the negotiation as a seesaw in which improving the relationship must result in a loss in the deal itself. Instead, imagine the two rising or falling in tandem. According to Ertel,

A strong relationship creates trust, which allows the parties to share information more freely, which in turn leads to more creative and valuable agreements and to a greater willingness to continue working together. But when a deal is struck that is not very attractive to one or both parties, chances are that they will invest less time and effort in working together, they will become more wary in communicating with each other, and their relationship will grow strained.[4]

Figure 4-2 illustrates Ertel's view of the deal-relationship cycle. In poorly handled negotiations, exploitation of the deal by one party creates a *vicious* circle of distrust and a withholding of information. Both the deal and the relationship eventually suffer. A zero-sum mentality eventually prevails. In skillfully handled bargaining, negotiators do not feel compelled to trade a good relationship for a good deal. As a result, they trade information and creative ideas more freely, expanding the possibilities of the negotiation. This leads to a *virtuous* circle of improved trust and deals that satisfy the core interests of all parties.

FIGURE 4-2

The Deal-Relationship Cycle

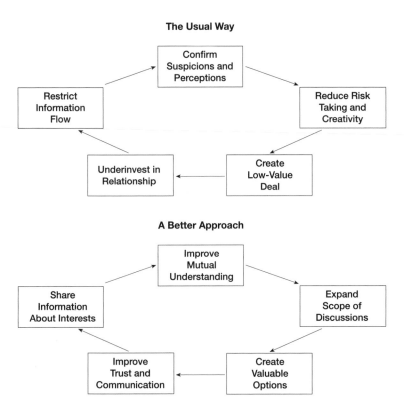

Source: Adapted with permission from Danny Ertel, "Turning Negotiation into a Corporate Capability," *Harvard Business Review*, May–June 1999, 64.

If relationships rank high among your organization's strategic goals, be forewarned that you could pay a personal price in pursuing them. Why? Because many companies still talk out of both sides of their mouths. On the one hand, they say that long-term relationships matter. On the other hand, they generally reward negotiators for delivering on monetary or other measurable values: the most advantageous settlement, the lowest-cost supplier contract, the most favorable contract terms, and so forth. We'll examine this problem—and its remedies—more closely later in this book.

Summing Up

This chapter examined the relationship value that plays a part in so many of today's agreements:

- Flatter organizations and companies' desire to build long-term links with suppliers are two important reasons why relationships matter in many of today's negotiations.

- Relationship value moderates extreme value-claiming behavior. Negotiating parties understand that trying too hard to claim value today means possibly losing opportunities to claim value in future transactions.

- Parties who perceive no relationship value will aggressively claim value.

- Even when both parties recognize relationship value, they may place unequal weight on that value. This can lead to a manipulative situation in which the party who values the relationship less pushes to claim more deal value from the party to whom the relationship matters more.

- Skillful negotiators separate the deal from the broader relationship and avoid making concessions in one category to save something in the other.

Leveraging Chapter Insights: Critical Questions

- Of all the parties with whom you regularly negotiate, which of the relationships do you value the most? What steps do you take, if any, to cultivate those relationships? What might you do differently to better maintain those relationships?

- Think of an upcoming, important negotiation you'll participate in. What are the deal issues related to that negotiation? What are the relationship issues?

CHAPTER FIVE

Four Key Concepts

Your Starting Points

Key Topics Covered in This Chapter

- *BATNA (best alternative to a negotiated agreement)*
- *Reservation price*
- *ZOPA (zone of possible agreement)*
- *Value creation through trades*

I N ALL YOUR negotiations as an HR professional, a negotiated agreement is advantageous only when a better option is not available. Consider this example: One of your best employees, Brian, is being courted by another company. Replacing him will be costly, but perhaps not as costly as negotiating some combination of financial inducements and work changes that will persuade Brian to stay and keep on contributing. Your mental calculator tells you that the cost of these inducements is less painful than your only other option—losing a star employee.

To successfully negotiate any agreement, you must know the following:

- Your best alternative to a negotiated agreement

- The minimum threshold of terms for a negotiated deal

- How flexible the other party is willing to be, and what trade-offs they're willing to make

Three concepts are especially important for establishing this framework: BATNA, reservation price, and ZOPA. This chapter develops these three concepts, using distributive negotiations as examples. It then expands the framework to include a fourth concept: value creation through trade, switching to integrative negotiations as examples. This switch also illustrates how the concepts of reservation price and ZOPA shift when you move from distributive to integrative negotiations.

BATNA

Your *BATNA*, or best alternative to a negotiated agreement, a concept developed by Roger Fisher and William Ury, is your preferred course of action in the absence of an agreement. Knowing your BATNA means knowing what you will do or what will happen if you fail to reach agreement in the negotiation at hand. Consider this example:

> *Thomas, an HR consultant, is planning to negotiate with Marta, a potential client, about a month-long assignment in which Thomas would prepare job descriptions for all the jobs in Marta's company. It's not clear what fee arrangement Thomas will be able to negotiate, or even if he and Marta will reach an agreement. So before Thomas meets with Marta, he considers his BATNA—his best alternative to an acceptable agreement. In this case, he defines his BATNA as spending that month developing employment-trend studies for an existing client—work that he calculates he can bill out at $15,000.*

Always know your BATNA before entering into any negotiation. Otherwise, you won't know whether a deal makes sense or when to walk away. The story in "A King Who Knew His BATNA" illustrates how having a clear BATNA can result in the best possible outcome. People who enter negotiations without defining their BATNA ahead of time put themselves in a weak position. When negotiators don't have a clearly defined BATNA, some will reject a good offer that is much better than their alternatives because they feel overly optimistic. For example, Fred has brought a damage suit against a former employer. That employer has offered to settle out of court for $80,000. But Fred wants more. "I know I'm in the right and can get what I want if I don't settle but go to court instead," he tells himself. Going to court is his best alternative to the $80,000 settlement offer. But how good is that alternative? Fred hasn't done a thorough job of estimating the probability of his winning in court or the size of a potential award. In other words, he has no real definition of this alternative. Therefore, he can't make an informed decision about how good the settlement offer is.

A King Who Knew His BATNA

Long before the acronym BATNA was invented, savvy negotiators kept their best alternatives in mind as they dealt with opponents. Consider France's Louis XI, one of the craftiest monarchs in fifteenth-century Europe. When England's Edward IV brought his army across the Channel to grab territory from his weaker rival, the French king decided to bargain. Knowing that his BATNA was to fight a long and costly war, Louis calculated that it was safer and cheaper to strike a deal with Edward. So Louis signed a peace treaty with the English in 1475, paying 50,000 crowns up front and an annuity of 50,000 crowns for the rest of Edward's life (which proved short). To seal the deal, Louis treated his royal counterpart and the English army to forty-eight hours of eating, drinking, and merrymaking. As an added token, he assigned the Cardinal of Bourbon to be Edward's "jolly companion" and to forgive his sins as he committed them.

As Edward and his army staggered back to their boats, ending the Hundred Years' War, Louis remarked: "I have chased the English out of France more easily than my father ever did; he drove them out by force of arms while I have driven them out by force of meat pies and good wine." Such is the power of negotiating when you know your BATNA.

In other cases in which negotiators fail to identify a BATNA ahead of time, there is some risk that they will accept a weak offer, one that is less favorable than what they could have obtained elsewhere if there were no agreement. ("I probably have some other options, but this seems like a good deal.")

Strong and Weak BATNAs

Your best alternative to a negotiated agreement determines the point at which you can say no to an unfavorable proposal, and how advantageous that point is to you will vary depending on the strength of your BATNA. If your BATNA is strong, you can negotiate for more favorable terms, knowing that you have something better to fall back on if a deal cannot be arranged. A weaker BATNA, on the other hand, puts you in a less powerful bargaining position. Consider the position of Thomas, the HR consultant in our earlier example. Suppose he had no other work lined up. In that case, his BATNA might consist of sitting around waiting for the phone to ring—a vulnerable position to be in while negotiating with a potential new client. A consultant in this sort of position would feel compelled to accept almost any offer— because he'd have no other prospects in the pipeline.

Whenever a negotiator has a weak BATNA (or hasn't taken the time to define a BATNA), it becomes difficult to walk away from a proposal—no matter how paltry its terms. Worse, if the other party *knows* that its opponent has a weak BATNA—has no other attractive options—the weak party then is in no position to negotiate. Not that this stops some BATNA-less people from trying to drive a hard bargain. For example, in late 2001, an organized group of unemployed men and women in France threatened to strike if the government failed to meet their demand for higher unemployment benefits. Needless to say, this group had little negotiating power.

Take a minute to think about your own best alternative to whatever negotiation you are currently preparing for. Do you have one? If so, is your BATNA strong or weak? Can you quantify it; that is, describe it in measurable terms?

Improving Your Position

A weak BATNA is not the end of the world. Whatever hand you've been dealt, you've got three strategies for strengthening your position:

1. Improve your BATNA.

2. Identify the other side's BATNA.

3. Weaken the other party's BATNA.

Let's examine each of these options more closely.

IMPROVE YOUR BATNA. Thomas, our HR consultant, has $15,000 of other work he can turn to if negotiations with Marta fail. But he might be able to expand that other work, thereby *improving* his BATNA and giving himself an even stronger hand during the negotiations. For instance, he might call his current client and say, "You know those employment-trend studies you asked me to develop? For a slightly higher fee—say, $5,000 more—I could expand the scope of those studies to include preparation of an employee handbook. Would you like me to do that?" If Thomas got the go-ahead to expand the project in this way, his new BATNA would be higher—$20,000.

Anything you can do to improve your BATNA will strengthen your negotiating position. Take a minute to think of ways you could do that, given your current circumstances.

If you have a strong BATNA—and if you are certain that it's much stronger than anything the other side can muster—don't be shy about it. Discreetly let the other side know that you're negotiating from a strong position.

IDENTIFY THE OTHER SIDE'S BATNA. Knowing the other party's BATNA further strengthens your negotiating position. Is their alternative to a deal stronger or weaker than yours? Do your best to estimate the other side's BATNA. For instance, Thomas would have a stronger bargaining hand if, by doing a little sleuthing, he found out that Marta would have to pay $25,000 to another firm for the same work she's considering having Thomas do. Twenty-five thousand dollars would thus be Marta's BATNA; knowing that would help Thomas bargain more effectively. Better still, a little more sleuthing might reveal that the consulting firms that make up Thomas's competition were booked solid for the next four months. If the work for Marta has to be done soon, she would have a very weak BATNA under these conditions. And Thomas could pursue negotiations with confidence: "My price is $30,000, and I can start the work later this month."

When measuring you BATNA against the other side's, you likely won't know exactly what the other side's BATNA is. It's important not to be swayed by your perceptions of the relative positions. "A Caution on BATNA Values" offers a guide to keeping things realistic.

Clearly, knowing the other side's BATNA can give you a decided edge in negotiating. But how do you obtain that knowledge? The other party won't tell you their BATNA unless it's very strong. They may even bluff about it, attempting to give the impression that its BATNA is better than it really is. Sometimes, however, you can gain information about the other party's circumstances. Asking questions during the negotiation can help you learn about the other side's BATNA, but you can also do some digging in advance of the bargaining. For example:

- Contact sources within your industry.

- Check potentially relevant business publications.

- Review annual reports (or public filings).

- Ask questions informally of the negotiator or others within his or her company.

A Caution on BATNA Values

Although it's essential that you define your own BATNA and try to estimate the other party's, be aware that most people don't estimate BATNA values accurately. For example, David Lax and James Sebenius describe an experiment involving estimating the value of a company that's up for sale. "Even given identical business information, balance sheets, income statements, and the like," the authors write, "those assigned to buy the company typically rate its true value as low, while those assigned to sell it give much higher best estimates. Neutral observers tend to rank the potential someplace in between."[a]

The lesson? Personal perspective can strongly influence the way people assign a value to their BATNA. To avoid this trap, view your potential BATNA as objectively as possible. And check your thinking with a neutral third party.

[a] David A. Lax and James K. Sebenius, *The Manager as Negotiator* (New York: Free Press, 1986), 57–58.

- Imagine what your interests, preferences, and needs would be if you were in the other party's position.

By estimating your negotiation counterpart's BATNA, you gain a clearer understanding of how far you can push for your best terms during the bargaining. But other knowledge is equally important. For instance, find out everything you can about the other party's broader concerns, industry, corporate structure, and other deals and goals. The more you know about these, the more you can find creative ways to meet *the other side's* interests—preferably at low cost to *you*.

WEAKEN THE OTHER PARTY'S BATNA. Anything that weakens the other side's alternative to a deal will improve your relative position. In some cases, you can weaken the other side's BATNA directly. For example:

> *PeoplePower, Inc., a large, Texas-based HR consulting firm, had been acquiring independently operated rivals in the northeastern United States and was in preliminary negotiations with Jim Norris and Barbara Stanley for purchase of BestHR, the company they had founded in central Connecticut. When those negotiations began, Jim and Barbara felt confident that BestHR could fetch a high price, because another interested party in the area, Bemis Associates, had been angling for years to buy Jim and Barbara out. "That's a fine business you have there," Daniel Bemis had told them repeatedly. "If you ever want to sell it, talk to me." Daniel had even hinted at $800,000.*
>
> *Jim and Barbara thought of $800,000 as their best alternative to negotiating a sale price with PeoplePower. "If we can play Bemis Associates off PeoplePower," Barbara told Jim, "we should be able to get a still better price—maybe $1 million." But things didn't work out that way. Later that week, Jim spotted a startling headline in the local newspaper: "Bemis Associates to Be Acquired by Texas-Based HR Giant." Jim and Barbara's attractive alternative had just evaporated, leaving them in a weak position to demand a handsome purchase price from PeoplePower.*

In this example, PeoplePower neutralized BestHR's alternative deal. By acquiring Bemis Associates, PeoplePower took Jim and Barbara's $800,000 BATNA off the table, leaving continued operation of the business as their only alternative to an offer from People-Power. In this way, PeoplePower strengthened its bargaining position by weakening BestHR's BATNA.

When You Have No Alternatives

Nothing puts a negotiator in a weaker position than having *no* alternative to a deal. In this case, the other party can dictate the terms of the agreement with impunity. The BATNA-less party becomes a deal *taker*, not a deal *maker*. If you find yourself in this dangerous situation, brainstorm alternatives. For instance, Jim and Barbara could consider enticing another potential acquirer into the game—perhaps a rival HR consulting firm.

Are you without an alternative in any of your current negotiations—with your boss, an employee, a vendor, a peer manager? If so, stop to think about how you could create a BATNA. Think, too, about which type of alternative would *most* strengthen your hand.

BATNA Is Not Always Simple

BATNA is a straightforward concept. But *applying* it isn't as simple as we've made it appear. Most business negotiations involve many variables, some of which the parties can't easily quantify or compare. This complexity can make BATNAs unclear. For example, suppose you're contemplating hiring a large research firm to design an employee-opinion survey. The firm wants to charge a fee of $26,000 and offers a 15 percent discount on a future engagement if you sign on for the current job. A friend of yours, however, is launching a new freelance business focusing on survey design. He offers to charge you $18,000 for the work. But because he's still operating on a shoestring, he's willing to offer only a 5 percent discount on a future engagement. In addition, he wouldn't be able to start the work for another two months. As you negotiate with the research firm, your friend's offer would seem to be your BATNA. But is it a *useful* benchmark of what you could achieve in the absence of an agreement?

If price were the only issue, the agreement with your friend *would* be your BATNA. However, there are substantial differences between the two potential agreements beyond just price. To be sure, you could get your friend to do the work at a lower price, and you like the idea of supporting his budding freelance business. In addition, you suspect that you may get more personalized attention from your friend during the project than you'd get from the people at the research firm. But you'd have to wait months for the friend to start work on the project. This worries you, because you've promised the vice president of HR that you'd have the survey ready in six weeks. And your friend doesn't have the track record of the larger firm. Most negotiations involve similar complexities.

In a transaction that involves price and various other factors, such as the survey example above, you can give your BATNA sharper definition by assigning a monetary value to the various non-price factors and adjusting the BATNA value by that amount. For example, you could assign a price penalty of $4,000 to your friend's offer to reflect the longer timeline for the work. At the same time, you could add a price premium of $500 to that same offer to reflect the fact that you'll likely receive more personal attention from your friend as the project progresses. Netting these adjustments, you have $3,500 (or $4,000 – $500). Add these to your friend's offer of $18,000, and you get $21,500—your new, more clearly defined BATNA. If the research firm offered to reduce its fee to $22,500, you'd be indifferent as to which deal you'd accept—at least theoretically.

Not all situations are amenable to price adjustments, for the simple reason that price isn't always the fulcrum of negotiated deals. Qualitative issues also matter. For example, a person who is negotiating the purchase of a small business may be concerned with *when* the transaction will take place and with the *level* of the current owner's involvement as a consultant. In these cases, the negotiator must be able to make trade-offs in both sizing up the deal and developing his or her BATNA.

You'll need to consider all of these issues when developing a strategy for negotiation. See assessment tool 5-1 to help identify your BATNA.

Assessment Tool 5-1
Identify Your BATNA

1. **What are your alternatives to a negotiated agreement?**

   List what your alternatives will be if the negotiation ends without agreement.

   1.

   2.

   3.

   4.

   Review the list. Which of these alternatives would be best?

2. **What could improve your BATNA? Consider . . .**

   Are there any better arrangements you can make with parties other than the party you're currently negotiating with?

   Is there any way to remove or alter any constraint that makes your current BATNA unfavorable? What? How?

   Is there any way to change the terms you bring to the negotiation that could improve your BATNA? What? How?

3. **Write what your new BATNA will be if you succeed in improving it.**

SOURCE: Harvard ManageMentor® Negotiating.

Reservation Price

Your *reservation price* or *position* (also referred to as your *walk-away*) is the least favorable point at which you will accept an agreement. Your reservation price *stems* from your BATNA but usually is not *identical* to the BATNA. If the negotiation in question centers on money, however, and a credible dollar offer is your BATNA, then your reservation price would be approximately equal to your BATNA. Consider the following example:

> *Thomas, our HR consultant, is currently paying $20 per square foot for suburban office space. The location is satisfactory, and he believes that the price is fair. But he wouldn't mind paying more to be closer to his downtown clients. While preparing to negotiate with a commercial landlord for an office lease in a downtown high-rise, he decides that he will not pay more than $30 per square foot. That's Thomas's reservation price. If the landlord insists on more, Thomas can walk away and attempt to lease space in a different building. Or he can stay where he is at $20 per square foot (his BATNA).*
>
> *At the end of a lengthy negotiation session, the landlord declares that she will not accept less than $35 per square foot—and she won't budge. Thomas graciously terminates the negotiation and walks away from the deal.*

In this example, Thomas's reservation price is different from his BATNA. His BATNA in this case is the current rent he's paying at the current location of his office: $20 per square foot. But the new location has different characteristics that enter into the equation. It's closer to customers, and it may be a more attractive space with greater workplace utility. Thomas would be willing to assume the added expense and the hassle of moving, even if it meant paying $30 per square foot. Anything more than that, however, he considers unacceptable. Note, then, that there's a subtle difference between a person's BATNA and his or her reservation price.

The fact that Thomas's prospective landlord would not take less than $35 per square foot suggests that $35 is *her* reservation price.

See assessment tool 5-2 for help on setting your reservation price.

Assessment Tool 5-2
Set Your Reservation Price

1. **Explore the variables that affect your reservation price, or "walk away."**

   What is the value to you of the current negotiation?

   How does this value compare to the value of your BATNA?

   What other values or stakeholders do you need to consider?

   If there is a dollar number involved in the negotiation, what is the lowest amount that you can consider?

   What are the minimum non-dollar terms that you would consider?

2. **Evaluate the trade-offs between issues and interests.**

   Which issue(s) or term(s) do you care most about in this negotiation?

   Are any of these issues or terms linked? (That is, does more or less of what you want on one issue give you more or less flexibility on any of the others?)

   How much of what you want on one issue or term would you trade off against another?

   Are there different package arrangements that would be equivalent in value to you?

3. **Articulate the parameters of your reservation price.**

   (The resulting terms create the context for you to evaluate alternative proposals.)

SOURCE: Harvard ManageMentor® Negotiating.

ZOPA

The *ZOPA*, or zone of possible agreement, is a third key concept to master as you hone your negotiation skills. ZOPA is the area or range in which a deal that satisfies *both* parties might take place. Put another way, it is the set of agreements that potentially satisfy both parties.

Each party's reservation price determines one end of the ZOPA. The ZOPA itself exists (if at all) in the *overlap* between these high and low limits; that is, between the parties' reservation prices. Consider this example:

> Sarah, HR director for Montana Enterprises, has received approval from the company's CEO and board to create Montana Enterprises University—a business school that will focus on executive development. She is preparing to negotiate a contract with EduServ, an educational-services firm, to help her set up and staff the university. She sets a reservation price of $275,000. "That's as high as I'm willing to go," Sarah tells herself. Naturally, she would prefer paying less if that opportunity arises. Unbeknownst to her, Charles, the account manager at EduServ with whom Sarah will be negotiating, has set a reservation price of $250,000. That is the least he'll take for the job. The ZOPA, therefore, is the range between $250,000 and $275,000, as shown in figure 5-1. Sarah and Charles might haggle a bit in reaching agreement, but an agreement that falls within this range would satisfy each of them. The haggling might unfold as follows:

Sarah: Our budget would accommodate about $255,000 for this project. What are your thoughts about that?

Charles: Thanks, but I believe that this kind of service is very much in demand these days, and I'm certain our other clients could meet our fees.

Sarah: Well, you may be right. But we'd like to get moving on this project. I'd be willing to go to $260,000 now if we could reach an agreement.

Charles: At $265,000, I think I could get agreement from my people.

Sarah: Then $265,000 it is.

Figure 5-1 illustrates the ZOPA in Sarah's and Charles's negotiation.

In this commonplace example, each party had a reservation price, and they bargained within the ZOPA. In doing so, each got a better price than his or her walk-away. We can assume here that neither knew his or her counterpart's reservation price. But as you might imagine, that knowledge would have been extremely valuable. For example, if Sarah had known Charles's reservation price, she might have driven a tougher bargain, holding out for something closer to $250,000.

Sometimes you can estimate the other party's reservation price. If, for example, Sarah knew that equivalent services were costing $260,000, she could assume with some confidence that Charles' reservation price would be close to that figure. Likewise, if investigation revealed that Charles was highly motivated to forge an agreement, Sarah could offer less.

Now consider what would happen if the numbers were reversed—that is, if Sarah had set a reservation price of $250,000 and Charles had set a reservation price of $275,000. That is, Sarah won't pay more than $250,000, and Charles wouldn't take anything less than $275,000. In this case, there would be no overlap in the ranges in which the two parties could reach agreement—no ZOPA. No agreement would be

FIGURE 5-1

Zone of Possible Agreement

Source: Adapted from *Harvard Business Essentials: Negotiation* (Boston: Harvard Business School Press, 2003), 24.

possible, no matter how skilled the negotiators—unless there were other elements of value to be considered or one or both sides' reservation prices changed. For example, suppose Charles learned that Sarah was also considering launching a new training series at Montana Enterprises. In this case, he might offer her a few hours of conversation about potential training programs with an EduServ trainer who has the time available because she's between engagements. That kind of "sweetener" doesn't cost Charles's company much, and might break the impasse in a case where he and Sarah had no ZOPA. This kind of information can enable two bargainers to create new value in what becomes an integrative negotiation.

Value Creation Through Trades

Another fundamental concept of negotiation is *value creation through trades*. This concept holds that negotiating parties can improve their positions by trading the values at their disposal. Value creation through trades occurs in integrative negotiations. It usually takes the form of each party *getting* something it wants by *giving* something else it values much less. Consider the following example:

> *William is the HR director for Starlight, a publishing company. He's negotiating starting salary and benefits with Lisa, a candidate for a position in Starlight's editorial department. The two can't seem to agree on a starting salary—Lisa insists on $50,000 a year, while William says he can't go higher than $40,000.*
>
> *However, as the discussion continues, Lisa mentions that she's taking continuing education courses in the evenings at a nearby university. William asks her how much she's paying for tuition, and she tells him, "A thousand dollars per course." As it turns out, Lisa wants to take five more courses. William realizes that if Starlight paid the tuition on the remaining courses, the company would be spending $5,000 less than if he agreed to Lisa's $50,000 starting salary. And, Starlight would save on payroll taxes by paying the tuition instead of the higher salary. The $5,000 paid by the company in tuition could be considered*

income for Lisa, and if so, she would have to pay income tax on it. Nevertheless, William suspects that Lisa would highly value the opportunity to take the additional courses without having to shell out any more cash.

William proposes the deal: Starlight will pay for the rest of Lisa's courses and pay her a starting salary of $40,000. Lisa accepts the proposal enthusiastically. Both feel extremely satisfied with the agreement.

In this case, two individuals were able to *create* value, not simply claim it. Both emerged from the bargaining feeling deeply satisfied with the outcome. This mutual satisfaction was possible because the terms exchanged had only modest value to their original holders, but had exceptional value to their new owners.

Think for a moment about the negotiations you're currently preparing for. Are you engaging in a tug of war with your counterparts in a win–lose framework? If so, think of ways that you might be able to satisfy the other side with something that would cost you very little. Consider the following:

- **You're negotiating terms with a potential new hire.** For the job candidate, the opportunity to work from a home office two days each week may produce great satisfaction while costing his or her employer nothing.

- **You're haggling over shared resources with the manager of another department in your company.** For that manager, greater value might be found in your offer of two high-powered workstations that your people rarely use. That manager may be able to offer something in exchange that you value more than he does—such as occasional use of extra office space in the other department.

- **You're negotiating with a vendor who will be providing your company with a series of training workshops.** The vendor may find greater value in an extended period for delivering the workshops. For you, spreading delivery of the series over several months might be of no great consequence. But for a vendor overwhelmed by training engagements, the extended schedule may have enormous value.

- **You're negotiating pay and other work conditions with the head of your company's union.** For union members, greater value may take the form of more rigorous safety measures on the shop floor, which might be relatively inexpensive for your company to install.

Few of the things that others value highly will have little value to you, and vice versa. But they do sometimes exist. With a little creative thought and probing, you can identify them. That's value creation. Just be sure that if you give something that other party values highly, then you ask for something in trade that *you* value highly.

Summing Up

This chapter has explained the fundamental concepts used by skilled negotiators.

- BATNA is the best alternative to a negotiated agreement. It is your preferred course of action in the absence of a deal. Knowing your BATNA means knowing what you will do or what will happen if you fail to reach agreement. Don't enter a negotiation without knowing your BATNA.

- If your BATNA is weak, do what you can to improve it. Anything that strengthens your BATNA improves your negotiating position.

- Identify the other side's BATNA. If it is strong, think of what you can do to weaken it.

- Reservation price is the price at which you will walk away from the negotiation. Always enter a negotiation with a clear reservation price.

- ZOPA is the zone of possible agreement. It is the area in which a deal will satisfy all parties. This area exists when the parties have different reservation prices, as when a property buyer is willing to pay up to $275,000 and the property seller is willing to take an offer that is at least $250,000.

- Value creation through trades is possible when a party has something he or she values less than does the other party—and vice versa. By trading these values, the parties lose little but gain a lot.

Leveraging Chapter Insights: Critical Questions

- Consider the negotiations you typically engage in at your company. In what percentage of these negotiations do you define a BATNA and a reservation price ahead of time? What steps can you take to ensure that you define a BATNA in *all* of your future negotiations?

- How do you go about estimating the other party's BATNA and reservation price before and during negotiations? Is your current process useful? If not, what might you do differently to form more accurate estimates in future negotiations?

- Think of a negotiation you're currently participating in at work. What forms of value, beyond price, would matter a lot to you in this particular bargaining situation? What forms of value do you think the other party might consider very important? What steps might you take to learn more about what the other party may value?

CHAPTER SIX

Preparing for a Negotiation

Nine Steps

Key Topics Covered in This Chapter

- *Defining a good outcome for you and the other side*

- *Identifying potential opportunities for value creation*

- *Identifying BATNA and reservation price*

- *Shoring up your BATNA*

- *Determining the authority levels of both sides in a negotiation*

- *Understanding your negotiation counterparts*

- *Preparing for flexibility*

- *Establishing criteria for fairness*

- *Altering the negotiation process in your favor*

EVERY IMPORTANT endeavor benefits from preparation. Negotiating is no different. In your negotiations as an HR executive, manager, or staff member, the more you know what you want, what you're willing to settle for, and what the other party values most, the more you improve your chances of negotiating a favorable agreement that benefits both parties. Consider the following example:

Laura, one of Phil's best employees, requested a meeting to talk about taking a six-month personal leave of absence that would not be covered under the Family and Medical Leave Act. She had expressed her interest in an extended leave several times over the past several months. Yet now she made a formal request for a meeting. Phil responded: "Let's meet a week from Tuesday at four o'clock to discuss it."

With so much going on in the department, Phil didn't want to think about how his unit would get its work done without Laura. So he avoided thinking about her request. "Maybe she'll change her mind or just forget about it," he mused. But she didn't.

When they finally met, Laura had carefully prepared for the conversation. She had picked potential starting and ending dates for her leave. She had checked with the HR department about leave policies and staffing issues. And she had anticipated the issues her boss would raise: Who will pick up the slack? How will deadlines be met? Who will take her place in team activities? Laura had prepared answers for each of these questions.

Phil, on the other hand, had done no such preparation. All he knew was that he didn't like the idea of extended leaves. "What if everybody decided to do this?" he muttered. "We'd have chaos around here." But whenever he raised an objection, Laura came back with an effective response. Phil wanted to suggest an alternative to such a long leave, but couldn't think of one.

In the end, Laura got her leave on her terms because she was prepared and Phil was not. Had he been prepared, Phil might have found common ground on which his unit's goals and Laura's goals could have been mutually satisfied.

For any negotiator, preparation means understanding your own position and interests, those of the other party, the issues at stake, and alternative solutions. It means learning as much as possible about the four concepts you read about in the previous chapter: your BATNA and reservation price and those of the other party's, the zone within which an agreement can be forged, and opportunities to create new forms of value. Preparation also means understanding the people with whom you'll be negotiating. In this chapter, we explore these and other preparation issues through nine steps.[1]

Step 1: Define a Good Outcome for You and the Other Side

Never enter into a negotiation without first asking yourself, "What would be a good outcome for me? What are my needs, and how do I prioritize them?" Then ask the same questions from the perspective of the other party.

In the example introduced earlier in this chapter, Phil, the manager, should have thought ahead to the outcomes that would have been good for him—outcomes that would allow his unit to achieve its goals. The most obvious would be for Laura *not* to go away for six months. But that isn't feasible, because the company does have a leave policy. And turning her down flat might prompt her to resign, creating a still bigger problem. But that's the extreme outcome. There are plenty of others that might enable Phil's unit to accomplish its work. For example:

- Negotiate a shorter leave.

- Schedule the leave for a slow part of the year.

- Ask Laura to develop a plan with her coworkers that clearly accommodates the unit's business needs.

Any of these outcomes might satisfy Phil.

But what about Laura's perspective? If she has any bargaining power, her concept of a good outcome will limit Phil's ability to produce the best outcome for himself. So as part of his preparation, Phil needs to put himself in her shoes and ask the same questions: "What would be a good outcome for Laura? What are her needs, and how does she prioritize them?" Logically, Phil can answer these questions only if he understands Laura and her motive in seeking a leave of absence in the first place.

Since Phil hasn't bothered to understand Laura's issues, let's play mind reader and find out what she's thinking.

I really need to spend more time with my son Nathan. He's a very unfocused teenager. And it shows in his school reports. He's not doing his homework, he's goofing off in class, and his grades are lousy. Someone needs to get him on track or he'll never get into a decent college or develop good work habits. Someone should be there when he gets home from school to enforce study habits and provide a family dinner during which we listen to each other. His father can't do it—he travels too much. And I can't do it with a full-time job. I don't get home until 6:30, and by then I'm pooped! That long commute is just killing me.

I need some time off to get that boy on track. Six months might do it. We really can't afford the lost income, but we can't let our son continue to drift either.

Had Phil prepared himself by learning why Laura wanted a leave, he would have been able to postulate one or more good outcomes from her perspective.

Without understanding your own and the other party's interests, you can't easily define a good outcome for yourself or postulate one for the other side. Yet it can be difficult to uncover the other person's interests, especially if the individual conceals them. Dialogue during a negotiation can sometimes reveal the two sides' interests, but not always—particularly in win-lose, distributive deals. If you can't identify the other side's interests, use every communication opportunity to probe for them. Assessment tool 6-1 provides an opportunity for you to brainstorm ways to gather these insights.

Assessment Tool 6-1
Assess the Other Side's Position and Interests

To learn as much as you can about the other side's interest and concerns, have you . . .

1. Contacted sources within the industry?

   Yes   No

2. Checked potentially relevant business publications?

   Yes   No

3. Reviewed its annual reports and public filings (if the other side is a company)?

   Yes   No

4. Asked questions informally of the negotiator or others (if he or she is representing a company)?

   Yes   No

5. Imagined what your interests, preferences, and needs would be if you were in the other party's position?

   Yes   No

Assess the other side's BATNA. What do you know . . .

About the other side's business circumstances?

How strong is the individual's or company's financial performance?

What is the company's strategy?

What are its key personal or corporate initiatives?

What competitive or other pressures does it face?

About the value this deal has to the other side?

How important is this negotiation to the other side at this time?

Is the negotiation necessary for the other side to meet a larger objective? (If so, describe the objective.)

About the availability of a replacement agreement?

Is what you're offering easy for the other person or company to find elsewhere?

Could the other side obtain it in time to meet its deadlines?

Has the other side already obtained bids from or initiated informal negotiations with anyone else?

Consider the terms the other side would like to see for the negotiation.

What broader business objectives would the other side like to see served by this negotiation?

What terms of this negotiation could hamper the other side's business growth?

What terms might you offer that would benefit the other side (at a low cost to you)?

SOURCE: Harvard ManageMentor® Negotiating.

Step 2: Identify Potential Value-Creation Opportunities

Once you understand what a good outcome would look like from your own and the other party's vantage point, you can identify areas of common ground, opportunities for compromise, and ways of making favorable trades. For instance, if Phil eventually recognized Laura's key issue as one of balance between work and family life, he could prepare himself with a handful of feasible alternatives that would enable both parties to attain most, if not all, of their goals. For example:

- **Reduced hours for Laura—9:00 a.m. to 2:00 p.m.** Phil reviews possible scheduling alternatives for Laura with the HR department before discussing them with Laura. He finds that a 9:00 a.m. to 2:00 p.m. workday has been offered in the past to employees in similar circumstances. This schedule would enable Laura to go home in time to be with her son, and Phil could use her salary reduction to hire a temp to fill the 2:00-to-5:00 p.m. time gap.

- **Telework from a home office from 8:00 a.m. to 3:30 p.m.** Likewise, Phil discovers through talking with the HR manager that the company has permitted other employees to telecommute. Working from her home from 8:00 a.m. to 3:30 p.m. would address Laura's interests with respect to her long commute, her desire to provide closer supervision for her son in the late afternoon, *and* her concern about losing significant income. In turn, Laura could address Phil's interests by developing a plan for timely delivery of all her work and participation in any meetings she would need to attend.

Indeed, Laura might see either of these alternatives as superior to her initial request for a six-month leave. Each option would have her at home in the early afternoon and still provide her with most—if not all—of her income. And neither would create serious problems for Phil's unit. In this sense, the negotiation would create new value. Laura would get the time she needed for work/life balance, and Phil would retain a good employee and keep his department running smoothly.

Any time negotiators create new value, they need to answer the question of who will claim that value. One party could claim 100 percent of it, or the two parties could share it in some way. Naturally, if you help create value during a negotiation, you'll want to claim a share—you're entitled to it. This is what sellers do in negotiated business acquisitions.

> *Wholesome Products, Inc., is being purchased by Conglomerated Foods in a friendly takeover. Although Wholesome's shares trade for $50 per share on the stock exchange, Conglomerated is willing to pay $65 per share. Why? Among other reasons, the acquirer sees valuable synergies in putting the two companies together. That extra value did not exist in Wholesome as a stand-alone company, and it might not exist if some other company were making the acquisition. But as Conglomerated sees it, adding Wholesome to its portfolio is equivalent to making two plus two equal five.*

In settling on a premium for the share price, both companies in this example are claiming their newly created value: Wholesome shareholders get more money. And even at the higher price, Conglomerated's managers thinks they have scored a success because of the anticipated synergies between the combined companies.

Step 3: Identify Your and the Other Side's BATNA and Reservation Price

The previous chapter discussed BATNA and reservation price at length. We mention these concepts again here because they constitute such important elements of preparing for a negotiation. To prepare for a successful negotiation, you need to define your strongest possible BATNA. (See "How Needy Are You?" for insights on how having a weak BATNA can undermine your position.)

How Needy Are You?

Author and consultant Jim Camp urges his readers to avoid appearing "needy," which he equates with having a weak BATNA. Shrewd bargainers will take advantage of any neediness they perceive in their negotiation counterparts. And tough negotiators will do whatever they can to encourage neediness in their counterparts:

> Tough negotiators are experts at recognizing this neediness in their adversaries, and expert in creating it as well. Negotiators with giant corporations, in particular, will heighten the expectations of their supplier adversaries, painting rosy, exaggerated scenarios for mega-orders, joint ventures, global alliances, all for the purposes of building neediness on the part of their adversary. . . . Then, when the neediness is well-established, they lower the boom with changes, exceptions, and . . . demands for concessions.[a]

How to avoid appearing needy? Build a strong BATNA—and let the other side know that you're prepared to walk away if it demands too many concessions.

For example, suppose you're negotiating salary with a highly qualified candidate for a hard-to-fill position in your company. In this case, you certainly don't want to let on that you've had a hard time filling the position. But you also need to build a strong BATNA. To illustrate, you could cast your net wider in attracting candidates for the position, so you'll have more than one highly qualified candidate to choose from. Or, you could think of creative ways your firm could accomplish the work defined in the position. For instance, you could redefine several employees' roles or redeploy people so that the activities described in the new job are covered by existing employees rather than handled by a newly hired person.

[a] Jim Camp, Start with No (New York: Crown, 2002), 22.

Getting back to the example of Phil and Laura, what is Phil's BATNA? The story doesn't give us enough details to know for certain, but it appears that Phil hasn't even thought about his BATNA. He doesn't have anyone waiting in the wings to replace Laura if he denies her request and she resigns. If he walks away from negotiating her leave request, he'll have to either (1) deal with a disgruntled employee if Laura stays, or (2) hire a replacement if she leaves. Neither is a pleasant prospect from Phil's viewpoint. If Laura surmises this during her preparation, she'll put herself in a better position to negotiate.

Laura's BATNA is also limited. If she doesn't negotiate with Phil, she'll likely get her leave, because company policy does provide for leaves. But saying, "Give me a leave or I'll sue" would undermine her standing in the company—something she doesn't want. So her best alternative to a negotiated deal may involve resigning and looking for a new job six months down the road. If Phil understands this, he'll be better prepared to bargain.

Step 4: Shore Up Your BATNA

As we saw in chapter 5, anything you can do to improve your best alternative to a negotiated deal will put you in a stronger bargaining position. In the case of Phil and Laura, Phil could have improved his BATNA while preparing for the meeting with Laura. How? He could have identified another employee who would be willing and able to step into Laura's shoes if she drove too hard a bargain. Laura's strongest bargaining chip is her importance to the smooth functioning of the unit. If she could be made "replaceable," that chip would lose its power.

Shoring up your BATNA is an important part of preparing for a negotiation, but it's not limited to the pre-negotiations phase. Good negotiators work to improve their BATNAs before *and* during deliberations with the other party.

Step 5: Anticipate Authority Issues

Conventional wisdom holds that your negotiation counterpart must have full authority to forge an agreement. Otherwise, you risk falling victim to the old "car dealer" trick, where just as you're about to reach agreement with the salesman, he says, "I'll have to clear this with my manager." In other words, car dealerships use the negotiation with the salesman to bring you to your bottom line; the second negotiation, with the manager, aims to push you beyond it.

When you negotiate with the person who has the power to sign on the dotted line, you have real advantages:

- All of your reasoning is heard directly by the decision maker.

- The benefits of the good relationship you've built during the bargaining will likely be reflected in the agreement and its implementation.

- You reduce the likelihood of disputes or misinterpretation of particular provisions.

- You avoid being subjected to the "car dealer" trick described above.

- If you want the other party to personally desire a deal with you, you'll stand a better chance of making that happen by ensuring that the real decision maker isn't somewhere in the background of the negotiation.

As an HR professional, you probably encounter some negotiation situations in which it's hard to discern who the real decision makers are. For example, if you're working to secure a contract with a large company that provides benefit-management or training services, the person the firm sends to talk with you about terms may not have the final say about how those terms read. To gain the advantages described above, you need to do whatever you can to identify the real decision maker. Don't be afraid to ask, "Who will make the decision about the final terms?" If that person is not already actively participating in the negotiation, suggest that he or she be included. "If Mr. Jones will be making the decision, wouldn't it be best if he participate in our meeting? That way we can avoid misunderstandings and save time." If *your* final decision maker is participating in the discussion, point out that fact. Then press the other side to reciprocate.

Also, try to find out *how* the other side will make their decision. Is the decision up to one individual? A team? A committee? Will the decision be kicked around the organization for a week or two? Don't be shy about asking point-blank, "What decision-making process do you use for an issue like this one?"

As a practical matter, you won't always be able to negotiate with the individual (or committee) who retains final authority. Even deals negotiated by the president of the United States—arguably the most powerful individual in the nation—must be ratified by the U.S. Senate. In that case, recognize that bargaining with negotiators who lack full authority offers advantages of its own. Specifically, these individuals may be freer to discuss their company's interests and to explore creative options. If you're negotiating with someone who does not have full authority, view this situation as an opportunity to refrain from committing to any agreement. But observe these cautions:

- Confirm the ground rule that neither side will be committing his or her company to any agreement during the negotiation. (If the other side isn't committing, you shouldn't have to either.)

- Suggest using the discussion to explore your respective interests and to come up with creative options and packages.

- When negotiating about price, leave yourself some *wiggle room* in case the final decision maker pushes harder in a second round of bargaining. If there's no wiggle room, strongly convey the message that this is your best offer.

Instead of insisting that your bargaining counterpart have full authority, it's more important that you *determine* the authority level of the person with whom you will be negotiating. That way, you can plan your strategy accordingly. Thus, try to ascertain answers to the following questions:

- Who will participate in the negotiations?

- What is that person's title and area of responsibility?

- How long has the other party's representative been with his or her company?

- How is the other company structured? For example, is it very hierarchical, with significant decision-making powers concentrated at the top? Or is it relatively decentralized?

- How is the other negotiator viewed within his or her organization? Is he or she generally respected and listened to, or not?

Granted, this information may be difficult to obtain, but it's well worth digging for. If you know other people in your negotiation counterpart's industry or business community, make an informal, off-the-record phone call or two to see what you can find out.

If you learn that the negotiator for the other side has very little formal authority and is not respected or listened to by the real decision makers, you've got a problem. Working with this person may simply waste your time. Your response? Try to get another representative to participate in the negotiations. One tactful way to do this is to suggest that you will be bringing a colleague to the deliberations—someone who has more formal authority than you or who can give the proceedings more weight by making a joint recommendation. Then request that the other party do the same.

As for your side, always know exactly how much authority you have in a negotiation. For example:

- Are you authorized only to commit to a predetermined range of terms for which you've received approval from a committee? What if you can negotiate something better? What would the committee consider to be better?

- Are you authorized to commit to an agreement that meets certain financial objectives, with freedom to structure other terms in the best way you see fit? Would your company prefer that you bring such an agreement back for formal review and approval?

- Is your authority limited to price but not to other creative options that have no major financial implications?

- Are you authorized to provide information about your company's needs, interests, and preferences if the other side engages in a good-faith, reciprocal exchange?

If you don't get the authority you seek in a particular negotiation, don't despair. The good news is that you won't unwittingly overstep your bounds. And again, less authority has its advantages. Checking with your superiors can be strategically helpful. It may also free you to exercise more of your own creativity in inventing options for a mutually beneficial agreement. See assessment tool 6-2 for help with anticipating authority issues during a negotiation.

Assessment Tool 6-2
Authority—Theirs and Yours

Their authority
(Learn as much as possible about the individuals on the other side.)

1. Who will be participating in the negotiation?

2. What are the formal titles and areas of responsibility of the person(s) with whom you will be negotiating?

3. What are their ages/how long have they been with the company/what other relevant experience do they have?

4. If you're negotiating with another company, how is the firm structured? (Is it hierarchical, with significant

decision-making powers concentrated at the top, or is it relatively decentralized?)

5. If you're negotiating with another company, how are members of the company's negotiating team viewed within their organization? (Are they generally respected and listened to, or not? Rely on contacts outside the organization, if available.)

6. What are the other party's additional interests outside of work? (Consider sports, hobbies, volunteer interests, political orientation, children, and other potential interests.)

Your authority
(Confirm in as much detail as possible.)

Which of the following kind of agreements are you authorized to make?
(Complete as appropriate.)

Only a predetermined agreement for which committee approval has been obtained? (If yes, describe. If you can also negotiate something "better" beyond the predetermined agreement, what does the committee consider "better"?)

Only an agreement that meets certain objectives? (What are the objectives? Do you have freedom to structure the agreement in the best way you can?)

The committee would prefer that you bring an agreement back for formal review and approval?

Your authority is limited on dollar issues but not on other creative options without significant financial implications?

You're authorized to provide information about your company's needs, interests, and preferences if the other side engages in a good-faith, reciprocal exchange?

SOURCE: Harvard ManageMentor® Negotiating.

Step 6: Learn All You Can About the Other Side

At its core, negotiating is an interpersonal activity. Seasoned negotiators understand this and make a point of learning as much as they can about the people with whom they'll be interacting. Who are those individuals? Are they experienced negotiators or novices? Are they aggressive or are they conflict-avoiding accommodators? Is the culture of their organization bureaucratic or entrepreneurial? Are they authorized to forge an agreement, or must they run back to their bosses for instructions and approval? Perhaps more important, what are they hoping to achieve and how critical is this negotiation to their business?

You need to seek answers to these questions not only while preparing for a negotiation but also during the deliberations themselves. You should, for example, ask the other side to provide the names and titles of its negotiating team members. Once you have those names, ask around your company or around the industry, "What can anyone tell me about these people? Has anyone dealt with them before?" Their job titles may shed light on whether they're authorized to approve the terms of an agreement.

If you're preparing for a negotiation with a single individual—a job seeker, an employee, a company executive, your boss, a one-person consulting firm—don't assume that you can forgo this stage of your preparation. To put yourself in the best bargaining position possible, you'll still need to anticipate that other person's interests, goals, concerns, and hopes—as well as how he or she perceives the significance of the upcoming negotiation. All these issues play just as crucial a role in the bargaining as the question of authority does. The more you know the person, the better your ability to fashion an agreement that serves both of you.

Step 7: Build Flexibility into the Process

Like most other aspects of life, negotiations don't always follow a predictable or linear path. Relationships sometimes sour. Unanticipated developments cause one party to withdraw or freeze talks. Newly discovered opportunities encourage the other side to drive a harder bargain. One negotiator is replaced by another. Such developments mean that both parties must prepare themselves to move forward without a clear roadmap. They must also exercise patience, because many negotiations unfold over a series of stops and starts. If you've earned your spurs in companies where "let's get it done now" is the watchword, you may not be naturally disposed to patience. But it's this very virtue that you'll need most in negotiating.

To build flexibility into your negotiations:

- Start with the assumption that the process will not unfold in a predictable, linear fashion.

- Be prepared for changes on both sides—including new people and unanticipated developments.

- Treat every change as an opportunity for learning.

Flexibility is important, particularly within the context of your larger goal. If, for example, your company's goal in a negotiation is to acquire a particular business, keep that goal uppermost in your mind if you're participating in the bargaining process. Alter the pace as needed. Be patient when unanticipated delays occur. But never allow these bumps in the road to make you lose sight of your firm's ultimate goal.

Step 8: Gather Fairness Standards and Criteria

In any negotiation, both parties want to believe that any agreement they reach will be fair and reasonable. And if the parties expect to have a continuing relationship, a sense of fairness and reasonableness carries that much more importance. Neither party should feel that it's been forced into a bad outcome.

In many industries, bargainers can use "objective" criteria to establish what's fair and reasonable. For example, let's revisit the example of an HR professional who's looking for a consulting company to provide services for a business school that her company is setting up. In this case, to establish standards of fairness and reason-ableness, she might say something like "I've spent some time re-searching the fee structures used by firms such as yours in the area. As you can see, for the kinds of services we're talking about, the fees are roughly in the ranges that my company has been offering to pay. Thus I believe that our offer is both fair and reasonable."

Because there are often many relevant criteria for fairness and reasonableness, you need to (1) research which criteria might best apply, (2) be prepared to show why those criteria *more* favorable to you are more relevant, and (3) figure out how to show why those criteria *less* favorable to you are less relevant. If you can convince the other side that a certain criterion or formula is fair and reasonable, that side will find it harder to reject a proposal incorporating that standard. Moreover, it will be more likely to feel satisfied with the final outcome.

Step 9: Alter the Process in Your Favor

Have you ever felt that your ideas were being ignored during meet-ings or formal negotiations? Does it ever seem that these meetings are rigged to produce a particular result—in spite of input by you or others? Many negotiators have this feeling—especially if they be-lieve that the people they're bargaining with have more power than they do. If you've found yourself in this situation, consider these pos-sible explanations:

- Whoever set the agenda did so with a particular outcome in mind—one that benefits that person.

- People are deferring to someone with greater organizational clout—your arguments notwithstanding.

- Yours is a "lone voice in the wilderness" and out of step with others.

Any of these explanations can shut you out of a negotiation and steer results in a direction that someone else favors—or has rigged.

The antidote? Take steps to change the negotiation process. Deborah Kolb and Judith Williams recommend making what they call "process moves." Don't address the substantive issues in a negotiation, they say. Instead, directly affect the hearing those issues receive: "The agenda, the pre-negotiation groundwork, and the sequence in which ideas and people are heard—all these structural elements influence others' receptivity to opinions and demands."[2]

If you've ever followed international conflict negotiations on the evening news, you've probably noticed that experienced diplomats don't jump right into the issues. Instead, they spend months trying to agree where the meeting will take place, who will participate, and even what the shape the negotiating table will have. These are all process moves. Kolb and Williams make these specific recommendations about process moves:[3]

- **Work behind the scenes to educate others on your ideas.**
  A formal meeting is not always a good venue for making a detailed case or for engaging in dialogue about a complex issue—especially when someone else controls the agenda. So educate other participants one on one *outside* formal meetings. Concentrate on people who are respected wielders of influence. Convince these people that your ideas have merit. They'll likely back you when others try to ignore your position during meetings. Better still, form a coalition of support outside the negotiations.

- **Reframe the process.** If you're been marginalized in a series of meetings or negotiations, the process may be the reason. Consider this example: A loud and brash department head has framed an upcoming meeting in terms of her need for more resources—resources that will have to come from your department. She's prepared to wrestle for as much as she can get, confident that others at the meeting will be neutral because they will not be affected. You could counter by reframing the discussion from "her needs" to "the company's needs." This would make you appear levelheaded and statesmanlike, and would help others recognize that the department head's resource grab also affects them. (We'll learn more about framing in the next chapter.)

As you prepare for a negotiation, recognize that the process requires time and careful thought. But rigorous preparation can boost your chances of getting the terms you want in the upcoming negotiation, as well as crafting an agreement that serves both parties' interests. See assessment tool 6-3 for a worksheet that will help you prepare for a negotiation.

Assessment Tool 6-3
Prepare for a Negotiation

Have you . . .

. . . Thought through what would be a good outcome?

What do you hope to accomplish through the negotiation?

What would the best result look like?

What outcomes would not be palatable?

Why would these outcomes not be palatable?

. . . Assessed your needs and interests?

What you must have

1.

2.

3.

What you would like to have

1.

2.

3.

. . . Identified and improved (if possible) your BATNA?

What is your best alternative to a negotiated agreement?

(See the "Identifying Your BATNA" worksheet.)

How might you improve your BATNA?

. . . Determined your reservation price?

(See the "Setting Your Reservation Price" worksheet.)

What is it?

. . . Evaluated the trade-offs between issues and interests?

Issues you care most about?

1.

2.

3.

Terms you care most about?

1.

2.

3.

. . . Assessed the other side's people, BATNA, and position?

(See the "Assessing the Other Side's Position and Interests" worksheet.)

The people representing the other side:

Their business circumstances:

The specific outcomes they want from this negotiation:

The value this negotiation has for them:

The availability of a replacement agreement:

... Anticipated the authority issue?

(See the "Authority—Theirs and Yours" worksheet.)

Summarize the following:

Your understanding of the level of authority of the representative(s) for the other side:

The kind of agreement you are authorized to make:

... Gathered the external standards and criteria relevant to the negotiation?

(In this negotiation, what standards and criteria are considered fair and reasonable?)

External standards:

Relevant criteria:

... Prepared for flexibility?

(Is there linkage between issues? If yes, which ones?)

SOURCE: Harvard ManageMentor® Negotiating.

Summing Up

The best bargainers take the time to prepare carefully for an upcoming negotiation. This chapter describes nine steps to preparing for a negotiation:

- **Step 1:** Know what a good outcome would be—from your point of view *and* that of the other side.

- **Step 2:** Look for opportunities to create value in the deal.

- **Step 3:** Know your BATNA and reservation price. Make an effort to estimate those benchmarks for the other side.

- **Step 4:** If your BATNA isn't strong, find ways to improve it.

- **Step 5:** Find out if the person or team you'll be dealing with has the authority to make a deal.

- **Step 6:** Know those with whom you're bargaining. Learn as much as you can about the people and the culture on the other side and how they've framed the issue at hand.

- **Step 7:** If a future relationship with the other side matters to you, gather objective standards and criteria that will show your offer to be fair and reasonable.

- **Step 8:** Don't expect any negotiation to follow a linear path to a conclusion. Be prepared for bumps in the road and periodic delays.

- **Step 9:** Alter the agenda and intended negotiation process in your favor.

Leveraging Chapter Insights: Critical Questions

- How do you typically prepare for a negotiation? Which of the nine steps described in this chapter do you usually follow?

- For steps that you tend *not* to follow, how might you ensure that you do follow them in future negotiations?

- Think about a negotiation in which you followed most or all of the steps described in this chapter. How did the negotiation turn out? How did the outcome compare to negotiations for which you didn't prepare as carefully?

CHAPTER SEVEN

Negotiation Strategies

How to Bargain Skillfully

Key Topics Covered in This Chapter

- *Getting the other side to negotiate*

- *Making a good start*

- *Conducting distributive (win-lose) negotiations: anchoring, counteranchoring, preparing for concessionary moves, using time to your advantage, devising package options, closing the deal*

- *Conducting integrative (win-win) negotiations: active listening, exploiting complementary interests, and taking your time*

- *General strategies: framing, continual evaluation, nonverbal cues*

I F Y O U ' R E a recent newcomer to the HR profession, you may be entering into negotiations with substantial concerns. You will have to make some early decisions about *strategy*. Should you be tough or collaborative? Should you hold firm to your terms or be prepared to make concessions? Is it best to fight hard for the most you can get, or to seek a fair outcome? Should you make the first offer or wait to counter it? If you're a seasoned professional, you have likely faced increasingly complex and high-stakes negotiations the further you've advanced in your career. However, you'll still need to address these questions about strategy. This chapter provides guidelines for resolving these and other questions in the context of both integrative and distributive negotiations.[1] Let's begin with strategies you can use to get the ball rolling—that is, to get another party to negotiate with you.

Getting the Other Side to Negotiate

Before we get into actual negotiating strategies, let's consider some approaches to getting another party to begin participating in a negotiation. In many cases, issues you may want to negotiate cannot move forward because one or more parties simply aren't interested in considering a change. The other side is satisfied with the status quo, so it sees no point in negotiating with you. And if the other party has greater organizational power than you, then you may be brushed off with these types of comments: "I don't think there's any reason to make a change—things are fine," or "We're so tied up with the budget that I won't be able to consider your proposal until next spring at the earliest."

Writing in the *Harvard Business Review*, Deborah Kolb and Judith Williams note: "Resistance is a natural part of the informal negotiation process." An issue or proposal will generally receive a fair hearing only when the other party believes two things: You have something desirable to offer, and the other party's own objectives will not be met unless they give something in return. "Willingness to negotiate is, therefore, a confession of mutual need."[2]

More precisely, resisters must conclude that they will be better off if they negotiate and worse off if they do not. Kolb and Williams suggest three things you can do to help reluctant bargainers reach this conclusion:

1. **Offer incentives.** What are the reluctant person's needs: money? time? your support? Determine those needs and then pose them as potential benefits of negotiations. For example, if your boss, the vice president of HR, is reluctant to give you time to work on a redesign of the company's payroll-processing system, explain how an improved system will help solve one of his problems: higher costs owing to the need to fix errors.

2. **Put a price on the status quo.** Spell out the cost of not negotiating. Kolb and Williams use the example of a woman whose boss promoted her and had her take on additional work, but was forever delaying discussion of a pay raise. Frustrated by his inaction, she found a way to get his attention—she secured a job offer from another company. The boss was suddenly very interested in dealing with her long-overdue pay raise. He had to negotiate or face the costly and time-consuming process of replacing an effective subordinate. In other words, he realized the price of the status quo.

3. **Enlist support.** Allies can sometimes accomplish what other measures cannot. For example, if the HR vice president

described earlier still will not give you time off to improve the payroll system, look for allies who have organizational power *and* a reason to favor your goal. The chief financial officer, for instance, will likely favor any plan to improve payroll management. The CFO knows that better payroll management means fewer errors and lower costs to fix those errors, which makes her look good. Once your manager has realized that the CFO is supportive of this project, he'll be more likely to bargain.

Use one or more of these strategies, and the other party will see the virtue of negotiating with you.

Making a Good Start

Once you've gotten another party to negotiate with you, it's important to get things off to a smooth start. Begin by relieving the tension that is often present in the early stages of a negotiation. In your opening remarks:

- Express respect for the other party's experience and expertise.

- Frame the negotiation positively, as a joint endeavor that will benefit both parties.

- Emphasize your openness to the other side's interests and concerns.

After these opening remarks, go over the agenda for the conversation. Make sure you and the other party have a common understanding of the issues to be covered. Then, explicitly discuss your assumptions about how the negotiation process will unfold. People often hold different assumptions about how the process should work. Some assume that the two parties will engage in haggling. Some expect one or both participants to present proposals at the outset, while others expect an open discussion of the issues to come first. Listen carefully to the other party's comments about process—

you'll likely learn a great deal about your counterpart's negotiating style. Also, offer to explain some of your interests and concerns first. This demonstrates that you are prepared to disclose information, provided that the other person reciprocates. If the other side does *not* reciprocate, be very cautious about providing more information. See "Tips for Establishing the Right Tone" for more guidelines on making a good start.

Tips for Establishing the Right Tone

The negotiating environment can affect the level of tension and openness that prevails. If you're interested in lowering tension and seeking collaborative discussion, follow these tips:

- Never underestimate the value of "breaking bread." In practically every culture, sharing a meal is a bonding ritual. So have coffee, soft drinks, and light snacks available.

- Use small talk at the beginning of the discussion to dispel tension, lower people's natural defenses, and begin building relationships. Even in a win-lose negotiation, small talk helps the different sides get to know each other and gauge each other's truthfulness. It may also loosen people up so that they begin seeking value-creating opportunities.

- See what the small talk reveals about the other negotiator's style and possible interests.

- If the other person is very formal, don't speak too casually—he or she may interpret this as a lack of seriousness on your part. If your counterpart is decidedly informal, speak in a more casual way. Consider using metaphors or analogies with which he or she is comfortable; for example, "We think of our business partners as family and want to do whatever we can to help each other."

Addressing Win-Lose Negotiations

In some negotiations, every gain by one side represents a loss to the other. Chapter 3 defined these as distributive negotiations. Not all negotiations pit one party directly against the other, but many do. For example, in your own work as an HR professional, you may find yourself participating in negotiations with labor representatives or with an employee who has filed a lawsuit against your company. Such situations are often viewed as win-lose, or distributive. The approaches described in this section will help you navigate these situations more skillfully.

Anchoring

Anchoring is an attempt to establish a reference point around which negotiators will make adjustments. In some cases, you can gain an advantage by putting the first offer on the table. That first offer can serve as a strong psychological anchor: It becomes the reference point of subsequent pulling and pushing by the participants in the bargaining. As described by Max Bazerman and Margaret Neale, initial positions "affect each side's perception of what outcomes are possible."[3] Consider this example:

> *Jake, a highly sought-after HR consultant, was negotiating with several potential clients to sell a new change-management methodology he had developed. The methodology was based on cutting-edge theory and included innovative, easy-to-use tools. "If I can charge $150,000, I'll be satisfied," Jake told himself. "If that's not possible, I'll hold onto the model for six months and see if I need to refine it further." Jake's business partner suggested that he tell all potential clients that he would want to charge a fee of $175,000 for delivering the methodology.*
>
> *In the weeks that followed, Jake's stated fee became the anchor point for subsequent negotiations with four potential clients, all companies from outside the area. Three of the four offered to hire Jake at slightly lower levels—$160,000, $165,000, and $170,000—hoping to arrive at an agreement with Jake somewhere in the middle. The*

*fourth company, sensing keen competition for Jake's time, offered to pay
the full fee.*

This example underscores the effect of anchoring. In the right
circumstances, the first party to put a price (or deal package) on the
table secures an important psychological advantage. In fact, studies
show that negotiation outcomes often correlate to the first offer.

When should you anchor? It may be wise to anchor when you
have a reasonably good sense of the other party's reservation price. If
you are very uncertain about that price, you might encourage him
or her to make the first move.

Where should you place your anchor? In a negotiation in which
claiming maximum value is the primary goal, you should peg your first
offer or proposal at or just a bit beyond what you believe is the other
side's reservation price. (Remember: You can determine that price
through pre-negotiation investigation or direct probing of the other
side.) Thus, if you had a sense of Jake's reservation price ($150,000),
you might make a first offer at $125,000 and allow him to score some
points in negotiating the deal up to $150,000 (assuming you think
that amount represents an acceptable price).

Wherever you place the anchor, be prepared to articulate *why* your
offer or proposal is reasonable or justifiable. "I believe that my fee of
$175,000 is fully justified by the unique benefits of this methodology.
It uses the latest change-management theory and includes tools that
your managers and employees will find innovative and easy to use. I
think you'll find that other change-management consultants who are
far *less* innovative are charging about the same for their services."

Anchoring with a price (or a proposal) has its advantages. But it
also creates two risks. First, if you set too aggressive an anchor, the
other party may conclude it will be impossible to make a deal with
you—and may also feel personally insulted by your proposal. Second,
if you've made an erroneous estimate of the other side's reservation
price, your offer will fall outside the zone of possible agreement. If
you incur either of these risks, shift to a less aggressive offer—and
have a different line of reasoning ready to support the change. For
example, "Because my business partner is traveling and wants to line

up engagements now for the upcoming quarter, he has authorized me to adjust our fee to . . . ."

The best safeguard against making an inept anchoring attempt is preparation *before* the negotiating starts, as described in the previous chapter. If you do your homework, you'll be much less likely to place an anchor at a point from which you'll be forced to beat an ignominious retreat.

Counteranchoring

If the other side makes the first offer, recognize that offer's potential power as a psychological anchor—and resist that power. Remember that anchors are most powerful when uncertainty is highest—for example, when no one has a clear idea what the price of a company or a piece of equipment should be. When no one has a clue as to the appropriate price, there is no basis for disputing the merits of the first offer.

You can reduce the other party's anchoring power by clearing up the uncertainty surrounding the issue that's up for negotiation. That means gathering and bringing objective information to the bargaining process.

Don't let the other party set the bargaining range with an anchor unless you think that anchor constitutes a sensible starting point. If you think the anchor suggests an unfavorable or unacceptable starting point, steer the conversation away from numbers and proposals. Focus instead on interests, concerns, and generalities. Then, after some time has passed and more information has surfaced, put *your* number or proposal on the table, and support it with sound reasoning.

To see how this might be done, let's replay the example of Jake and his attempts to sell his new methodology. But this time, let's assume that only one potential client, Flow Industries, steps forward to discuss the possibility of hiring Jake. The negotiator for Flow is named Carla.

Jake has just explained to Carla that his fee for delivering the methodology is $175,000, confident that that number would serve as a firm anchor point for all negotiations with potential client companies. But he hasn't counted on dealing with Carla. She has thoroughly researched a number of change-management consulting firms over the past few *months, so she is familiar with the fees they are charging, the unique characteristics of their approaches, and the feedback from their current and previous clients.*

During her first meeting with Jake, Carla explains how she has been researching her options. Without making any reference to Jake's $175,000 stated fee, she cites three examples of change-management consulting services delivered to companies like hers during the past year, indicating how those services were more or less similar to Jake's: "These three are very comparable to your services in terms of delivery schedule and quality, scope of project, and ease of use," she tells Jake as she shows him her research notes. "Those services were delivered for fees of $125,000, $130,000, and $145,000, respectively, within the past ten months. Factoring in cost-of-living increases for consulting professionals this year, that makes your service worth about $150,000 at the most, which is what I'm prepared to pay you today."

Here, Carla has placed her own anchor on the board. Instead of focusing on what Jake wants from the agreement, she ignores his initial fee, substituting a new fee supported by market data. That relevant data gives her anchor greater authority than Jake's, and makes it easier to push his aside. In the absence of other potential clients—particularly companies whose agents hadn't done their homework—Jake has to negotiate with Carla in terms of *her* stated offer. In effect, she has substituted her anchor for Jake's.

The lesson of this tale is to avoid direct comparison between the other party's initial offer and your own. If the initial offer is not serious or realistic, you can safely ignore it; there's a good chance that the other side will do the same. If the initial offer *was* serious, and the other side refers to it again, you should respectfully ask the other party to explain why the offer is reasonable. "Why are you asking for $175,000 in this market? Could you explain how you are justifying that fee?"

Be Prepared for Concessionary Moves

Once an anchor point is on the table, the parties generally engage in a set of moves and countermoves that they hope will end in an agreeable price or set of arrangements. For example, if Carla in the previous example offered $150,000 for Jake's services, Jake more than likely would respond with a counteroffer of, say, $165,000:

> *"I appreciate the research you've done, Carla, but I don't feel that the other consulting services you've used as benchmarks are really comparable to my service. After all, the service I'm proposing is the only one that uses this new methodology in this particular fashion. Moreover, I can deliver the methodology in far fewer workshops than other consultants can. Taking those factors into account, I think that my proposal is worth substantially more than your offer, and I believe that other companies will share my view. However, in the interest of getting things wrapped up, I'm willing to lower my fee by $10,000 to $165,000."*

Negotiation experts generally interpret a large concessionary move as an indicator of significant additional flexibility. Give a large concession, and the other side will think that you're capable of making additional large concessions. Thus, Carla may think "If Jake is willing to come down $10,000 in this first counteroffer, he's probably prepared to come down at least another $10,000." A small move, on the other hand, is generally perceived as an indication that the bidding is approaching that party's reservation price, and that further pushing will result in smaller and smaller concessions.

These assumptions are not always true, especially when the other side is in no hurry, and when they feel confident that other parties may come forward with attractive prices or conditions—that is, when they have a strong BATNA. This may be the case with Jake. A $10,000 concession on his part isn't a huge concession, even though Carla's bid has satisfied his $150,000 reservation price. We can almost hear Jake's voice as he mulls over the negotiation to himself:

> *"I'm happy that I have an offer of $150,000 already. I could live with that. But I may get a better offer in the next week or so, either from Carla or from another potential client. Actually, I'd expect Carla to up her bid to $160K. If she does that, should I push for a bit more? Should I say, 'Give me $165K and we'll have a deal?' Or should I sit on her offer and hope to get a better one?"*

Jake's uncertainty about how far to push Carla in this example is a function of his uncertainty about her BATNA and reservation price. If he could estimate these with confidence, he could drive a harder bargain. In this case, Carla's BATNA may be the price of similar consulting services. He could come up with a list of those services, their key characteristics, and their associated fees. Those might represent the set of Carla's alternatives.

The best advice about concessions is to resist the impulse to make them. Few of us like negotiating, so we want to get it over with as quickly as possible. And as social creatures, we want other people to like us, and to view us as reasonable. These factors often make inexperienced negotiators too ready to make concessions. If you find yourself in this category, consider these tips:

- Look to your BATNA before you consider making a concession. If your BATNA is very strong (especially relative to the other side's), a concession may be unnecessary for arriving at an agreement.

- If you're impatient to get the negotiating over with because the process is stressful, take a break before you consider making a concession. If the other side is expecting a $10,000 concession on a fee you're proposing, think about how difficult it was for you to earn that $10,000. Think about the good things you could do with the $10,000 that other party would like you to give away. Ask yourself, "Is getting rid of a little stress worth $10,000?"

- If your need to be liked or seen as a reasonable person is causing you to make a concession, forget about it. The other side is more likely to view you as an easy mark if you concede too readily. Remember, too, that negotiation isn't *only* about making friends.

The Ticking Clock

In a buyer-seller negotiation, such as the Jake and Carla example, time can serve as an important tool. From the buyer's perspective, the seller should never be allowed to feel that he can indefinitely sit on the buyer's most recent bid while he awaits a better offer. The seller will simply use the offer to improve his BATNA. The remedy is to attach an expiration date to the offer to buy. Negotiators sometimes refer to this tactic as an *exploding offer*. If Carla decided to counter Jake's latest offer ($165,000) with a bid of $160,000, she might stipulate that "this offer is good until 9 p.m. on this coming Saturday, September 23." That expiration date would put a fire under Jake and force him to make a decision. In the absence of an expiration date, Jake would simply tell himself, "Now that I have an option to sell my services at $160,000, I can wait for a better offer."

Package Options for a Favorable Deal

Offering alternative proposals (two or more) is often an effective negotiation strategy. For example, suppose Carla wasn't happy with the way the negotiations with Jake were going, and that the consulting services Jake was proposing consisted of classroom training as well as online, self-paced learning modules. Carla's not as interested in the online learning modules, so she might say something like, "I'm willing to pay $160,000 for the classroom and online training as a package, or $130,000 for the classroom alone. What's your preference?"

Package options have dual benefits. First, people don't like to feel pushed into a corner. A single proposal may feel like an ultimatum—take it or leave it. But when presented with alternative proposals, people may compare the proposals to each other instead of to their original goals. In addition, when a negotiating counterpart won't discuss their interests, you can often infer those interests by noticing which proposal the person prefers.

But before presenting alternative proposals, do the following:

- Assess the value of each option to each negotiator.

- Consider whether the diminution of one option would be offset by an enhancement of another.

- If you prefer one of the alternatives, adjust at least one of the proposals so that you feel equally positive about at least two of them.

Closing the Deal

Assuming that things go well, you'll eventually reach a point where you're fairly satisfied with the negotiation and you want to wrap things up. The other side may or may not be at the same point. Here are four recommended steps for closing the deal:

1. **Signal the end of the road before you get there**. If you have been negotiating back and forth, showing flexibility on various issues, and then suddenly announce you're at your bottom line, the other party may challenge you or not take you seriously. So as you approach the parameters of what you would like in a final deal, say so. Repeat the warning, not as a threat but as a courtesy—particularly if the other negotiator seems to expect a lot more movement in his or her direction.

2. **Allow flexibility if you anticipate going beyond the final round.** If you are aware that the other negotiator lacks final authority, leave yourself some flexibility, or wiggle room, in the final terms. More specifically, don't give the other side your best and last offer. Instead, save that in case you have to bend a little during the final round. Nevertheless:

   - Don't create *so* much flexibility that the the other side's decision maker rejects the agreement.
   - Consider whatever final trade you would be willing to make if you end up requesting significant adjustment in the final terms.

3. **Discourage the other side from seeking further concessions.** If you appear to have reached a final accord that is acceptable to the other side (and perhaps also favorable to you), discourage further tweaking in the other party's favor.

   - Express your willingness to accept the total package, without changes.
   - Explain that adjustment in the other side's favor on one term would have to be balanced by adjustment in your favor on another. For example, "If we open that issue, then we'll have to reopen the whole deal for it to work for me."

4. **Write down the terms.** If your negotiation time has been well spent, don't risk ruining it by failing to record and sign your agreement. People's memories of an agreement's details will inevitably diverge. So record the terms to avoid future disputes and confusion. Recording also provides closure to the negotiation process. Even in situations where an attorney will draft official documents for an agreement, write an informal agreement in principle. Decide whether it is binding or not, and say so in the document. If your informal agreement is nonbinding, it will still serve as a common reference for both parties as future, good-faith questions arise.

Managing Integrative Negotiations

As you saw in chapter 3, integrative (or win-win) negotiations are those in which the parties enlarge the "pie" through trades and the creation of new forms of value. As an HR professional, you may find yourself in these bargaining situations while negotiating salary with job seekers, making counteroffers to existing valued employees who have received an offer from another firm, negotiating budgets with other departments during the budgeting process, and discussing potential agreements with vendors and consultants.

Integrative negotiations like these require a different set of strategies, beginning with a slower, more exploratory opening. They rely on greater collaboration and information exchange. Unlike the win-lose tactics described earlier, where the focus is on claiming value, well-handled integrative bargaining enables the parties to both create *and* claim value.

Getting Started

As you begin your negotiations, don't start with numbers. Instead, talk and listen. Observe the suggestions offered earlier in the section "Making a Good Start" and the "Tips for Establishing the Right Tone" box. They apply equally here. Frame the task positively, as a joint endeavor from which both sides should expect to benefit. Emphasize your openness to the other person's interests and concerns.

As you learn about the other party's concerns and interests, don't make a proposal too quickly; a premature offer won't benefit from information gleaned during the negotiation process itself. If you are the buyer, such information could alert you to the seller's desperate financial situation, thereby leading you to make a lower initial offer than you otherwise might have. On the other hand, the information could reveal that the seller is not desperate at all, thereby suggesting that you should *not* make a low initial offer that might insult the seller.

Instead of hastily throwing out an offer, try these techniques:

- Ask open-ended questions about the other side's needs, interests, concerns, and goals.

- Probe the other side's willingness to *trade off* one thing for another. For example, "Do you care more about X or Y?"

- Inquire about the other side's underlying interests by asking why certain conditions—for example, a particular delivery date—are important.

- Listen closely to the other side's responses without jumping in to cross-examine, correct, or object.

- Be an active listener. The more the other person talks, the more information you're likely to get. (See "Tips for Active Listening" for more information on this.)

- Express empathy for your negotiation counterpart's perspective, needs, and interests. Empathy is especially important in highly charged situations. It takes active listening one step further, confirming that you can connect with the speaker and the underlying tensions or emotional issues.

- Adjust your assumptions based on what you've learned. The assumptions you've made about the other side's interests and circumstances when you were preparing for the negotiation may turn out to be wrong. If so, you'll need to revisit your strategy.

- Be forthcoming about your own business needs, interests, and concerns. It's just as important to assert what you need and want (and why) as it is to listen carefully to the other side. Indeed, striking a balance between empathy and assertiveness is essential to effective negotiating. If you are too empathetic and insufficiently assertive, you may shortchange your own interests. If you are too assertive and insufficiently empathetic, you risk missing out on a satisfactory accord and escalating negative emotions. But don't barrage the other side with all of your interests at once.

- Work to create a two-way exchange of information. Stay flexible about who asks questions and who states concerns first. If the other person seems uncomfortable with your initial questions, offer to talk about one or two of your most important points—and explain why you consider these points important.

- Continue your relationship-building efforts even after the negotiating has begun. Show empathy, respect, and courtesy throughout the proceedings. Always remember that the other "side" consists of human beings with feelings, limits, and vulnerabilities.

- Refrain from personal attacks. Don't accuse or blame. Maintain a sense of humor.

- When an issue seems to make the other negotiator tense, acknowledge the thorniness of the issue.

- Don't feel pressured to close a deal too quickly. Instead, generate options that offer mutual gain.

Look for Options That Exploit Differences

During any negotiation, you are confronted with the other party's positions and come to understand the interests underlying those positions. You hope that the other person will understand your positions and interests just as well. The challenge now is to arrive at an

Tips for Active Listening

There's a big difference between keeping your mouth shut while your negotiation counterpart is talking and what communication experts refer to as "active" listening. Active listening helps you capture what the other side has to say while signaling that you are alert and eager to hear what the person has on his or her mind. The following active-listening tips can help you in any type of negotiation.

- Keep your eyes on the speaker.

- Take notes as appropriate.

- Don't allow yourself to think about anything but what the speaker is saying.

- Resist the urge to formulate your response until *after* the speaker has finished.

- Pay attention to the speaker's body language.

- Ask questions to get more information and to encourage the speaker to continue.

- Repeat in your own words what you've heard, to ensure that you understand and to let the speaker know that you've processed his or her words.

outcome that satisfies both parties' interests. One place to look for a mutually satisfying outcome is in the *differences* between the parties.

People know intuitively to build on their shared interests. Less obvious sources of value can be hiding in the differences between them. By trading on differences, you create value that neither party could have created on its own. In particular, look for differences in these places:

- **Access to resources.** For example, Martha, who works for a company that owns two office buildings, is negotiating with an interior designer for his services in renovating one of the buildings. She agrees to pay a somewhat higher price than planned for the renovation design; in exchange, the designer will order fixtures and furnishings for the other building at his trade discount. Martha would not otherwise have ready access to these discounts—yet providing them costs the designer nothing. Value has been created for both sides.

- **Future expectations.** For example, the current owner of a business is selling it. He demands a high price because he predicts that the market for his product will increase over time. The potential buyer is unwilling to pay that high price; she does not share the owner's rosy outlook. Within this difference of opinion, they see an opportunity. They agree to a base sale price, plus 20 percent of the company's increased revenues over the next five years—if any—with the current owner providing advice and assisting with marketing and distribution plans over that period. Under this arrangement, the buyer will get a lower price, and the seller will be able to capture the upside growth in the business he anticipates.

- **Time preference.** The timing of a deal can present a barrier to a mutually satisfactory conclusion. For example, Jonathan is happy with the CEO's plan to promote him to vice president of HR, but unhappy that he must play a waiting role until the incumbent retires six months from now. The CEO, however, has arranged for the current HR VP to use that time to finalize several large projects. "He engineered these projects and has close personal ties to key players on the other side," the CEO tells Jonathan. "I want him to wrap up the projects." Within these differences, however, the CEO finds a solution: He will put Jonathan in charge of a team that is working on the plan to implement the projects. That satisfies Jonathan and benefits the company.

- **Risk aversion.** What is highly risky for one party is often less risky for another. Parties often have different risk tolerances. In these cases, a negotiator can create value by shifting risk to the party better able to bear it—in exchange, of course, for higher potential returns for the party assuming the risk. For example, Jeff is negotiating with Jones Properties, a developer, for the purchase of a newly built office building for his company. For Jeff's firm, which is new and struggling with cash flow, the office building would be an enormous, risky investment. "What if business takes a bad turn and we had to sell the building sometime soon?" Jeff ponders. "If the commercial real estate market were depressed at the time of sale, we'd take a heavy loss." Jones Properties, on the other hand, owns hundreds of commercial properties around the country. Its risk of ownership is highly diversified. And the negotiator from Jones poses a solution: As part of the sales agreement, it will agree to buy back Jeff's company's office building at any time within two years of purchase at 95 percent of the purchase price less transaction costs.

Take Your Time

Don't be tempted to close a deal too quickly—when the first acceptable proposal has been presented but you and your counterpart have exchanged little information. Spend a bit more time finding a deal that's even better for both sides. Signal that the current proposal is worth considering, but that you believe it could be improved if the two parties learned more about their respective interests and concerns. Then, begin the search for mutually beneficial options.

Here are several more suggestions for generating integrative solutions:

- Move from a particular issue to a more general description of the problem, then to theoretical solutions, and finally back to the specific issue.

- Pay special attention to shared interests and opportunities for cooperation.

- Consider joint brainstorming with the other side—it can be a very fruitful way of generating creative alternatives. Set ground rules that encourage the participants to express any and all ideas, no matter how wild or impractical they may seem. Be careful not to criticize or express disapproval of any suggestion. At this stage, such judgments inhibit creativity, making people reluctant to offer further suggestions—and more likely to criticize any ideas you volunteer.

We've covered a lot of ground in these previous two sections. See assessment tool 7-1 for a checklist of techniques that you might consider using during your next distributive or integrative negotiation.

Assessment Tool 7-1
A Checklist of Negotiation Techniques

Are you contemplating a difficult negotiation or embroiled in one already? If so, use this tool to assess possible techniques you might use to boost your chances of success as the negotiation unfolds.

If you're having trouble getting another party to negotiate, have you . . .

Offered incentives, such as your support or time?

Yes   No

Put a price on the status quo by spelling out the cost of *not* negotiating with you?

Yes   No

Enlisted support from allies whose opinions the other party values?

Yes   No

If you're involved in a distributive (win-lose) type of negotiation, have you . . .

Established the right tone by using small talk, refreshments, and reassuring comments to dispel tension and encourage discussion?

Yes   No

Used research to estimate the other side's reservation price, and set an anchor point just a bit beyond that price?

Yes   No

Articulated why your offer is reasonable or justifiable?

Yes   No

Decided whether an anchor point set by the other party (if he or she named a price first) is reasonable?

Yes   No

Redirected the conversation away from numbers and proposals and toward interests, concerns, and generalities if the other party's anchor point seems unreasonable?

Yes   No

Identified the potential for flexibility in large concessionary moves from the other party?

Yes   No

Resisted the impulse to make large concessions yourself?

Yes   No

Used time to your advantage; e.g., by attaching an expiration date to your offer?

Yes   No

Offered alternative proposals, such as packages of options, if the negotiation seems to be stalling?

Yes   No

Signaled that you're approaching your final terms?

Yes   No

Recorded and signed your agreement once it has been reached?

Yes   No

If you're involved in an integrative (win-win) negotiation, have you . . .

Used open-ended questions and active listening to probe for the other side's needs, interests, concerns, and goals?

Yes   No

Assessed the other party's willingness to trade off one thing for another?

Yes   No

Expressed empathy for the other person's perspective, needs, and interests?

Yes   No

Been forthcoming about your own business needs, interests, and concerns?

Yes   No

Cultivated a two-way exchange of information by remaining flexible about who asks questions and who states concerns first?

Yes   No

Looked for a mutually satisfying outcome in the differences between you and the other party—such as access to resources, time preferences, or tolerance for risk?

Yes   No

Resisted any temptation to close the deal quickly?

Yes   No

General Strategies

Whether you're engaged in a distributive or integrative negotiation, you'll generate the best results if you adopt any one of the following tactics: making process moves, framing, continually evaluating the negotiation process, reading body language and other nonverbal cues, and understanding the impact of personal negotiating styles. You can use these strategies while discussing agreement terms with another negotiator or while you're taking a break from the bargaining to firm up your approach. You learned about process in chapter 6, so this section focuses on the other general strategies.

Framing

You're probably familiar with tried-and-true test of whether you're an optimist or pessimist: Fill a glass of water halfway to the top. Now, if you described this glass to someone else, would you say it was half empty or half full? Whichever way you describe the glass, you are framing the situation. In negotiations, if the other person accepts your frame without question, subsequent discussion will proceed within that frame. This could be advantageous to you. Consider these examples.

- **The glass is half empty.** A labor negotiator tries to frame upcoming wage and benefit talks with a company:

  "During the past three years, hard work by our members has helped this company to triple its revenues and almost double its profits. Management salaries have grown substantially as a result, and key executives have rewarded themselves with record-breaking bonuses. And what is management willing to share with rank-and-file employees? A mere 25 percent increase in wages over the next three years! That, we contend, is a slap in the face to the people who have created this company's good fortunes."

  This negotiator is maintaining that a fair sharing of the wealth created by the employees should frame wage negotiations.

- **The glass is half full.** A manager makes the company's pitch to labor:

> *"We are pleased to offer our rank-and-file employees a salary increase of 25 percent over the next three years. That increase is one-third higher than what our main market competitors have offered their employees. It will put the average annual wage of our people some $3,000 above the industry average, and will allow the company to retain sufficient funds to reinvest in the technology it needs to ensure job security and future wage increases."*

This negotiator is arguing from within a frame that emphasizes financial constraints and the company's desire to ensure job security and higher future incomes.

Like an anchor, a frame can determine how negotiations will ensue. It orients the parties and encourages them to examine the issues within a defined perspective. The labor union frame described above would put management on the defensive and encourage negotiations around a framework that stressed "fair distribution" of the profit pie. The management frame is based on its generosity relative to peer group companies and the benefits workers may receive in the future, thanks to profit reinvestment. (Note how the company manager has used external criteria—as described in chapter 6—to establish the fairness and reasonableness of its offer.) Whichever side can get the other to buy into its frame will have a negotiating advantage. As Bazerman and Neale put it, the way in which options available in a negotiation are framed, or presented, can strongly affect a party's willingness to reach an agreement.[4]

Effective framing taps into preexisting mental models of how we should behave under various conditions. Thus, how one side frames a solution can determine how others decide to behave. Marjorie Corman Aaron, a consultant and trainer with many years of experience in mediation, negotiation, and dispute resolution, gives the example of a bank officer faced with demands by local community activists to provide more generous lending arrangements. In advising the bank's board on a course of action, the officer could adopt any one of several frames:

He could frame the demands to the board of directors as a "shake-down," thereby invoking a mental model that resists "knuckling under to pressure." But if he framed it as a business problem—the need to earn the goodwill of the community—the board might be persuaded to fund some programs. If he framed the bank's circumstances as "wrestling with a 500-pound gorilla," the board would probably do whatever it would take to get the gorilla off its back, and quickly.[5]

So, if you frame your position in terms of a mental model the other side can embrace, you'll have less trouble moving toward agreement. More generally, you can use these frames:

- Frame your proposal in terms that represent a gain instead of a loss. Instead of saying "My current offer is only 10 percent less than what you are asking," say "I've already increased my offer by 10 percent."

- Tap into people's natural aversion to risk. Risk aversion has two consequences:

  1. People who are very risk averse will often accept smaller losses today rather than facing the possibility of incurring larger losses in the future. This explains why many employers choose to settle lawsuits before they go to trial, rather than risk potentially huge damage awards by a jury if the case goes to court.
  2. Most people prefer "a bird in the hand rather than two in the bush." In other words, they prefer the certainty of a smaller offer to the *uncertainty* of a larger future gain. "I know that you want $400,000 for that office building, and you may get it someday. However, I'm willing to pay $340,000 for it today. Can we make a deal?"

Continual Evaluation

Normally we think of negotiating as a linear process of preparation, negotiation, and eventual agreement or failure. The first step takes place away from the negotiation conversations; the rest take place during those conversations. In simple interactions, this model often holds true. But many other negotiations are complex and can take place in succeeding rounds and involve several different parties. New information can appear at various points, casting fresh light on the issues at stake. Different parties can offer concessions or heighten their demands. This more complex dynamic suggests a nonlinear approach to the preparation process, as shown in figure 7-1. Here preparation is followed by negotiation, which produces outcomes and information that require evaluation. The outputs of evaluation then feed into a new round of preparation and subsequent negotiation. Round and round it goes until agreement is reached or the parties call it quits.

Michael Watkins, author and expert on the subject of negotiations, suggests that the ambiguities and uncertainties associated with complex deals should caution negotiators to give less attention to pre-negotiation preparation and more attention to what he calls "planning to learn."[6] Learning must be ongoing. After all, the infor-

FIGURE 7-1

Nonlinear Negotiating Process

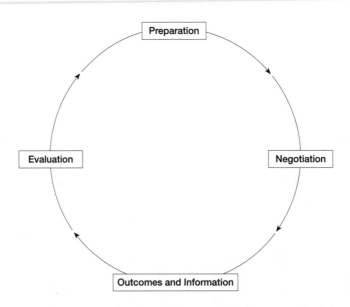

Source: Harvard Business Essentials: Negotiation (Boston: Harvard Business School Press, 2003), 66.

mation available to negotiators before they begin the process is bound to be limited and may even be inaccurate. So instead of setting your course based solely on pre-negotiation information, consider doing the following:

- Take small steps, gathering more detailed and reliable information as you proceed.

- Continually learn from new information and the other party's behavior and comments.

- Use that learning to adjust and readjust your course as you move forward.

Evaluation is another important element of the process, and should be part of your approach. Periodically, put a little distance between yourself and the negotiations and ask: How are things going? Are negotiations proceeding along a track that will eventually serve my goals? Is the other party playing my game, or am I playing theirs? Whose frame dominates the talks? If I were representing the other side, how would I answer these same questions?

Answering these questions objectively isn't easy—and it doesn't come naturally to most of us. To generate these insights, you have to imagine yourself a neutral stranger and adopt an outside-looking-in stance.

Reading Body Language and Other Nonverbal Cues

In any negotiation, the other party's facial expressions, body postures, gestures, and other nonverbal behaviors can reveal much about his or her thoughts and feelings, as well as intentions, concerning the bargaining. But the meaning of nonverbal behavior can vary enormously across cultures. For example, in one culture, a smile may indicate enjoyment of what is going on around the person. In another, a smile might mean that the person feels uncertain or embarrassed. In addition to cultural differences, duplicitous efforts on the part of another negotiator may cause confusion over the meaning of that person's body language and facial expressions. For example, it's easy to paste on a smile to tone down internal feelings of hostility. However, some behaviors and their interpretations are fairly common across cultures and individuals. Table 7-1 shows several of these.

To boost your chances of reading the other party's nonverbal cues accurately, research any cultural differences before the bargaining begins. Do some additional research during the negotiation if you have the sense that you've misread a particular behavior. If you're negotiating with a group of individuals, evaluate one person's body language in conjunction with that of his or her colleagues. That way, you can get an average reading of the group's *collective* mood. And learn to trust your instincts about others' nonverbal behaviors. We human beings have a sharp instinctual sense for these things, based on eons of evolution. If you have the sense that the other party is bored, hostile, or open, you may well be correct in your interpretation.

TABLE 7-1

Reading Nonverbal Behaviors

Behavior	Possible Meaning
Leaning back	Hostility
Crossed arms	Disbelief
Leaning forward	Attentiveness
Open expression	Interest
Direct eye contact	Positive thoughts and feelings
Hand on chin	Thoughtfulness
Inattentive gaze	Lack of concentration
Fiddling with pen or other object	Distractedness
Open arms	Indecision
Wide eyes and warm expression	Willingness to be persuaded
Averted gaze and touching of ear or other body part	Lack of conviction about the other party's position
Steely gaze and head tilted to the side	Boredom
Wide eyes and tense jaw	Exasperation

Source: Tim Hindle, *Negotiating Skills* (London: DK Publishing, Inc., 1998), 40–43.

TABLE 7-2

Negotiating Styles and Coping Strategies

Style	Defining Behaviors	Strategies for Coping
The "Tank"	Is pushy and ruthless; loud and forceful	Command respect by: • Remaining calm • Interrupting aggressive behavior by saying the person's name repeatedly • Restating the person's main point • Concisely summing up the current status of the negotiation
The "Sniper"	Identifies your weaknesses and uses them against you	Bring the person "out of hiding" by: • Asking a question that exposes the sniping behavior, such as "What does that have to do with our negotiation?" • Suggesting an alternative behavior for future negotiating sessions that will better benefit both parties
The "Know-It-All"	Is reluctant to listen to your ideas; persists in pushing his or her ideas	Open the person's mind to new information by: • Being prepared and "knowing your stuff" • Summing up what the person has told you to indicate that you've heard him or her • Presenting your views indirectly, using softening words such as *maybe, perhaps, this may be a detour, what do you suppose*; using *we* or *us* instead of *I* and *you*
The "Nothing Person"	Reveals nothing	Persuade the person to talk by: • Building abundant time into the negotiation process • Asking open-ended questions expectantly; for example, "What are you thinking?" "Where do we go from here?" • Using humor to ease any discomfort that may have caused the person to clam up

Source: Dr. Rick Brinkman and Dr. Rick Kirschner, *Dealing with People You Can't Stand: How to Bring Out the Best in People at Their Worst* (New York: McGraw-Hill, 1994).

Understanding the Impact of Personal Negotiation Styles

Each negotiator has his or her own personal bargaining style. Some styles can make bargaining even more stressful or difficult than it already is. In such cases, your job is to identify your negotiation counterpart's style and devise ways for effectively dealing with it. Table 7-2 shows several typical styles that can exert the most destructive impact on negotiations, along with strategies for dealing with them. Of course, just as you might try to identify destructive negotiating styles in others, watch that you don't exhibit such styles yourself!

Summing Up

This chapter described the first two essential negotiation strategies:

- Get the other side to the table. This won't happen unless the other side sees that it is better off negotiating than going with the status quo. Encourage negotiation by offering incentives, making the status quo expensive, and by enlisting the help of allies.

- Once you've gotten the other side to the table, get things off to a good start by relieving tension, making sure that all parties agree with the agenda and the process, and setting the right tone.

   Several tactics are particularly useful in distributive (or win-lose) deals:

- Establish an anchor, an initial position around which negotiations make adjustments.

- If an initial anchor is unacceptable to you, steer the conversation away from numbers and proposals. Focus instead on interests, concerns, and generalities. Then, after some time has passed and more information has surfaced, put *your* number or proposal on the table, and support it with sound reasoning.

- Make concessionary moves if you must. But remember, many interpret a large concessionary move as an indicator that you're capable of conceding still more. A small concession, on the other hand, is generally seen as an indication that the bidding is approaching the reservation price and that any succeeding concessions will be smaller and smaller.

- Package options for more favorable deals. Offer two or more alternative proposals. Presenting multiple options has several benefits. It helps people feel that you're not pushing them into a corner, and enables them to compare the proposals to each other instead of to their original goals. In addition, it helps you infer their interests by revealing which proposal the other party prefers.

Tactics for integrative (win-win) negotiations are fundamentally different from those just described, since value creation is one of the goals. So concentrate on these tactics:

- Practice active listening, showing genuine interest in building a positive relationship with the other party and paraphrasing or summing up to indicate your understanding of what your counterpart is saying.

- Exploit complementary interests. Often, differences in interests can spark ideas for creative agreements that satisfy both parties.

- Take your time. Rushing the process only prevents you and the other party from identifying the fullest possible range of opportunities to craft a mutually satisfying agreement.

Finally, the chapter offered tactics usable in any context:

- Frame the negotiation in a way that speaks of opportunities and gains rather than problems and losses.

- Continually evaluate the information you're uncovering during the negotiation, and be willing to revisit outcomes based on new information.

- Read body language and other nonverbal cues to discern how your negotiation counterpart is responding to the ideas you're exploring together.

- Understand the impact of personal negotiating styles, and apply strategies for counteracting destructive styles.

Leveraging Chapter Insights: Critical Questions

- What strategies have you used to participate in distributive (win-lose) negotiations? How have those strategies worked? What changes, if any, do you believe would improve the outcomes of such negotiations for you?

- Likewise, what strategies have you used to participate in integrative (win-win) negotiations? How have those strategies worked? What changes, if any, do you believe would improve the outcomes of such negotiations for you?

- Do you ever have trouble getting another party to negotiate with you? If so, what might you do in the future to encourage others to participate in an important negotiation?

- What steps do you tend to take in order to get a negotiation off to a good start? What additional strategies, if any, might you use to improve your abilities in this area?

CHAPTER EIGHT

Frequently Asked Tactical Questions

Answers You Need

Key Topics Covered in This Chapter

- *FAQs about money*
- *FAQs about process*
- *FAQs about people*

I N T H E P R E V I O U S chapter, you learned about strategies you can use in the various types of distributive and integrative negotiations that can arise for HR professionals. This chapter follows up with answers to frequently asked questions (FAQs) about negotiating strategies.[1] For convenience, we've organized the questions and answers under three broad categories: money, process, and people.

FAQs About Money

Should I ever state my acceptable range in a negotiation?

Some negotiators will ask you to state a range of what you're willing to pay for a service or product you're considering purchasing. If this happens to you, do not comply with the request. This would give away your reservation price. For example, if you tell an HR services provider that you would pay $20,000 to $25,000 for the provider to design a survey assessing workers' understanding of corporate strategy, rest assured that you will end up paying *at least* $25,000. Why? The other party will think, "That's the reservation price," and it is the only number he or she will pay attention to. It is much better to work in terms of *your* bottom line, or "the best I can do."

The only time it makes sense to mention a range is toward the end of the negotiating process, when you want to discourage the other person from pushing you beyond that range. For example, suppose that after several rounds of back and forth on a dollar figure, you are at $23,000. The other side is at $30,000 and seems to be pushing for a deal at $28,000. You could say, "My range walking in here today was $20,000 to $23,000, but not above $25,000." Revealing your range may make it easier for the other negotiator to accept $25,000, because he will feel that he has pushed you to the top of what you'll be willing to accept.

Should I ever tell the other side my real bottom line?

You can reveal your bottom line, but only if you've reached it (or are about to). If you do reveal your bottom line, make sure you call it just that—with appropriate emphasis or firmness. Otherwise, your negotiation counterpart may not take you seriously. Moreover, he or she may view that number or proposal as just another step on the way to a final deal.

Suppose that the other side opens with an incredibly unreasonable number. Should I counter with an equally unreasonable number, or decline to counter at all?

Consider one of the following strategies:

- Make a joke to indicate that you don't consider the number a serious offer: "Right, and the moon is made of green cheese. Now, let's get serious."

- Clearly state that the other side's number is entirely out of the range you had imagined for the deal. Go back to talking about interests. Ask about a specific issue of some importance. Explain your perspective on the deal—how it might have value to you or others similarly situated. (You will, of course, be describing value that falls in an entirely different ballpark.) Let some time and discussion go by. Then suggest a number or proposal that you can justify as reasonable and that is in the favorable end of your range (or close to what you estimate the other person's reservation price is, whichever is better). Do *not* refer to the other person's initial number or proposal. Ignore it. If you counter with an equally unreasonable number, you will either contribute to the impasse or make the road to agreement longer and more difficult.

- Indicate that the offer is entirely out of range. Then express your concern that a deal may not be possible. Try to get the other party's negotiators to bid against themselves by saying something like: "That offer is so out of range that we can't even consider it. Why don't you confer with your people and get back to me with something more realistic? I'll be in my office all afternoon."

FAQs About Process

Is it ever acceptable to bid against myself—to make two moves in a row?

It's not a good idea. Just say, "Wait, you seem to be asking me to make another move here. I made the last offer; I don't want to bid against myself. Give me your offer." This usually elicits at least a token move from the other side.

If it doesn't—if the other person is stuck and the only way to make progress is for you to move again—announce your awareness of what you are doing. State that your action should not be considered a precedent. Make your next move in good faith, to a proposal or number you can justify as reasonable. Explain your reasoning, and ask the other side to do the same. If they don't, you may have reached an impasse.

To bridge the gap, consider broadening the discussion of the parties' interests, and formulating other creative options, perhaps through joint brainstorming. You might also bring in a third-party facilitator.

Is it smart or fair to bluff?

Is *bluffing* during a negotiation okay? Sure. One man's puff is another's positive spin. One woman's bluff is another's best foot forward. Lying about a material fact, however, is almost certainly grounds for legal action. In certain circumstances, creating a false impression or failing to disclose material information may constitute legally actionable fraud or misrepresentation. Nevertheless, as long as what your side offers has real value, you need not reveal all the circumstances that make you willing to conclude a deal.

Consider a situation in which you're negotiating the terms of an offer you've received to head up the HR department in a large corporation. There is nothing wrong with describing the major projects for which you have been responsible in the past and your likely next step on the corporate ladder in your current company. Neither is there any shame in describing your achievements in the most positive light possible. At the same time, you need not mention that the CEO at your current company is impossible to deal with—and that that's part of the reason you're looking for another job.

In a complex deal, is it better to reach agreement issue by issue or wait until the end?

Every deal is different, but it's generally better to aim for tentative agreements, or agreed-upon ranges, for each issue, one at a time. This will give you the flexibility to make value-creating trade-offs between issues later on and to create alternative packages of different options. The downside of negotiating each issue in serial fashion is that you lose opportunities to create value through trades.

Is it better to deal with difficult or easy issues first?

In general, dealing with easier issues will build momentum, deepen the parties' commitment to the process, and enable the participants to become familiar with each other's negotiation and communication styles before hitting the tough stuff.

In some instances, however, you may want to deal with a more difficult issue as a threshold matter. If you cannot reach tentative agreement on the difficult issues, then you will not have wasted time on the smaller matters. It is also true that once the most difficult issue is resolved, smaller ones often fall more easily into place.

What if there is an unexpected turn in the road—before or after an agreement?

Unexpected developments can endanger potential agreements. They can also undermine agreements already made. Consider this example:

You have signed a fixed-price contract with Info Tech, a software firm that will develop and install a new, multi-application HR information technology system for your company. The contract specifies use of several particular off-the-shelf software applications, which Info Tech will inte-grate as part of its services for your company. But after the contract is signed, the maker of the most important application doubles the price on the product.

Under your negotiated agreement, Info Tech is to bear the risk of fluctuation in material costs. If you insist on that term, Info Tech may try to make up some of the cost in other ways, perhaps by taking shortcuts. If you agree to renegotiate, absorbing some or all of the addi-tional cost (or choosing a different application), Info Tech will be more likely to do a high-quality job for you.

A month after the new system is up and running, you discover that one minor function is less user-friendly than you now realize your company needs. This was not part of the original contract, but you want Info Tech to take it on as soon as possible and at a reasonable price. If you've treated the company well during the price-hike situation, they'll be more likely to treat you well during this stage of implementation of the contract. In other words, what goes around comes around.

Similar events can happen while you're in the process of negoti-ating a deal. In both cases, analyze how the unexpected development affects the decision to go forward. Determine if a deal still makes sense, or if you need to undo the deal that has been negotiated. Also, when a surprise surfaces:

- Contact the negotiator(s) on the other side immediately.

- Acknowledge the unexpected nature of what has happened.

- Affirm your commitment to working on the problem (if you are in fact committed).

- Jointly discuss the underlying principles and intent of the deal as originally negotiated, and agree on what issues or provisions are affected by the unexpected development.

- Pick up the negotiations again.

FAQs About People

What happens when you pit a collaborative negotiator against a positional hard bargainer?

A positional bargainer aims to win at the other side's expense. He or she will agree that "compromise is what will get us to a deal," then expect *you* to make all those compromises.

As an effective collaborative negotiator, you should be able to deal with this type of negotiator *if* you recognize the situation for what it is. After all, you will have analyzed your BATNA, set a reservation price, and considered both opening and first-offer strategies. If the positional hard bargainer refuses to disclose information and begins to use any disclosures against you, that's a clear signal that the outcome of the bargaining will not likely be equally satisfying for both parties. In this case, seek reciprocity or refrain from providing additional information.

The real question is whether you, the collaborative negotiator, will be able to "convert" the hard bargainer, at least enough to create some value in the eventual outcome. The answer is "maybe." If you're effective and resourceful, you should be able to tease out some of the interests underlying the hard bargainer's positions. You may then suggest different options and packages for meeting both parties' interests. Even the most recalcitrant hard bargainer can recognize when it benefits his or her interests to join in creating value.

How should I respond if the other side seeks to change something in its offer after a deal has been reached?

Chances are the people on the other side are afflicted with the *winner's curse*: Whenever they reach a deal, they are cursed with the thought that they could have gotten more.

If the other party tries to change an agreed-upon term of the final negotiation, express surprise or disappointment. Explain that if the change must be made, then the other side must understand that you will want to open up other issues as well. Say something like: "I agreed to a total package. A change on one issue affects the entire package. Are you willing to renegotiate other issues?" If the answer is yes, then the other side's negotiators were sincere, and you should proceed with the renegotiation. If they reconsider and withdraw the request for a change, then assume that they were just testing you. If they insist that they must have this change and no others, express dismay, then decide whether the adjusted deal has sufficient value for you to agree.

What should I do when the negotiator on the other side has a temper tantrum?

Don't respond in kind. Instead, help him or her regain control. The right response will depend on how angry or upset you feel, the value of the deal, and whether you want to proceed. Consider these alternatives:

- Sit quietly. Say nothing. After a few moments, resume the negotiation with a calm voice.

- Stop. Say, "This is getting us nowhere. I'm inclined to leave and let you cool off. Is that what you want?"

If the other party is using shouting to get you upset and throw you off-balance, don't reward that strategy by losing your focus—or your nerve. Also, keep in mind that you have some control over whom you will negotiate with. If you're negotiating with someone from an organization, consider contacting another person from that organization to suggest that a different negotiator be assigned to the deal.

I don't believe what the other side is saying. What should I do?

Suppose you suspect that members of the other team are lying or bluffing. At best, perhaps they're just telling you what they think will prompt you to arrive at an agreement, and they have no intention of following through on their promises. If this is the case, here's how you might respond:

- Make sure the other party understands that the deal is predicated on his or her accurate and truthful representation of the situation. For example: "If you can't provide delivery of this executive-development training on the schedule we've described, it's best to tell me right now."

- Require that he or she provides back-up documentation, and that the deal be explicitly contingent on its accuracy.

- Insist on enforcement mechanisms, such as a penalty for non-compliance (or perhaps positive incentives for early performance). For example: "We expect the final agreement to contain a late fee of $100 per day for every day that milestones are not met. On the other hand, we are willing to pay you a bonus of $2,000 if you can have the work done on or before July 20 of the coming year."

When, if ever, is it appropriate to negotiate over the telephone or by e-mail? Or is a face-to-face meeting essential?

It is far better to negotiate face-to-face, especially when personal, nonverbal cues matter. For example, is this a negotiation in which the other side might be tempted to lie or shade the truth? Are the parties professionally or emotionally invested in what's at stake? These situations often reveal themselves through nonverbal cues.

Some research indicates that people are less likely to lie in person, perhaps because they fear that the other side will detect their deception. Indeed, in a face-to-face negotiation, you can see the sideways glances of members of the other negotiating team. You can also sense when they are becoming uncomfortable. And you pick up the nonverbal cues indicating that something is more important than their words suggest.

Anecdotal evidence indicates that e-mail or other written messages may have a greater tendency to lead to disputes and impasses. For example, imagine sending an e-mail (or fax) to someone who interprets a comment in the message negatively—even when you didn't intend it that way. Because you're not there to see the recipient's offended facial expression or hear his or her exclamation of dismay, you can't correct the wrong impression. Moreover, when the recipient sends you a nasty-sounding reply, you may be tempted to respond in kind—further escalating the bad feelings.

On the other hand, the fact that e-mail communication is devoid of verbal and nonverbal cues, such as tone of voice and facial expressions, can be a big plus for an inexperienced negotiator. If you're just now developing your negotiation skills, you may be less likely to get emotionally whipsawed by an aggressive negotiator on the other side if the bargaining takes place in writing. And since e-mail makes it possible to reflect on a message before hitting the Send button, you're less likely to give away vital information to the other side. Unwarranted disclosure can be a problem in face-to-face discussions, because some people talk too much. Either through thoughtlessness or an effort to make themselves seem important, they give away vital information without realizing how that behavior damages their position in the negotiation. Such negotiators are less likely to do this when e-mail is the medium of communication.

You can remove some, but not all, of the problems associated with e-mail simply by using the telephone. We human beings are pretty good at interpreting one another's tone of voice to keep communications on track. However, the phone makes it more difficult for conversation participants to propose creative ideas. You can't write those ideas on a chalkboard or easel and review them together. And some recent research indicates that people are more likely to bluff over the telephone. On the other hand, if the negotiation centers on a simple issue in which personal communication is not likely to matter, the most efficient method works best.

How should I react when the other side challenges my credentials, status, or authority to make a deal?

Ask yourself, "Why are they challenging me? Are they just trying to make me defensive or put me off-balance? Or do they have genuine concerns?"

In this situation, your best approach is to shift the discussion to general ground rules. Say something like this: "Right. We should be clear about whose approval is needed for a deal—both on my side *and* yours. I am authorized to complete the deal within these parameters: *x*, *y*, and *z*. I need formal approval for any agreements outside those parameters. Now, what about you? What are you authorized to do?"

If the other party challenged your authority to make you feel defensive, the responses described above will enable you to demonstrate that such strategies won't succeed.

Summing Up

This chapter covered frequently asked questions in three areas:

- **Money:** the dangers of stating your acceptable range, smart ways to reveal your bottom line, and ways to respond to unreasonable offers

- **Process:** guidelines for making multiple moves in a row, bluffing, deciding whether to negotiate issue by issue during a complex deal, weighing the advantages of dealing with difficult or easy issues first, and handling surprise developments

- **People:** advice for negotiating with positional hard bargainers, negotiators who seek to change something after an agreement has been reached, people who throw temper tantrums, and negotiation counterparts who you believe aren't telling the truth; the pros and cons of negotiating face-to-face or by e-mail; and what to do when the other party challenges your credentials, status, or authority

Leveraging Chapter Insights: Critical Questions

- In your negotiations, do you generally find dealing with money matters, process matters, or people matters most challenging? Which of the techniques described in this chapter do you think would be most helpful for strengthening your abilities in these areas? How will you practice or implement these techniques?

- Think of an upcoming negotiation. In your view, which money matters, process matters, and people matters do you anticipate will pose the most daunting challenges for you in this negotiation? What steps might you take to prepare for dealing with these challenges?

- What might you do to help other managers in your company to effectively handle the most common money, process, and people issues that come up in their negotiations?

CHAPTER NINE

Manipulative Negotiation Ploys

How to Recognize and Respond to Them

Key Topics Covered in This Chapter

- *Descriptions of the more common manipulative negotiation ploys*

- *A three-step process for steering the negotiation process in a more principled direction*

- *Skills you'll need to reshape the negotiation process*

I N C H A P T E R 7, you saw some examples of negotiating styles that can make the bargaining process unstable or unpleasant, and discovered strategies for dealing with these styles. In this chapter, we take a look at highly manipulative negotiation ploys—tactics that may be at the very least unpleasant or unethical and at most outright illegal. Unfortunately, no matter what types of negotiations you find yourself involved in as an HR executive, manager, or staff member, you may run into an unprincipled bargainer who uses such tactics.

This chapter shows you how to recognize manipulative negotiation ploys and how to respond to them in ways that help you maintain your composure and stay focused on the desired outcome of the bargaining: a mutually satisfying agreement.

A Plethora of Ploys

Unscrupulous negotiators have a wide variety of manipulative tactics at their disposal—from lying and verbally abusing their negotiation counterpart to using various forms of pressure to make you feel uncomfortable (so you'll want to end the negotiation as soon as possible). Table 9-1 lists common tricky tactics.

TABLE 9-1

Common Tricky Negotiation Tactics

Tactic	Examples
Deliberate deception	• Misrepresenting facts (lying) • Misrepresenting authority (giving you the impression that he or she has the power to approve an agreement when that isn't so) • Misrepresenting intention to comply with agreed-upon terms
Psychological attacks	• Setting up the physical environment in ways that create stress and discomfort for you • Saying things that make you feel uncomfortable, pressured, or threatened (e.g., "I'll convince my people to strike if you don't concede" or "You've got twenty-four hours to decide on my proposal") • Making you wait, or refusing to listen to or make eye contact with you • Interrupting the conversation to talk with others • Using aggressive body language, such as pounding the table, pushing objects away, and leaning forward
Lock-in ploys	• Publicly committing to a position before the bargaining starts, in an attempt to force you to be the one to make any concessions
Calculated delays	• Postponing coming to a decision until a time he or she thinks favorable (e.g., a labor leader delays making a decision on a proposal until the last few hours before a strike deadline)
"Dividing and conquering"	• Exploiting potential disagreement among members of your negotiating team by appealing to the person most sympathetic to his or her case
Emotional appeals	• Accusing you of acting unfairly in not agreeing to his or her terms • Stressing his or her sacrifices • Expressing offense at your lack of trust • Asking you to give up more than you should to preserve the two parties' relationship
Deliberate deepening of differences	• Introducing an issue he or she knows will cause the parties to choose sides and stay there
"Good cop/bad cop"	• Staging a disagreement with his or her fellow negotiation team member in which one person acts agreeable while the other acts disagreeable—then using the "bad cop" to retract an agreement or propose something so harsh that the "good cop's" offer seems generous

Sources: Roger Fisher, William Ury, and Bruce Patton, *Getting to Yes: Negotiating Agreement Without Giving In*, 2nd ed. (New York: Penguin Books, 1991), chapter 8; Rollin Glaser and Eileen Russo, *Dealing with Tough Negotiators Workbook* (King of Prussia, PA: HRDQ, 1998); and Tim Hindle, *Negotiating Skills* (London: DK Publishing, 1998), 36–39.

Focus on the Negotiation Process

Most people respond to a manipulative tactic by putting up with it in the hopes that the manipulator will be appeased, or by responding in kind. Though these responses might be understandable, neither one gets the negotiation back onto a principled footing. As Roger Fisher, William Ury, and Bruce Patton explain in *Getting to Yes: Negotiating Agreement Without Giving In* and *Getting Past No: Negotiating Your Way from Confrontation to Cooperation,* the best way to handle a manipulative negotiator is to focus on and change the negotiation *process*—not the detailed terms under discussion or the character or integrity of the other party. These authors recommend three steps for seizing control of the process and turning it in a more principled direction:[1]

Step 1: Know When the Other Side Is Using a Tricky Tactic

Many of us instinctively sense when someone else is trying to manipulate us, take advantage of us, or make us feel uncomfortable. Our stomachs may clench, our palms sweat, or our faces flush. Or we simply feel that something has gone wrong. By noticing such natural reactions, you can more easily detect manipulative moves coming from the other party. You can also spot these tactics more readily by learning more about them—which you're doing by reading this chapter.

Step 2: Raise the Issue Explicitly During the Negotiation

After you've recognized that the other party is trying to manipulate you, bring it up frankly and respectfully. Say something like, "Mary, I may be wrong, but I have the sense that these numbers aren't accurate. I hope you'll understand that I'll need to verify these figures." When you openly discuss the tactic, you reduce its power to unnerve you. And, you may cause the other person to worry about offending you so much that you'll walk away. He or she almost certainly doesn't want you to do that—otherwise, the person wouldn't bother using a ploy!

Step 3: Change the Negotiation Process

To steer the negotiation in a more principled direction, focus on procedure rather than the substance of the bargaining—or the desire to "teach that jerk a lesson." It's far easier to change the negotiation process than to reform the other party. Fisher, Ury, and Patton recommend these strategies for altering the negotiation process:

- **Separate the person from the problem.** If you realize that the other negotiator has deliberately sat you in a chair facing the sun (a sleazy but often-used tactic), don't say, "You've done this on purpose to distract me." Instead, say, "I'm finding the sun in my eyes distracting. Should we revise the timetable for today so that I can be more focused?"

- **Focus on interests, not positions.** Suppose you're negotiating wages with a labor leader, and she has told her constituency that she won't accept less than a 3 percent wage increase during her negotiations with you. She brings this up during her conversation with you as a way of locking herself into her position—and trying to set up the "game" so that you're the one who has to make concessions. In this case, you might say something like, "Why are you committing yourself to an extreme position? Are you trying to protect yourself from criticism? Or from changing your position? Is it in our mutual interest if we both use this tactic?"

- **Insist on using objective criteria.** Frame the principle underlying each tactic as a proposed "rule" for the "game." For instance, "I'm assuming that we'll take turns sitting in the chair that gets all the sun." Don't be afraid to use humor; for example, "I'd like to propose that we alternate spilling coffee on each other each day."

Skills for Reshaping the Negotiation Process

In order to reshape the negotiation process as described above, you need a handful of skills. Rollin Glaser and Eileen Russo (in their

Dealing with Tough Negotiators Workbook) define several skills and provide suggestions for honing them.[2]

Maintaining Your Composure

Manipulative negotiators create an emotionally heated environment in hopes of upsetting you so you're not thinking clearly. By maintaining your composure in spite of the heat, you can evaluate the other person's behavior and statements with a level head and better encourage him or her to focus on the goal of the negotiation: a mutually beneficial accord.

We each use our own techniques to maintain our composure during stressful situations. Here are some ideas to consider:

- Think for a moment about something good in your life—a happy memory, a favorite oceanside cottage, anything that helps you distance yourself from the discussion.

- Lighten up the situation with humor if you think the other person will appreciate a good chuckle or laugh.

- Mentally take inventory of your own interests and needs in the negotiation.

- Take a moment to sum up the goals of the negotiation for the other person.

Gaining Time to Think

When you sense a manipulative ploy, you'll need time to think about how to respond. Consider these techniques for gaining time:

- Pause and say nothing for several or many seconds.

- "Play back" the conversation; for example, "Let me just make sure I understand what you're saying."

- Take careful notes about what your counterpart is saying.

- Suggest a quick break.

- Resist any urge to make important decisions on the spot.

Developing Data

When you find yourself up against a manipulative negotiator, you need to accumulate as much objective knowledge about the situation as you can during the proceedings. These strategies can help:

- Use "feelers" (e.g., "What do you think about this idea?") instead of presenting direct or firm offers to gather insights about the other person's intentions or preferences and prevent a deadlock.

- Make notes about your bottom line on important issues and refer to them during the bargaining.

- Ask the other person what his or her priorities are—time? cost? reputation?

- Pay attention to the other person's body language. What does it suggest about his or her attitudes toward the bargaining so far?

Refocusing the Discussion

When the discussion starts focusing on irrelevant topics or emotional issues that can't be resolved, refocus it on objective information and the underlying needs of both parties. Here are some ideas:

- Ask problem-solving questions that prompt you and the other person to collaborate to address an issue.

- List the underlying needs of each goal and brainstorm ways of meeting those needs. For example, if the other side has a goal of hiring additional staff, see if the underlying need is to accomplish work more effectively. If so, there may be other ways of meeting that need.

- Stop and recall your own needs.

- Bring outside, objective data into the discussion.

- Work together to list all the common interests you can think of.

Handling Information Strategically

Most unprincipled negotiators don't communicate openly during the discussion. In such cases, how you release and ask for information becomes just as important as the information itself for making the other person feel comfortable exchanging information. Consider these ideas for handling information thoughtfully:

- Give the other person reason to trust you by revealing some information. But *don't* reveal it all at once in the earliest stages of the bargaining.

- Give the person enough time to digest new information you're introducing.

- Provide one or two strong reasons for a proposal you're making, rather than listing as many reasons as possible, including weak ones.

- Watch your counterpart for signals that he or she feels positive about the direction the bargaining is taking.

- Gather objective information to verify the validity of the other person's statements.

"The Case of the Manipulative Negotiator and His Savvy Counterpart" shows some of these strategies for dealing with a manipulative counterpart in action.

The Case of the Manipulative Negotiator and His Savvy Counterpart

Lisa is an HR staff member at Anderson & Sons, a large shipping company. She is negotiating with John, a representative of the company's Employee's Quality of Life Committee, over several issues. Over the previous year, the two have engaged in several bargaining sessions with one another. Today, they get together to focus on a specific list of issues: an employee lounge, flex time, and the building's ventilation system. Lisa is in a good mood as the two settle into their chairs in the conference room. But she thinks John seems a bit agitated.

Roughly halfway through the negotiation, John brings up the one issue that he and Lisa have really clashed on in the past: employee drug testing. John has always been totally against the practice, while management has always believed that the company has every right to test employees for drugs. In preparing for the negotiation, John had decided to introduce this sore subject into the conversation, in the hopes of polarizing himself and Lisa. He believes that by deepening the differences between their positions on the issue, he might be able to make her so uncomfortable that she will offer concessions on the drug issue. In a further attempt to manipulate her, he tells Lisa that he has promised his committee members that he would gain her agreement on a no-drug-testing policy. And he insists that she make a decision on the issue by the end of today's discussion.

John's tactics frustrate Lisa, and it takes all her self-control not to snap at him. But she puts her negotiating skills into action. To maintain her composure, she counts to ten silently (a technique that always works for her). Her silence gives John the signal that he may have taken unfair advantage of the situation. Lisa also moves to refocus the discussion, by gently reminding John about the goals of this particular meeting. She suggests that they

Continued

write the three goals on a flipchart. Finally, she asks John to rank the importance of reaching agreement on each of the issues.

Lisa's responses to John's attempts at manipulating her pay off: As the two begin writing their original goals for the meeting on the flipchart and discussing the relative importance of each, John starts mulling over the various issues relating to the employee lounge, flex time, and the ventilation system. Soon he and Lisa are talking in detail about possible solutions to problems associated with these issues, and the issue of drug testing doesn't come up again.

SOURCE: Adapted from Rollin Glaser and Eileen Russo, *Dealing with Tough Negotiators* (King of Prussia, PA: HRDQ), 36.

Summing Up

In this chapter, you saw numerous examples of manipulative ploys unprincipled negotiators have at their disposal—including psychological attacks, deception, emotional appeals, and other tactics.

You also learned about a three-step strategy for responding to such tactics:

1. Recognize that a manipulative ploy is being used.

2. Bring the ploy into the open with the other party.

3. Redirect the negotiation process so that it's back on principled footing.

To use this three-step strategy, you need a handful of skills:

- Maintaining your composure

- Gaining time to think

- Developing data

- Refocusing the discussion

- Handling information strategically

Leveraging Chapter Insights: Critical Questions

- Think of negotiations you've handled in the past in which the other party has used manipulative tactics. How did you handle these situations? What was the outcome? What might you do differently in the future if you run into the same kinds of ploys?

- What are your "hot buttons"—the trigger points that manipulative negotiators can press most easily? For example, are you particularly susceptible to being made to feel ignorant or mistrusted? Are you most vulnerable to aggressive body language and loud voices? How might you desensitize yourself to these hot buttons so that you won't be quite as susceptible while bargaining with an unprincipled negotiator?

- Have you ever tried to use manipulative negotiation ploys? If so, why? What would it take for you to commit to avoiding such tactics?

CHAPTER TEN

Barriers to Agreement

How to Recognize and Overcome Them

Key Topics Covered in This Chapter

- *Die-hard bargainers*
- *Spoilers*
- *Lack of trust*
- *Informational vacuums*
- *Communication problems*
- *The power of dialogue*
- *Cultural and gender differences*
- *Structural impediments*

I N Y O U R W O R K as an HR professional, you may have been involved in some negotiations that couldn't reach completion for the simple reason that one or another party had better alternatives elsewhere. For these parties, negotiations were not in their best interest; it was better to walk away. But you may also have participated in other negotiations that failed even though there *was* a zone of potential agreement, a ZOPA. We need only examine geopolitical history to note the many conflicts that could have been worked out had the parties been more objective and less driven by pride, impatience, stubbornness, or ignorance of the facts. The same unfortunate development happens in business and interpersonal negotiations. This chapter examines barriers to successful negotiations and offers guidelines for overcoming or eliminating them.

Die-Hard Bargainers

They're out there: the *die-hard bargainers*, for whom every negotiation is a test of wills and a battle for every scrap of value. Unless you're willing to play the same game—or lack other options—negotiations with these people may be fruitless. Here are some ways of making the most of this type of situation:

- **Recognize the game they're playing, and don't be thrown off balance by it.** Anticipate low-ball offers, grudging concessions, and lots of bluffing and puffing along the way. Don't let these antics prevent you from analyzing your BATNA and setting your reservation price and aspirations. Try to assess theirs, and proceed accordingly.

- **Be guarded in the information you disclose.** You're dealing with highly acquisitive people who will take whatever information you reveal and use it against you—and give nothing in return. So, disclose only information that the other side *can't* use to exploit you.

- **Test the other side's willingness to share information.** If you're unsure about the other person's attitude, let slip a minor piece of information and see what the individual does with it. Does he or she use it against you? Or respond by offering information to you? If the answer is "yes" to the first question and "no" to the second, be guarded with any further information.

- **Try a different tack.** Suggest alternative options: "Here are two alternatives for solving this problem." Ask which the other side prefers, and why. That will throw the ball into the other party's court, tempting him or her to respond. If the other party won't respond, ask if it would be better or worse if you added or eliminated one of the options. Continue in this manner. The idea is to get the other party to show more of his or her hand.

- **Be willing to walk away.** Clearly, the other side sees some value to reaching an agreement, or there would be no need to negotiate. The other party will be less overbearing if he or she knows that the behavior creates the risk of no deal at all.

- **Strengthen your BATNA.** If your position is weak, the other side can bully or ignore you with little risk. But if your BATNA is strong—or growing stronger over time—your negotiating counterpart will be more respectful of your interests. (See "Speak Softly but Build Your BATNA.")

Speak Softly but Build Your BATNA

In the years following the French Revolution, tensions mounted between France's new government (the Directory) and the fledgling United States. The Directory closed French ports to U.S. shipping, and its navy captured many American trade vessels in what became known as the Quasi-War. Envoys sent to Paris to negotiate a peaceful relationship and open trade were turned away.

The Quasi-War at sea, and popular revulsion at the murderous excesses of the revolution, turned American opinion against its former ally, and many clamored for war. President John Adams stood squarely against the urge to declare war, seeing only danger and damage that would result from such a move. He sought, instead, a peaceful settlement of disputes and a resumption of trade, and he kept up a diplomatic campaign over several years to secure both.

France had clear advantages in its dispute with the United States. It did not need U.S. friendship and trade as much the United States needed these things from France. And once Napoleon Bonaparte came to power, France became the most formidable military power in the Western world. It could afford to treat the small North American country in high-handed fashion—and it did.

Undeterred, Adams kept pushing for negotiations. But at the same time he strengthened his position (i.e., his BATNA) by building up the American navy from a handful of vessels to fifty ships, including state-of-the-art frigates. That maritime clout helped break the impasse. "Adam's insistence on American naval strength," wrote biographer David McCollough, "proved decisive in achieving peace with France" in 1800.[a] A century later, another American president, Theodore Roosevelt, followed Adams's example, summing up his diplomatic approach with the slogan "Speak softly but carry a big stick."

[a] David McCullough, *John Adams* (New York: Simon & Schuster, 2001), 366.

Spoilers

Particularly in multiparty negotiations, certain stakeholders may prefer "no deal" as the outcome. Let's call them spoilers. These individuals may have the power to block or sabotage your negotiations. They may be directly involved in the negotiation, or they may not. For example, the president of the United States may negotiate a trade deal with a foreign nation, but two or three powerful senators who view the deal as contrary to the interests of their constituents may block ratification in Congress. An influential executive who has the ear of key board members can sometimes accomplish the same result.

You can anticipate this barrier to an agreement by identifying all key stakeholders, their respective interests, and the power of each to affect the agreement and its implementation. Then identify potential spoilers and consider whether you need to "sweeten" the negotiation in a way that would neutralize their incentive to sabotage an agreement. See "Tips for Dealing with Spoilers" for additional strategies.

Tips for Dealing with Spoilers

Many internal negotiations aim to create change within the organization. Change is a necessary condition of vitality, but it often creates winners and losers. And those who see themselves as potential losers do what they can to resist or undermine change.

"The reformer has enemies in all those who profit by the old order," Machiavelli warned his readers. And what held true in sixteenth-century Italy remains true today. Some people clearly enjoy advantages that—rightly or wrongly—they view as threatened by change. They may perceive change as a danger to their livelihoods, their perks, their workplace social arrangements, or their status in the organization.

Anytime people perceive themselves as losers in the outcome of a negotiation, expect resistance and possible sabotage. Resistance may be passive, in the form of noncommitment to the goals and

Continued

the process for reaching them, or active, in the form of direct opposition or subversion. Here are some tips for dealing with resistance and possible sabotage:

- Always try to answer the question, "Where and how will this change create pain or loss in the organization?"

- Identify people who have something to lose, and try to anticipate how they will respond.

- Communicate the "why" of change to potential resisters. Explain the urgency of moving away from established routines or arrangements.

- Emphasize the benefits of change to potential resisters. Those benefits might be greater future job security, higher pay, and so forth. There's no guarantee that the benefits of change will exceed the losses to these individuals. However, explaining the benefits will help shift their focus from negatives to positives.

- Help resisters find new roles—roles that represent genuine contributions *and* mitigate their losses.

- Remember that some people resist change because it represents a loss of control over their daily lives. You can return some of that control by making them active partners in your change program.

- Build a coalition with sufficient strength to overpower the spoilers.

Lack of Trust

Agreements are difficult in the absence of mutual trust. "How can we negotiate with these people?" is a common refrain in bargaining situations in which trust is missing. "We cannot believe a thing they tell us. And if we were to make a deal, how could we be sure that they'd hold up their end of the bargain?"

The importance of trust was cited by Dominick Misino, a retired New York Police Department hostage negotiator, in the *Harvard Business Review*. Trust, he said, begins with civility and respect:

> *When I'm dealing with an armed criminal, for example, my first rule of thumb is simply to be polite. . . . A lot of times, the people I'm dealing with are extremely nasty. And the reason for this is that their anxiety level is so high: A guy armed and barricaded in a bank is in a fight-or-flight mode. To defuse the situation, I've got to try to understand what's going on in his head. The first step to getting there is to show him respect, which shows my sincerity and reliability. So before the bad guy demands anything, I always ask him if he needs something.*[1]

The sincerity and reliability cited by Misino are the building blocks of trust.

Given the choice of negotiating with an untrustworthy party, people with realistic options will turn to their alternatives, or they will hedge the agreements they make with these parties by making them more narrow or limited than they would otherwise be. Negotiation scholars refer to these as *insecure agreements*. But don't give up too quickly if you suspect the other side is not entirely trustworthy.

Emphasize that the negotiation is predicated on their accurate and truthful representation of the situation.

- **Require that they provide back-up documentation,** and that the terms of the accord be explicitly contingent on the documentation's accuracy.

- **Structure the agreement** in a way that makes future benefits contingent on current compliance and performance.

- **Insist on** *compliance transparency*—the ability to monitor compliance from the outside. You want to craft an easily monitored compliance mechanism that assures you that the other party is honoring the terms of the agreement. For example, if you've agreed to license a proprietary technology in return for royalty payments, build into the agreement your stated right to examine the other side's books on a regular basis to ensure the proper calculation of royalties.

- **Require enforcement mechanisms**, such as a security deposit, escrow arrangement, or penalties for noncompliance (or perhaps positive incentives for early performance).

You can also help to foster a climate of greater trust by building relationships between people and by improving the channels of communication between the organizations involved in the negotiations. Joint ventures, for instance, require substantial trust between independent organizations. Experienced managers of joint ventures give key personnel of the different parties opportunities to know each other and to collaborate in making decisions. They arrange meetings within which people from both organizations can communicate about and address problems, opportunities, and workplace frictions. These mechanisms create opportunities for people to build the trust needed for the venture's success.

Information Vacuums

Negotiators have difficulty connecting with each other when they have little or no pertinent information about their counterparts' interests. In the absence of illuminating information, they pass by each other like ships sailing in darkness. Consider this example:

> *PeoplePro, a small HR consulting firm, had just won a big contract from a major new client to deliver a series of executive-development workshops over the next twelve months. PeoplePro often hired independent consultants to take on large projects. Jarrod, a project manager at PeoplePro, was scrambling to identify the right independent consultants for the new contract and set up contracts with them. To deliver the workshops, PeoplePro needed to sign contracts with consultants who had strong leadership-training and change-management backgrounds and skills. Unfortunately, all of the people Jarrod had in mind were backlogged with other work. Then he found Levin Associates, a small, new HR consulting group near the city in which PeoplePro operated.*

Neither of the two companies knew much about the other. More-over, Jarrod and Polly, the representative from Levin Associates, had reasons for not sharing certain information. For example, Jarrod didn't want Polly to know how desperate he was to find the right personnel to deliver the workshops for PeoplePro's new project. Without them, PeoplePro's agreement with the new client might founder. "If the people at Levin Associates knew this," Jarrod told himself, "we'd be in a poor bargaining position and bound to get gouged on the price. They'd know that they had us over a barrel." Meanwhile, Polly also felt that her company was in a poor bargaining position. "If PeoplePro learned that we're having severe cash-flow problems," she told her boss, "they'd demand a rock-bottom fee—and we'd probably give it."

Though PeoplePro and Levin Associates need each other for important business reasons, neither realizes it. Each fears to reveal information about its situation. And if neither Jarrod nor Polly speaks up, the two could easily fail to negotiate a deal. Operating in the dark, PeoplePro's offer to engage Levin Associates' personnel at particular rates and Levin's proposed fee for hiring out its consultants might be so far apart that each party would be encouraged to withdraw.

This situation is symptomatic of what scholars call the negotiator's dilemma. In this dilemma, both sides could create value if *both* offered information about their needs and their business situations. But either will suffer if only *one* shares such information and the other does not. Consider the possible outcomes shown in figure 10-1. Here it's clear that both companies will make modest gains if both are open and truthful. It's also clear that either party stands to make a major gain if it conceals information or misleads when the other is open and truthful.

In the negotiator's dilemma, a party puts itself at risk by being the first to disclose important information. It stands to benefit most by keeping quiet and encouraging the other side to open up. If both sides maintain silence, however, both will ultimately lose.

So how can negotiators resolve this dilemma for mutual benefit? The best answer is cautious, mutual, and incremental information sharing. Here, the people on one side take a small risk: They reveal a minor piece of information about their interests. They follow this revelation with a query: "Now, tell us something about your interests."

FIGURE 10-1

The Negotiator's Dilemma

		Levin Associates	
		Be open and truthful	Conceal or mislead
PeoplePro	Be open and truthful	Both companies make modest gains.	Small gain for PeoplePro; major gain for Levin Associates.
	Conceal or mislead	Major gain for PeoplePro; small gain for Levin Associates.	Neither company gains. Negotiations may fail.

Source: Adapted with permission from Michael D. Watkins, "Diagnosing and Overcoming Barriers to Agreement," Class Note 9-800-333 (Boston: Harvard Business School Publishing, revised 8 May 2000), 4.

Reciprocity by the other side helps create a climate of trust in which the two sides can safely share still further information. As trust and sharing continue, the parties put more of their key cards on the table in turn—and identify opportunities for mutual value creating and value claiming.

Communication Difficulties

Communication is the medium of negotiation. You cannot make progress without it. Poor communication renders the simple treacherous and the difficult impossible. Communication problems cause deals to go sour and disputes to ripen. When you suspect that communication is causing the negotiation to go off track, try the following tactics:

- **Ask for a break.** Replay in your mind what has been communicated, how, and by whom. Look for a pattern. Does the confusion or misunderstanding arise from a single issue? Were important assumptions or expectations not articulated? After the break, raise the issue in a nonaccusing way. Offer to listen to the other side's perspective on the issue. Listen actively, acknowledging their point of view. Explain your perspective. Then, try to pinpoint the problem.

- **Have someone else act as spokesperson.** If the spokesperson of your negotiating team seems to infuriate the other side, assign someone else to take this role. Ask the other side to do the same if the spokesperson for that side drives your people up the wall.

- **Jointly document progress as it is made.** This is particularly important in multiphase negotiations. It will solve the problem of someone saying, "I don't remember agreeing to that."

The Power of Dialogue

Dialogue is a powerful mode of communication. It is a time-tested form of communication in which parties exchange views and ideas with the goal of reaching amicable agreement. Dialogue is usually the best way to peel back the layers of problems, bring undisclosed concerns to center stage, develop solutions, and reach common understandings.

Though the practice of dialogue between two or more individuals undoubtedly has roots stretching far back into human history, it was Plato, through his Socratic dialogues, who helped the Western world appreciate its power. Plato's purpose was not to tell us what *he* thought directly, but to teach us how to toss ideas back and forth in a logical process that eventually leads to the truth and common understanding. That same logical process makes negotiations run more smoothly, draws out the best ideas, and builds agreement around those ideas.

Dialogue can also help you give direction without telling people what to do in so many words—which is what many of us in today's participatory organizations must learn to do. For you and other HR professionals, negotiating with people is as important as directing them. For example, instead of saying, "Have the workforce turnover report on my desk at 3 p.m. tomorrow," try something like this:

You:	What progress have you made on the turnover report?
Your staff member:	It's almost ready. I only have one section to complete.
You:	Good. Do you see any problem in getting it all wrapped up by tomorrow afternoon?
Your staff member:	No, not if you need it by then.
You:	Yes, I do need it by 3 p.m. at the latest.
Your staff member:	You can count on it.

What works between managers and their direct reports can also work between negotiating parties if they start slowly, practice active listening, and gradually develop the level of trust that problem solving requires.

Cultural and Gender Differences

Our language, thought processes, perceptions, communication styles, and personalities are formed by a web of culture, including national, gender, and social dynamics. Culture is a cluster of tendencies that are more prevalent in one group than another—how people behave and think. We tend to attribute any mystifying behavior in other people to, say, an individual's national character, the ways of women, the personality of lawyers, or even the culture of a certain company.

But culture does not determine or predict any *single* individual's behaviors or choices: There are always great variations within given populations. Thus, an Italian engineer may have more in common with a German engineer than with an Italian artist. A female lawyer may have more in common with a male lawyer than with a female musician.

People often attribute a breakdown or difficulty in negotiation to gender or cultural differences, when these may not be the cause of the problem at all. They throw up their hands and say, "The problem is that she's a woman and can't deal with conflict." Or, "He's late because that's how Argentinians are with time." Don't make these mistakes. By attributing problems to gender or culture, you may miss the fact that the female negotiator is signaling her company's resistance point. Or you may fail to pick up on production problems at the Argentinian company. Rather than making assumptions, use the following techniques to analyze differences that arise in negotiation:

- If you're negotiating with someone from a culture very different from your own, and if you're experiencing problems understanding or dealing with each other, look for a pattern in these problems. Ask yourself: What kinds of issues are always tripping us up? What types of misunderstandings are we having? If you find a pattern, analyze it together.

- If you have the time, review any available literature about the other negotiator's culture and how it compares with yours. How is it different? Does this explain the pattern of problems you have had?

- Different cultures sometimes bring different, unspoken assumptions to the negotiating table. These can create barriers to agreement. Michael Watkins refers to assumptions as "the deeper, often unspoken beliefs that infuse and underpin social systems. These beliefs are the air that everyone breathes but never sees."[2] Look in particular at assumptions about who should make decisions, what is of value, and what will happen if agreement is reached.

- Differences in organizational culture may also lie behind the problems plaguing negotiators. For example, if your meetings with a joint venture partner seem to be going nowhere, the difference between your organizational culture and that of the other party may be causing the problem. This is especially true when one company is highly entrepreneurial ("let's get this done") and the other is highly bureaucratic ("we must follow established procedures"). This was the problem with an R&D alliance between Alza, a small, entrepreneurial start-up based in California, and Ciba-Geigy, the giant Swiss pharmaceutical firm. As described by Gary Hamel and Yves Doz:

[Alza's founder] believed deeply in the value of an informal, egalitarian environment in which unique talents could bloom through self-structuring teams. Alza's teams worked quickly and informally to integrate the many technologies needed to develop advanced trans-dermal drug delivery systems. Ciba-Geigy, on the other hand, was a two-hundred-year-old company. . . . It was the epitome of a traditional, disciplined, dedicated European company. And as a large multinational company, Ciba-Geigy was formally structured and bureaucratic.[3]

As this excerpt suggests, deep historical, cultural, and organizational differences made collaboration and agreement between these companies very difficult. The Alza people expected their partner's people to work at a Silicon Valley pace, while Ciba's people wanted things to move more gradually. To make matters worse, the trust needed to bind the partnership together never developed. The Alza people were always fearful that their larger partner would usurp the one thing they had of value: their technology. This distrust resulted in collaboration along very narrow lines.

Structural Impediments

In some cases, the road to agreement is blocked by structural impediments. Here are a few typical examples:

- **Not all the right parties are involved in the process.** For example, several colleagues are negotiating a work schedule for developing a new product. The people from research and development and marketing are there, but no one invited the manufacturing people, whose input is critical.

  Remedy: Get the right people on board.

- **Other participants in the negotiation don't belong there.** They're not only unnecessary—worse, they're getting in the way.

  Remedy: Get the group to confront the individual or individuals who are blocking progress and ask them to step aside. If a person resists, appeal to a higher authority.

- **A participant or party is acting in bad faith.** One or more participants who legitimately belong at the table are deliberately blocking progress toward an agreement.

  Remedy: If you have the organizational clout to prevail, tell this person or persons to ease off. If you lack that clout, form a coalition of other negotiators to deliver the same message.

- **No one feels a sense of urgency.** Without this spur, negotiations drag on and on.

  Remedy: Add what Michael Watkins calls an action-forcing event, such as a deadline or progress meeting. For example, "We are giving your company an exclusive opportunity to bid on this work. However, if we cannot reach a mutually satisfactory agreement by March 15, then we will have to seek other bids." If a time component was not part of ongoing negotiations, consider adding one. "Since we are in agreement that things are moving too slowly, I suggest that we adopt a timeline that provides for completion of our negotiations by March 15."

- **A contingent negotiation is blocking agreement.** Agreement on this deal is predicated on agreement in another separate negotiation that's going nowhere.

  Remedy: If it makes sense or is feasible, decouple the different deals. If that is not possible, consider adding a time constraint to the other deal.

Summing Up

This chapter examined typical barriers to negotiated agreements and strategies for overcoming or eliminating them.

- Die-hard bargainers will pull for every advantage and try to make every concession come from you. Handle these people by understanding the game they are playing, withholding useful information from them (they'll only use it against you) unless they demonstrate a willingness to reciprocate, and making it clear that you don't mind walking away. If you don't want to walk away—or cannot—do whatever you can to strengthen your position and your alternative to a deal.

- Spoilers are people who block or undermine negotiations. You saw several tips for neutralizing or winning over these individuals, including creating winning coalitions.

- Lack of trust severely impedes any negotiation. Nevertheless, agreements are possible if you take precautions, require enforcement mechanisms, build incentives for compliance into the deal, and insist on compliance transparency.

- It's difficult to arrive at a mutually satisfying agreement—and impossible to create value—in the absence of information. What are the other side's interests? What do they have to offer? What are they willing to trade? Ironically, fear of giving the other side an advantage encourages parties to withhold the very information needed to create value for both sides. Each is reluctant to be the first to open up. This is the negotiator's dilemma. The solution to this dilemma is cautious, mutual, and incremental information sharing.

- Communication problems can also create barriers. You can diffuse these barriers by insisting that each team be led by an effective communicator. Also practice active listening, document progress as it is made, and establish real dialogue between parties. Dialogue is a time-tested communication form in which parties exchange views and ideas with the goal of reaching amicable agreement.

- Cultural and gender differences can block agreement, particularly when one party brings to the negotiation a set of assumptions that the other side fails to notice: assumptions about who will make key decisions, what is of value, and what will happen if agreement is reached. Negotiators who represent organizations with conflicting cultures (e.g., entrepreneurial versus bureau-cratic) may also experience problems in reaching agreements.

- Structural impediments include the absence of important parties at the table, the presence of others who don't belong there and get in the way, and lack of a sense of urgency to move toward an agreement. But each of these impediments has a remedy.

Leveraging Chapter Insights: Critical Questions

- Of all the barriers to agreement described in this chapter, which ones do you encounter most often while participating in negotiations? What steps might you take to surmount these barriers?

- In what ways might you encourage more dialogue during upcoming negotiations that you'll be handling?

- In what ways might you cultivate trust during upcoming negotiations?

CHAPTER ELEVEN

Mental Errors

How to Recognize and Avoid Them

Key Topics Covered in This Chapter

- *Escalation*
- *Partisan perceptions*
- *Irrational expectations*
- *Overconfidence*
- *Unchecked emotions*

I N CHAPTER 10, you learned about the kinds of interpersonal, communication, cultural, and structural barriers that prevent willing parties from forging mutually beneficial agreements. This chapter describes mental errors that many people commit during the negotiating process. When we commit one or more of these errors, we make it harder to arrive at accords that satisfy both parties. The good news is that each of the errors you'll learn about below is amenable to self-correction. Learning to identify—and correct—these errors during a negotiation will help you continue honing your skills as an HR professional.

Escalation

In their book *Negotiating Rationally*, Max Bazerman and Margaret Neale point to "irrational escalation" as an error committed by otherwise levelheaded businesspeople when they get into difficult and competitive negotiations. In their definition, *irrational escalation* is "continuing a previously selected course of action beyond what rational analysis would recommend."[1] We might also think of this mental error as "overcommitment." Bazerman and Neale cite the example of Robert Campeau's ill-fated 1987 acquisition of Federated Department Stores, parent company of Bloomingdale's, as a case of irrational escalation. Campeau wanted Bloomingdale's for its inherent earning power and its potential to anchor various shopping malls he planned to develop. He pursued his quarry boldly despite strong competition from Macy's. This rival also desired the company and put in a high bid. Not to be outdone, Campeau bid some $500 million above Macy's last offer. With that bold stroke, he won the contest—and plunged his own organization into bankruptcy.

The lesson of the Bloomingdale's story, as Bazerman and Neale artfully point out, is that even a good strategy will produce a bad result if it is escalated beyond the point of making sense. Bloomingdale's was a great prize, but not at the price Campeau paid. Paying too much is a lesson that people have learned throughout business history.

Why do normally shrewd individuals fall into the escalation error? Here are possible reasons—and possible remedies.

- **Their egos cannot abide "losing."** Many highly accomplished people are accustomed to getting what they want. And they don't want to be seen coming home empty-handed from a negotiation, particularly when that outcome is highly visible. So, when winning requires paying more than every rational measure says is smart, their egos tempt them to pay. They then point to "future synergies" or other nebulous values as justification for their behavior.

- **Auctions and other bidding contests that pit individuals against each other encourage irrational behavior.** As one consultant put it, "Collectors in particular do not exhibit rational price behavior."[2] In the absence of any particular price expectations, they are more likely to bid up to a price they can afford than to a price they know an item is worth. The urge to have something—and to win out over other bidders—overcomes business sense.

- **A principal/agent problem is at work.** In general, negotiators who spend to win beyond the point of rationality do so with OPM (other people's money). Agents, in particular, can be susceptible to this tendency, because they're negotiating for principals (such as shareholders or corporations). Many agents who fall victim to this error take credit for the "win" and charge the costs to their principals. It's unlikely that they would be so bold, or so reckless, if they were spending their own hard-earned savings.

How to combat escalation? Consider these remedies:

- Get a firm handle on your alternatives to the deal *before* you negotiate. Remind yourself that money you don't throw away on an overpriced deal is money you'll have available to invest in those alternatives. Remember, too, that the money your competitor is using to defeat you is money they won't have at their disposal when the next deal comes down the pike.

- Before the bargaining begins, *objectively* set a price beyond which good sense dictates walking away. Seek agreement and mutual support within your negotiating team regarding that price: "Then we are agreed that we will not offer more than $350,000? Does anyone have a different view?" Agreement by many people regarding a price will reduce the temptation to escalate.

- Set clear breakpoints at which you and your team will stop and assess where you are in the negotiations and where you are headed.

- If, during negotiations, new information suggests raising your walk-away price, apply objectivity in recalculating that price.

- With respect to the principal/agent problem, the best solution is to align the negotiator's rewards with the economic interests of shareholders. (You learned more about this topic in chapter 2.)

Partisan Perceptions

Partisan perception is a psychological phenomenon that causes people to perceive the world with a bias in their own favor or toward their own point of view. For example, loyal fans of either team in a sporting event perceive that the referee was unfair to their side. Democrats and Republicans watching the same presidential debate perceive that their candidate "won." A panel of engineers representing two joint venture partners fails to reach a conclusion as to how well one of the companies has performed its part of an agreement.

Effective negotiators know how to stand outside a situation and see it objectively, thus avoiding partisan perceptions. They can also get inside the minds of the other parties and see their unique—and partisan—viewpoints. You can do the same by applying the following guidelines:

- Recognize partisan perception as a phenomenon to which we all fall prey.

- Put yourself in the other side's position. How would the issue look to you then?

- Pose the issue to colleagues (without revealing which side you are on) and solicit their opinions.

To convey your position to the people in the other party:

- Try to pose the problem as it appears to you, and ask how *they* view it.

- Use an analogy or a hypothetical situation to frame the problem as you see it.

Another technique for reducing partisan perceptions is for the opposing sides to reverse their roles, as in the following example:

When Oscar, an HR director, proposed a new performance-evaluation methodology to the managers of the company's major functions, one of the managers, Carla, objected. "This methodology is going to mean a lot more paperwork for us," Carla argued. Several other managers began objecting as well. "That's not necessarily true," responded Oscar. "And we really need to take steps to boost productivity in this competitive market. I believe this methodology can help us."

Faced with stiff resistance from the managers, Oscar formed a fact-finding committee to investigate the various merits and demerits of the proposed methodology, with all interested parties represented. Each side presented its facts—on the costs of the methodology, on the potential impact on workforce productivity, on the degree of administrative tasks associated with introducing and using the methodology, and so forth. Still, neither Oscar nor the resisting managers would accept the other's facts or interpretations of the information. Tensions rose.

Sensing that the conversation would continue to go around in circles, Oscar suggested that he and several of the managers reverse their roles—each of them representing the "facts" gathered by the other side, and vice versa. Moreover, each would develop a coherent and compelling case using the other side's facts.

By the end of the role reversal exercise, both Oscar and the managers had a greater appreciation for one another's point of view. And though they continued to disagree on some points, they eventually arrived at an agreement for a new performance-evaluation process that addressed each of their concerns.

Irrational Expectations

Negotiators find it difficult to reach agreement when one or more of the parties have expectations that cannot be fulfilled. Irrational expectations eliminate any ZOPA, or zone of possible agreement. Many people commit this mental error as they enter into negotiations. Consider this example:

Marie, an HR director, had received approval from her executive team to explore options for outsourcing her company's payroll processes. To get a sense of the potential costs, she talked with HR directors at other companies who had begun doing this sort of outsourcing when the human resource business-process outsourcing (HR BPO) industry had first emerged. Several people told her that their HR BPO provider had charged them about $25,000 for basic payroll services. Of course, Marie expected that her company would have to pay somewhat more than that. After all, in the early years of the HR BPO industry, when lots of new competitors were entering the marketplace, many providers were offering services at lower fees to gain a foothold in the market. So Marie decided that she could expect to pay at most $50,000.

But the first provider that Marie met with to discuss fees surprised her. "For basic payroll services, our rates are $100,000," the account rep told her.

"You've got to be kidding," Marie said. "That sounds way too high, in my opinion."

After some tense words with the account rep, Marie moved on to another provider, where she got the same reaction to her statement of what she expected to pay. "This seems like highway robbery," she thought to herself.

Puzzled, Marie called Paul, another HR colleague, to get his thoughts. "Look, Marie," Paul counseled over the phone. "This industry has changed dramatically in the past few years. There are fewer providers and less competition, and the quality of services—even for basic payroll processing—has really improved. So costs have gone up accordingly. Have you thought about the possibility that your expectations may be out of line?"

Indeed, Marie's expectations were out of line with reality as each of the providers she spoke with saw it. Nor did she have the bargaining power to force them to accept her point of view. The only way she could hope to negotiate a contract with an HR BPO provider would be to reconsider her expectations about costs.

Cases like this one are not uncommon, but they are not insoluble. In Marie's case, her irrational expectation resulted in no ZOPA, as described in chapter 5. With providers' reservation price somewhere around $100,000 and Marie's somewhere around $50,000, there was simply no overlap in which agreement could be struck. This sorry situation might have been remedied if the parties had provided one or both of the following:

- **Educational dialogue.** One of the HR BPO account reps might have had a calm, heart-to-heart conversation with Marie in which he shared industry pricing trends showing that his company's fees were in line with the market. This bit of education might have induced Marie to rethink her reservation price substantially.

- **New information.** Marie might have provided information (if she had it) to encourage one of the account reps to change his reservation price—and his expectation of future business. For example: "Here's an article I recently read in *HR Today*, which says that corporations can expect to pay less for outsourced payroll services if they also sign on for additional services with one provider."

Either of these tactics would have defused the problem caused by irrational expectations.

As you consider upcoming negotiations in which you'll be involved, ask yourself what your expectations are as you prepare to negotiate with your boss, a peer, a vendor, or an employee. Are those expectations realistic? Will the other side have similar expectations on key negotiating points? If your expectations and theirs are significantly at variance, you may find it impossible to arrive at an accord. Think about ways to bring both parties' expectations in line with fact-based reality.

Overconfidence

Confidence is a good thing. It gives us the courage we need to tackle difficult and uncertain ventures—such as negotiations. *Too much* confidence, however, can set us up for a fall. How? It encourages us to overestimate our own strengths and underestimate those of our negotiation counterparts. Consider the example of the American Civil War. Each side expected to "whip" the other quickly and "have the boys home" within a few weeks. Four years and hundreds of thousands of casualties later, the contending sides were still slugging it out—and on a scale that neither side could have envisioned. Leaders of the Imperial Japanese Navy made a similar error on the eve of the Battle of Midway. They dismissed the U.S. Navy as incompetent and unwilling to fight. That overconfidence encouraged them to take a tactical risk that resulted in heavy losses and a turning of the war's tide in the Pacific. Overconfidence can mar negotiations in both business *and* interpersonal disputes, where one or both parties reject settlement in favor of litigation: "We are very confident that the court will find in our favor. The lawyers say that we have a very strong case."

Overconfidence can blindside negotiators to dangers and opportunities alike. It is reinforced by a related mental error known as *groupthink*. The late Irving Janus, the Yale psychologist who coined the term, defined groupthink as "a mode of thinking that people engage in when they are deeply involved in a cohesive in-group, when the members' strivings for unanimity override their motivation to realistically appraise alternative courses of action."[3] Groupthink stems from the convergence of thinking around a norm. Unfortunately, that convergence is driven less by objectivity than by social and psychological pressures. In the end, opposing views are repressed in favor of homogeneity and an illusion of certitude. Those who "think otherwise" are either reeducated or pushed out. Here are some symptoms of groupthink:

- An illusion of invulnerability exists.

- Leaders are insulated (protected) from contradictory evidence.

- Group members accept confirming data only.

- Those holding divergent views are censured.

- Participants don't consider alternatives.

- Members of the "out" group are discounted or demonized.

Do you see any of these symptoms in your negotiating team? If you do, consider this suggestion for getting rid of them before groupthink leads to critical thinking errors: Empower a team of bright and respected people to find and objectively represent the relevant data. This same team should examine and report back on every one of your key assumptions.

Unchecked Emotions

People tend to assume that unchecked emotions occur only in personal negotiations, such as divorces, but rarely in business. Not so.

Business partnership and relationship dissolutions are called "divorces" for a good reason: They involve tremendous anger and personal vitriol. See "Fairness Matters" for an illustration of how making one party angry can destroy what might have been a beneficial outcome for both negotiators.

Fairness Matters

Anger and irrational behavior are often triggered by an offense to one party's sense of fairness. People will sometimes forgo tangible personal gains rather than be party to an agreement that treats them unfairly. Consider how most people would behave in the following situation, which we've adapted from a story told in Bazerman and Neale.[a]

Stephanie and George are having lunch in the company cafeteria. Their boss sits down and says, "I have $100 in my pocket, which I'm willing to give to you. There are only two conditions." Looking at George and showing him a stack of $1 bills, he says, "The first condition is that George must decide how the $100 will be split between you. The second condition is that I will keep the money if you two cannot agree on how the money will be divided."

Stephanie and George are both amazed by the offer, but not entirely surprised, since their boss is always pulling stunts like this. George thinks to himself that any amount he allocates to Stephanie is money she would not have otherwise. Rationally, she should be willing to agree to any split he offers. "Okay," he says. "Here's the deal. I'll give Stephanie $20 and keep $80 for myself."

"Keep your lousy $20," Stephanie says, leaving the table. "That's really unfair."

The boss laughs and returns the wad of bills to his pocket, leaving George empty-handed.

The lesson of this little story is that rationality can be trumped by one party's offended sense of fairness. George wrongly assumed that Stephanie's rationality would get her to accept the $20/$80 split.

[a] Max H. Bazerman and Margaret A. Neale, *Negotiating Rationally* (New York: Free Press, 1992), 116.

Bad things happen when anger takes control of a negotiation. The parties stop focusing on logic and rational self-interest. Inflicting damage on the other side becomes the goal, even when doing so damages one's own interests. For example, if Oscar had let his frustration over the initial impasse with Carla and the other managers over his proposed performance-evaluation methodology get out of hand, he may have resorted to nasty behaviors, such as challenging the managers' commitment to the company's best interests. At best, their relationship could have soured; at worst, Oscar could have decided that he was up against an impossibly resistance corporate culture—and resolved to look for more satisfying work elsewhere.

Negotiators cause huge damage when they allow their emotions to run rampant. This error often comes up in closely held family businesses in which the founder tries to retire and turn the reins over to a hand-picked successor. In some cases, siblings turn on each other and their parents and practically destroy the business through interpersonal warfare and expensive lawsuits.

If you see this happening in yourself or others during a negotiation, try the following:

- **Agree to a cooling-off period.** Call for a break and suggest that the combatants go to their separate corners.

- **Determine what is making the other negotiator angry.** What does this deal or this dispute mean to him or her? Listen very carefully when the person expresses anger. Search for clues.

- **Acknowledge the problem.** Respond to what appears to be the emotional problem. Express empathy for what the problem means to the other person.

- **Keep the focus on issues and processes.** Remember that people are most often angered and frustrated at a personal level by perceived deception, unfairness, humiliation, or loss of pride and lack of respect. Avoid these land mines by focusing the negotiation on the issues and the problems instead of on individuals and their personalities.

If none of these suggestions works, you might try to arrange to work with a negotiator who is less emotional, if that is possible. Otherwise, suggest that the negotiations proceed with a neutral, third-party facilitator: An objective moderator who has the best interests of the contending parties at heart may be able to dampen emotions, act as a medium of communication, and provide the "adult supervision" necessary during subsequent negotiations.

Summing Up

Mental errors by negotiators can result in no agreement—or an outcome that satisfies neither party. This chapter has examined five common mental errors.

- Irrational escalation is the continuation of a previously selected course of action beyond the point where it makes sense. Some people commit this error because they cannot stand losing. Others fall prey to "auction fever."

- Partisan perception is the psychological phenomenon that causes people to perceive reality in their own favor or in ways that confirm their own point of view.

- Irrational expectations can eliminate zones of possible agreement.

- Overconfidence encourages negotiators to overestimate their own strengths and underestimate those of the other party. It is reinforced by groupthink, a mode of thinking driven by consensus that tends to override the motivation to realistically appraise alternative courses of action. The antidote to both overconfidence and groupthink is to have one or more objective outsiders examine your assumptions.

- Unchecked emotion can crop up in business negotiations, and generally result in damage to your own position. Remedies include a cooling-off period and the use of an objective moderator.

Leveraging Chapter Insights: Critical Questions

- Of the five mental errors described in this chapter, which (if any) do you feel you're most susceptible to making? What steps might you take to reduce your tendency to commit these errors in future negotiations?

- Have you found yourself in negotiation situations in the past where the other party committed one or more of these errors? If so, how did you respond? What was the outcome? What might you do differently during future negotiations to turn such negotiations in a more positive direction?

CHAPTER TWELVE

Negotiations with Job Seekers and Employees

Handling Agreements About Salaries, Counteroffers, and Legal Arrangements

Key Topics Covered in This Chapter

- *Agreeing on starting salaries and benefits packages with job seekers*

- *Negotiating a counteroffer with a valued employee*

- *Determining legal agreements*

A s an HR professional, you may well find yourself engaging in a wide range of negotiations with job seekers, employees, your boss, peer managers, union leaders, vendors, and other parties. Each of these negotiations presents its own challenges. To handle these situations successfully, you need to approach them with unique strategies and techniques. Chapters 12–17 explore this world of HR negotiations, offering examples and insights into how to approach these situations.

In this chapter, we'll focus on negotiations you might typically engage in with job seekers and employees—from working out starting salaries and benefits packages to negotiating a counteroffer to a valued employee who is considering leaving the company. These situations may also include negotiating legal agreements such as offer letters, covenants not to compete, and confidentiality agreements with new employees, or separation agreements with discharged employees.

Working Out Starting Salary and Benefits Packages with Job Seekers

In negotiating starting salary and benefits packages with job seekers, you play a central role in staffing for your company. When the labor market is tight or the economy is struggling, your skill at handling such negotiations becomes even more crucial. Why? Only by attracting employees with essential knowledge and expertise can your firm compete successfully against rivals. And in a tight labor market, you'll be competing with other companies for the same talented job seekers. When the economy is struggling, your organization needs to hire at the best possible terms, but still attract the best talent.

Happily, negotiations with job seekers involve many benefits beyond just salary—giving you numerous opportunities to fashion a mutually satisfying agreement. And, you can probably obtain a detailed set of guidelines from your organization explaining how best to handle such negotiations. According to the results of a SHRM/ CareerJournal.com survey, many organizations have developed a formula or policy for "negotiating the same top five negotiable points job seekers believe could cause them to reject an offer if it is not negotiated to their satisfaction."[1] These five points are:

- Salary

- Time off

- Payment for relocation costs

- Salary reviews with an option for increases

- Bonuses and other incentives

If your firm has developed such guidelines, familiarize yourself with them. If it hasn't, you'll need to go into these negotiations with as much knowledge as possible about the unique challenges you may face. See table 12-1 for additional statistics about negotiable points during hiring.

TABLE 12-1

Statistics About Negotiable Points During Hiring

Did you know that . . .

- 58% of job seekers consider negotiation of a total compensation package "extremely important"?

- 30% of HR professionals rate themselves as "extremely comfortable" with negotiations with job seekers, while only 6% of job seekers describe themselves in the same terms?

- 19% of HR professionals say they "always" engage in negotiations, while just 8% of job seekers say the same thing?

Source: Negotiating Rewards Poll, Society for Human Resource Management and CareerJournal.com, July 2001.

According to Paul Falcone in *The Hiring and Firing Question and Answer Book*, several special issues can arise during hiring negotiations:[2]

- **Salary negotiations are the most misunderstand portion of the hiring process.** Assuming that the salary offer represents their perceived value to the organization, many job candidates see negotiations over salary as the "ultimate swing factor" in accepting or rejecting an offer. Yet some candidates may not understand the forces shaping salary offers—such as "internal equity" considerations (the need to "slot" a salary offer among other existing employees on the team) and budget considerations.

   Your strategy for handling this issue? Discuss salary from the outset in your candidate screening and interviewing process. If your firm has set a cap for a particular position's salary, share that fact with candidates up front. And avoid quoting salary *ranges*— you'll only direct candidates' attention to the highest end of the range. If you or someone else inadvertently mentions a range but your company can't pay the highest end of that range, explain the importance of internal equity considerations so candidates will understand the reasons behind the cap. Finally, after offering this explanation, gently "tug the offer away" by saying something like, "We understand if you'll need to pursue opportunities with other companies." This technique enables you to assess whether the candidate is still interested in your firm.

- **You're competing against another company that has made an offer to the same candidate.** In some job-offer situations, the candidate has agreed to a salary and benefits package but then receives a better offer from a different company just as you're about to extend the formal offer. The person makes it clear that he or she is hoping you'll match the better offer.

   What do you do? First, decide how much you want the candidate. Second, examine the internal equity situation and see where the person's overall compensation (if you matched the other firm's offer) would place him or her relative to existing employees. If offering the better deal would upset the balance, the move may not be worth it. (It's only a matter of time before other employees find out about inequity.) If you *can* afford to improve your offer somewhat, but not match the competing offer, be open and fair to minimize any perceptions that you're willing to engage in back-and-forth, incremental negotiations.

Also, find out what other forms of value the candidate might be interested in besides salary. Say something like, "I believe tug-of-war negotiations start employment relationships off on the wrong foot. I'd like to make you a good faith offer above what we originally agreed on, but this will conclude our negotiation. If the new offer isn't acceptable, I'll understand. And before I share the revised offer with you, let's compare the two companies and jobs. I'd like to get your thoughts about which position might be the best logical move for you from a career-development standpoint." The candidate may well decide that your company would provide him or her with better career opportunities than the other firm could.

See "Negotiating with Job Seekers: Do's and Don'ts" for further guidelines.

Negotiating with Job Seekers: Do's and Don'ts

- *Do* familiarize yourself with any guidelines your organization has developed for negotiating salary and benefits with job seekers.

- *Don't* assume that job candidates are interested only in salary.

- *Do* be as open and direct as possible in all your communications with candidates, including during the earliest screening and interviewing stages. Explain the reasons behind salary and benefits offers.

- *Don't* respond to competing offers carelessly. Think through how much you want the candidate, how a matching offer might impact internal equity, and what forms of value (such as career-advancement opportunities) may help you "sweeten the pot" even if you can't match the competing offer.

Negotiating a Counteroffer with a Valued Employee

In every company, it's inevitable that other firms will try to hire away talented employees—especially when labor markets are tight. And some professions, such as IT in recent decades, seem to stimulate more brutal "talent wars" than others—with rival companies offering lavish salaries and perks to lure valued employees away from competitors.

Though you and your firm's affected managers may feel terrible when an employee gives notice to go elsewhere, resist any knee-jerk impulse to make a *counteroffer*. As Paul Falcone explains, counteroffers should *not* become common practice, "because an employee who has gone through the mental process of deciding to terminate employment may have experienced an attitudinal separation [from your company] that can't be overcome readily. In addition, [throwing] dollars at people to keep them aboard . . . could be perceived as desperation by the company . . . and poor career management by the employee [if the counteroffer is accepted]."[3] Moreover, most employees who accept a counteroffer end up leaving in six months anyway, so the counteroffer merely delays the unavoidable. Finally, most people who leave companies do so because of a poor relationship with their supervisor. In such cases, persuading the person to stay by making a counteroffer won't get at the root of the relationship problem.

So when *should* you make a counteroffer? Do so when a top performer gives notice—someone without whom the firm can't function well. As Chris Velissaris notes, these are individuals "who are part of the core competencies the firm needs to complete projects."[4] Replacing such employees is expensive, and sometimes it's easier to pay more salary or offer better benefits to existing key employees than to start hunting for a replacement whom your firm will have to train.

If you've decided that a counteroffer is appropriate, Falcone recommends a structured approach based on genuine concern for the employee's needs. Though money may be important to the person, remember that he or she may value many other opportunities and perks as well—such as a career growth and development, a promotion, a new title, more challenging and interesting projects, a chance to work as a manager, club memberships, leased cars, and so forth. Initiate a counteroffer discussion by letting the person know how much the company values him or her. Ask what prompted the individual to look elsewhere for work and which criteria he or she used to select the firm that has extended the offer. Is it that the other company offers a better title? More opportunities for the person to enhance his or her skills? New contacts with people who can help the individual advance his or her career? More flexible hours or other valuable perks? Ask, "What would have to change here for you to stay with us?" Then say, "If we could make those changes, would you consider staying with us?"

Then express the desire to provide some of the same opportunities at your company. If you can't match everything the other firm has offered, be honest about that. Then explain what you *can* offer. Look way beyond salary. For example, one HR professional's counteroffer contained the opportunity for the employee to enroll in a graduate-level two-year marketing certificate program at the company's expense. The offer also contained two one-week assignments for the employee at corporate headquarters in the coming year—which promised to open new communication channels that might lead to career-development opportunities in the future.

As Falcone explains, even if this approach doesn't culminate in the employee's decision to stay with your firm, "word will get out that you handled the matter professionally, that you put the individual's career interests above your own needs, and that you were 'cool and classy' about the whole thing."[5] A stellar reputation for handling such negotiations can only serve your company in the future.

Falcone also recommends taking a proactive approach to counteroffer situations. *Before* people give notice or threaten to leave, work out a strategy for how you'll keep key players in place. Decide *now* who your company's most important employees are. Then role-play what your firm will do should they ever give notice. Even a proactive conversation with these employees today about their career needs can help you avoid getting into a counteroffer situation in the first place. "Counteroffering Do's and Don'ts" offers further tips.

Counteroffering Do's and Don'ts

- *Do* take steps now to fend off the counteroffer dilemma.

- *Don't* assume that every employee who gives notice should be lured back with a counteroffer.

- *Do* think in broad terms about key employees' career interests in shaping a counteroffer.

- *Don't* emphasize your own, the affected manager's, or your company's needs while discussing possible counteroffers; emphasize the employee's needs instead.

Negotiating Legal Agreements

You likely participate in numerous negotiations related to legal agreements while fulfilling your HR role. These legal agreements may range from job-offer letters, noncompete covenants, confidentiality agreements with new hires, and employment contracts to separation agreements with employees who have been laid off or dismissed.

Of course, with such agreements, there are always some terms that are open to negotiation—such as the starting date for a new job or the span of time covered by a confidentiality agreement. But these agreements also have a "bottom line": the point beyond which you and the other party can't negotiate, because it's illegal to do so. And because employment law is a vast subject involving numerous complex federal and state regulations, you'll want to consult your company's legal counsel to make sure you understand where that bottom line is, versus which terms are negotiable. The best way to successfully negotiate such agreements is to know as much of the law as you can—and to leverage any agreements your company's legal department has already developed.

Let's examine some of these agreements in greater detail below.

Noncompete Agreements

As Debbie Rodman Sandler points out, whenever your firm brings on a new employee, it gives that person access to its most valuable assets: people, customers, ways of doing business. "Given that the average American will change jobs seven times over a work life," Sandler writes, "chances are high that some of that information will eventually find its way to a competitor."[6] For that reason, more and more companies are asking new hires to sign *noncompete agreements*. In some hiring situations, the question of whether the job candidate will sign such an agreement may become a matter of negotiation (i.e., the candidate may not want to sign a noncompete). Thus it's up to you and/or the hiring manager to either insist on the agreement as a condition of being hired, or to negotiate a job offer that's attractive enough to make the candidate want to sign on—noncompete and all.

According to Louis K. Obdyke, noncompete agreements "limit the employee's ability to obtain employment of a same or similar nature within a geographical limitation and for a set period of time."[7] Some noncompete agreements also limit employees' ability to call on your company's customers or clients if they leave your firm—especially if the employees have gone to a competitor or have started up a new company of their own. Finally, noncompete agreements may stipulate against luring other employees away from your firm once an employee has left.

Once signed, noncompete agreements may present additional negotiation challenges if an individual is perceived to have violated them. In such situations, your company may end up at a disadvantage. Why? In the United States, many state courts don't like noncompete agreements. In the courts' view, such agreements overly constrain individuals' ability to earn a living in the field of their choice. As Sandler explains, "Courts faced with having to decide whether to enforce a [noncompete] will consider the following factors: Does the employer have a legitimate interest in being protected from this employee's competitive activity? Is the restriction reasonable in light of all the circumstances? Is the restriction reasonably limited in time and geography? Will enforcing the restriction harm the public interest [as in constraining the activities of a doctor, lawyer, or some other highly specialized professional]?"[8] In addition, during times of high employee turnover, savvy employees will often refuse to sign a noncompete. To negotiate noncompete agreements success-fully, Sandler offers the following recommendations:

- **Avoid the temptation to write a tough, all-inclusive non-compete.** Instead, target the restriction to cover your most important concerns only. For example, limit former sales reps' professional activities only to those accounts with which they had an actual sales relationship during their employment with your firm—rather than restricting their sales activity in the entire territory. To identify your key concerns, ask yourself, "Exactly what activity do we need to prohibit? How long would it take us to overcome competitive harm caused by a defecting employee? What harm will we suffer if the competi-tive activity isn't stopped? Is there a sum of money a former employee could pay that would compensate us for the harm incurred if he or she engages in the prohibited activity during the restricted period?" Also, avoid defining an overly long period of restriction; most courts won't accept it.

- **If you insist on a noncompete, enforce it consistently.** If your company doesn't enforce the agreement in some instances but does so in others, a court may decide that the firm has no compelling interest that needs protecting.

- **If your firm has a noncompete, be cautious in hiring employees coming from other firms that use a noncompete.** If your company hires a competitor's employee, ask the person up front if he or she is subject to any restrictions. Then have the individual sign a statement saying that he or she is not subject to any noncompete or other restriction. If the new hire *did* sign a noncompete, get a copy of it and have your firm's legal counsel review it to see whether it applies to the activities the new hire will be performing at your firm.

Confidentiality Agreements

Also called *nondisclosure agreements* or secrecy provisions, confidentiality agreements prohibit people from disclosing trade secrets or confidential information while they're employed by your firm and for a specified time period after they've moved on to another employer. These agreements protect your firm from damage that can occur if current or former employees share information with competitors about your firm's projects, practices, technologies, strategies, and current or potential customers.

Like noncompete agreements, confidentiality agreements rarely find favor among state courts because of their restrictive nature. Yet according to Attison L. Barnes III and Tara M. Vold, companies now have a new way to protect vital information: the judicially created "doctrine of inevitable disclosure."[9] This doctrine applies to certain people who leave their employer and accept jobs with rival companies of their former employer. Because of the nature of the knowledge that some employees acquired during their tenure—such as information about the company's strategies, processes, and so forth—these employees will inevitably disclose that knowledge to perform their new job. Under the inevitable disclosure doctrine, your company can prevent a former employee from working for a competitor—even if you didn't ask him or her to sign a noncompete or confidentiality agreement, or he or she never threatened to disclose trade secrets. Actual disclosure of such information isn't required for the doctrine to be invoked.

As Barnes and Vold explain, if your company is seeking an injunction under this doctrine, it will need to prove (1) that the former employee's new position strongly resembles the one he or she held at your firm, (2) that the rival company uses processes or methods substantially similar to those of your firm, (3) that the employee's knowledge of your company's strategies and processes have value for your firm's competitors, and (4) that the confidential information is still valuable despite the passage of time.

Barnes and Vold note that this doctrine has been invoked primarily by technology and start-up companies. All organizations, they maintain, should avoid relying on it as the sole means of protecting trade secrets. To limit sharing of confidential information, consider these strategies when negotiating hiring and employment conditions:

- Require employees to sign *reasonable* nondisclosure agreements.

- Create a policy of disseminating sensitive information on a need-to-know basis.

- Restrict employees' access to file drawers and offices containing proprietary information.

- Develop a document retention and destruction policy.

- Routinely inventory confidential information.

- Conduct exit interviews with departing employees to gain a sense of their new positions and to repossess or delete any important company information on employees' home computers.

- Make sure that any job candidate you're considering hiring is not bound by a nondisclosure agreement with his or her former employer.

Separation Agreements

Losing employees through layoffs or firing is always painful—for both employers and affected employees. And as Stephen Roush warns, "Whatever the combination of reasons for elimination of work and regardless of the [separation] packages that are offered, this is a traumatic time and it has the potential to generate litigation." [10] For this reason, many companies negotiate separation agreements with dismissed employees that stipulate severance pay and other possible benefits. According to Francis T. Coleman, "Providing severance packages [also] constitutes good public relations. It creates a good impression in the eyes of the public as well as instilling goodwill on the part of the remaining workforce...." [11]

Yet separation agreements stem from more than just public relations motives on the part of companies. Employers can also negotiate important protections for themselves in return for severance packages to departing employees. To gain these protections for your company, ensure that the separation agreements you and other managers negotiate include the following:[12]

- **Waiver and release of all employment-related claims** the employee may have, beyond certain statutory claims such as unemployment compensation and the right to file charges with government agencies such as the National Labor Relations Board, the Equal Employment Opportunity Commission (EEOC), or state and local civil rights agencies

- **Confidentiality** regarding all the terms of the separation agreement to third parties, including damage provisions in the case of breach of this protection

- **Nondisparagement** in oral or written form about the company

- **No reemployment** of the person by the company or its parent or affiliates

- **"Stay pay"** for laid-off employees who agree to remain on board for a specified period of time

- **Use of arbitration instead of litigation** to resolve any claims arising from or breach of the separation agreement

Separation agreements may also include restrictions often found in the other agreements discussed above—such as return of company property, nondisclosure of trade secrets and other sensitive information, nonsolicitation of the company's customers and employees, and noncompetition. In addition, such agreements may contain clauses specifying the award of legal costs to the prevailing party if either party breaches the agreement.

The key in negotiating a separation agreement is to tailor the agreement as best you can to your organization's needs. Coleman advises HR professionals to "decide to which group or groups the policy will apply. It is permissible to have one policy for one category of employees and a different policy for others as long as such differences are not based on illegally discriminatory motives. . . ."[13] Also, involve your firm's employment attorney early and often in designing a separation agreement. See assessment tool 12-1 for a checklist that can help you negotiate effective separation agreements.

Assessment Tool 12-1
Negotiate Effective Separation Agreements

Use this tool while negotiating a separation agreement with an employee. Or provide this tool to a manager in your company who is negotiating such an agreement. For each statement below, circle "Yes" or "No." Review your responses to determine how you might improve the protections provided in the separation agreement you're negotiating.

In negotiating the terms of the separation agreement, have you . . .

Included a waiver and release of all employment-related claims that the employee may have?

Yes   No

Required that the employee not confide any of the terms of the separation agreement to third parties?

Yes   No

Included terms preventing the employee from disparaging your company orally or in writing?

Yes   No

Stipulated that the employee will not be reemployed by your company or by the company's parent or affiliates?

Yes   No

Included "stay pay" for laid-off employees who agree to remain on board for a specified period of time?

Yes   No

Required the use of arbitration instead of litigation to resolve any claims arising from or breach of the separation agreement?

Yes   No

Included terms specifying the return of company property?

Yes   No

Specified nondisclosure of trade secrets and other sensitive information, if your firm and the employee have not signed a confidentiality agreement?

Yes   No

Specified nonsolicitation of your company's customers and employees and noncompetition if your firm and the employee don't have a noncompete agreement?

Yes   No

Employment Contracts

Most states in the United States recognize employment-at-will—the doctrine that an employee is deemed terminable at any time, for any reason, or for no reason at all. Some states also have judicial rulings that any employment arrangement that doesn't specify a term of employment is terminable at will. (Of course, there are many restrictions on employment-at-will in various states, including implied contract and public policy exceptions, whistle-blower laws, and protections under civil rights laws and collective-bargaining agreements.) On the surface, then, it may appear that the typical organization doesn't need *employment contracts*.

However, as Louis Obdyke points out, many firms have begun negotiating such agreements while hiring specific kinds of employees (such as executives, sales and marketing representatives, and people with special technical skills). The purpose? To ensure the employment of a particularly desirable person for a period of time. Employment contracts tend to be broad—covering the term of employment, compensation and benefits, the employee's duties and expected performance and behavior, and restrictions on the sharing of confidential information and competitive activities during and after the term of employment.[14] As such, many employment contracts contain some or all of the kinds of legal agreements discussed above. According to Obdyke, most employment contracts comprise the following content:

- **Term of the agreement:** the time period covered by the document, including under what conditions the contract is terminable, who can terminate the agreement, and how the contract can be terminated

- **Employee's duties:** for example, "those duties customarily performed by the vice president of marketing."

- **Confidentiality provision:** prohibits disclosure of sensitive information during and after the contract term

- **Compensation and benefits:** salary, sick leave, holidays, fringe benefits, commissions, and so forth

- **Noncompete provision:** limitations on the employee's ability to contact customers or employees after he or she has left your company or to engage in a competitive business while employed by your firm

"Legal Agreement Do's and Don'ts" offers further information. As with other such legal agreements, employment contracts must follow numerous complex federal and state laws. For that reason, always involve your firm's legal counsel in formulating and negotiating such agreements.

Legal Agreement Do's and Don'ts

- *Do* always consult your company's legal counsel in preparing, negotiating, and finalizing any employment-related legal agreement.

- *Don't* assume that legal agreements will be easy to enforce in court.

- *Do* take advantage of standardized agreements your company has developed, rather than "reinventing the wheel."

- *Don't* hire new employees without finding out if they are bound to restrictive covenants such as noncompete and nondisclosure agreements signed with their former employer.

- *Do* familiarize yourself as much as possible with the federal and state laws that affect employment-related legal agreements.

Summing Up

This chapter examined several types of negotiations that HR professionals engage in with job seekers and employees, and explored practical guidelines for handling these situations successfully. The topics covered included:

- Determining starting salaries and benefits packages with job seekers

- Making counteroffers to valued employees who have received job offers from competing companies

- Shaping legal agreements such as employment contracts and noncompete or nondisclosure provisions

Leveraging Chapter Insights: Critical Questions

- How have you typically approached negotiating starting salaries and benefits packages with job seekers? What has worked well during these kinds of negotiations? What has not worked as well? What might you do differently in future negotiations about salaries and benefits packages to forge more satisfying agreements for your company?

- How do you and other managers in your company generally respond when a valued employee receives a job offer from a competing firm? Is the outcome to such situations usually favorable to your organization? If not, what might you and other managers do differently to ensure a more favorable outcome?

- How familiar are you with the "bottom line" in negotiations involving legal agreements, and with the terms that *are* negotiable in such agreements? What might you do to increase your familiarity with these boundaries?

CHAPTER THIRTEEN

Negotiations with Your Boss, Peer Managers, and Other Senior Executives

Exerting Your Influence Effectively

Key Topics Covered in This Chapter

- *Getting your boss's support*

- *Negotiating HR policies with peer managers*

- *Obtaining executive approval for HR projects or expenditures*

- *Participating in your company's strategic planning*

I N THE WORLD of HR negotiations, some of the bargaining situations you engage in may not be nearly as formal as
those involving legal agreements and salary offers. Instead,
they may entail persuading your boss to approve an HR initiative or
support your career development, or negotiating HR policies with
peer managers in your organization. Or they may involve getting
executive approval for HR expenditures (such as new technology or
training) or expanding HR's role in formulating and implementing
corporate strategy. These sorts of negotiations hinge far more on
your ability to influence others than on any formal authority or legal
concerns. Below we examine these situations more closely.

Getting Your Boss's Support

In your day-to-day work and career planning, you'll often find that
you need your supervisor's support to launch an HR initiative or
take on more challenging duties as you advance in your career. At
times you may need to negotiate with your boss over the details of
these efforts. For example, will your supervisor approve the budget
you need for that employee-recognition project you want to implement? Or will he or she agree to promote you to a new level of
responsibility and give you the pay increase you want?

To successfully negotiate in these situations, you need to draw
on all the skills you've learned so far in this book. But you can fur-

ther strengthen your position—and boost your chances of getting your boss's support—by building your credibility and gaining your boss's trust. Here's how:[1]

- **Build a strong relationship with your boss.** Take steps to make your relationship with your supervisor as positive as possible. In straightforward, businesslike conversations, express your desire to work well together. Talk about what you need to do your job well. Take a problem-solving tone, while inviting your supervisor's input. For example, "I've got a few ideas on how we can reduce turnover that I'd like to get your thoughts on." After your boss responds, say something like, "I think those ideas have a lot of merit. Here are some other alternatives I've been thinking about." Always be prepared to make the business case for the resources or other forms of support you need, and keep your boss informed about what you're working on. And if you run into difficulty getting approval for a project or a promotion, keep any frustration or other emotional reaction under wraps. You'll get a lot further by demonstrating savvy business understanding and self-control.

- **Get the "big picture."** Develop a crystal-clear understanding of your company's strategic objectives and the ways in which you can help it meet those goals. Show that you're willing and able to make tough but necessary decisions (such as downsizing or dismissal of a problem employee) as efficiently and effectively as possible. Equally important, develop your awareness of how things work in other areas of the company by serving on committees and task forces comprising individuals from different functions. And cultivate a large network of professional contacts by participating in local trade and industry groups, attending HR- and industry-related conferences and conventions, and taking part in online industry forums.

- **Practice continuous improvement.** Take responsibility for enhancing your own skills by attending seminars, taking classes, and reading trade and professional journals regularly. Stay up-to-date on the trends and issues that exert the most impact on HR and your company's industry. Make it clear that you want to learn and grow. In addition, constantly seek ways to improve the service you provide to others in your company—for instance, streamlining operations or cutting costs.

- **Share your successes and goals.** Don't wait for your boss to notice your accomplishments. From time to time, remind him or her of your achievements; for example, by sending a simple e-mail telling about the results of a task force you recently led, or sharing articles you found interesting. Mention your accomplishments casually during hallway conversations. Also, don't be shy about letting your boss know that you want to advance in your career. He or she can't support you if you don't communicate your intentions.

Negotiating HR Policies with Peer Managers

As an HR professional, you know from direct experience that workforces are changing in response to shifts in demographics, the economy, and business practices. As Stephen Rubenfeld and James Laumeyer maintain, today's employees need flexible work schedules and opportunities to telecommute in order to balance hectic work and family lives.[2] And companies are managing far more ethnically diverse workforces than ever. Finally, younger generations of employees are demanding to be evaluated and rewarded based on their contributions rather than their years of service.

All these issues point to the need for new HR policies that meet employees' needs—and thus enable your organization to retain the talent it needs to compete. These new policies may include more time off, a wider range of benefits choices for employees, and performance-based pay systems. Additional changes might involve team- versus individual-oriented rewards, broader job descriptions, off-site work options, and training in technology.

In addition, with more people working off-site and on self-managed teams, HR professionals must take steps to get buy-in from managers and employees on any new or changed HR policies. As Mary Jo Case, president and COO of HR consulting firm Alliance Resources, explains, "To interpret and administer new policies, managers need to feel that they've participated in developing those policies, and that their concerns have been heard. More and more policies are being written in language that speaks to a policy's impact on organizational culture, and managers will have input into that."[3] Though inviting and responding to input on HR policy changes from peer managers can take more time, Case maintains that this collaborative approach results in better, stronger policies that benefit a wider range of employees *and* provide more solid legal protection for the company.

To gain buy-in for HR policy changes, Case recommends explicating which policies can be negotiated and which cannot, owing to legal implications. In inviting input on a proposed policy change, she also advises presenting managers with a written draft that they can build on and work from. "For most people, that's easier than starting off with a 'blank slate.'" Finally, Case suggests taking time to build positive, trusting relationships with peer managers long before introducing HR policy changes:

> *Get to know their hot buttons and viewpoints by proactively contacting them and asking how you can help them with the issues they're facing. Drop by unannounced or schedule more formal appointments—whatever works best for the people involved. When you ask managers how they see a proposed policy change affecting them and their staff, and what their key issues and concerns are related to the proposal, you'll be more likely to get their trust and their honest feedback if you've already taken time to build relationships with them. You also send the message that HR policies are for everyone's benefit—not just the HR director or particular managers and employees.*

Such strategies, Case adds, require the ability to listen carefully to what managers seem to be saying, and to set aside your sense of ownership of an HR policy.

Nancy Campbell agrees that "change is hard, sometimes excruciating."[4] She explains that anyone seeking to negotiate the details

of a new policy with other managers may well encounter stiff resistance in the form of comments such as, "But we've never done it that
way before!" Often, resistance stems from fear of losing control or
autonomy with the addition of "too many rules and regulations." To
persuade other managers in your firm to accept new or revised HR
policies, you need to make the business case for such changes, as well
as lay the groundwork for policy-related negotiations early. Campbell recommends the following techniques:[5]

- **Make sure policy changes are sound.** Examine your ideas for
  new or changed HR policies for flaws, ensuring that they're
  reasonable and fair and that they support your company's strategy. For example, if your firm has decided to encourage team-
  based achievement, the reward system you're proposing should
  emphasize collective, not individual accomplishments. Ask if
  your idea is workable in practical terms.

- **Involve people early.** As soon as you have ideas for new or
  changed HR policies, involve other managers up front in discussions about these ideas. Get their perspective on the kinds of
  issues your ideas are intended to address—whether it's high
  turnover of staff, employee burnout, or some other problem.
  Probe for concerns about the policy change you're exploring.
  For example, will a new policy mean more work for a manager
  or require more of his or her time? Get these concerns into the
  open. Also look for hard-core resisters, so you can identify with
  whom you may need to take a firm stand later.

- **Continually educate.** As you take further steps in developing
  HR policy changes, keep talking about your ideas with other
  managers. Run additional ideas by them, and periodically
  update them on the status of the changes. Keep soliciting their
  input, listening carefully to their responses. And test possible
  new approaches on them. You'll end up with stronger, sounder
  policies, and you'll boost your chances of successfully negotiating the details of those policies with managers throughout your
  organization.

- **Provide grace periods.** If your negotiations with other managers over a new or changed HR policy have been difficult, consider giving people time to get used to the notion of a policy change and to adopt it gradually before formal enforcement of the policy begins. For example, suppose you're recommending a new performance-evaluation system that's scheduled for implementation in October, but you know that the affected department managers will need several months to start using the system consistently. Announce that any discrepancies between the previous and new system will be handled informally during October; during November, you expect people to begin using the new system more consistently. And by December, you anticipate that the new system will be firmly embedded in the relevant departments.

Obtaining Executive Approval for HR Projects or Expenditures

You've got a great idea for a new HR project—such as a database that you're certain will help your company operate more quickly and efficiently and boost profitability. But the technology is so expensive that you anticipate encountering difficulty getting the go-ahead from the CFO. You're not alone: Many HR projects (particularly those involving costly technology) face numerous roadblocks—including lack of clear financial benefits, competing initiatives, an overly complex business case that others find hard to understand, lack of funds, and lack of a progressive management culture.[6]

If this describes your situation, how might you boost your chances of negotiating successfully for the necessary approval and funding for your project? Your best strategy is to help the individuals who have a say over whether your project moves forward to understand the benefits that HR projects can offer the entire organization. That means *you* need to grasp your company's future goals and the ways in which your projects can support those plans. Julie Britt offers several guidelines achieving both:[7]

- **Demonstrate your knowledge of industry drivers.** These include the forces that most powerfully influence your firm's performance—such as talent management, technology, globalization, deregulation, and leadership development.

- **Study HR trends.** Find out what analysts are saying about HR trends, then use your knowledge to persuade executives to support your initiatives. Startling trends might include increased spending on HR technology, greater adoption of new performance-management methodologies, and so forth.

- **Assess your project's potential strategic impact.** Ask yourself, "Where does HR stand in my firm? Where does my company stand in relation to its competitors? And where could my project take the company in relation to our rivals?"

- **Demonstrate the project's strategic impact.** Explain your project's potential strategic value to your firm and the measurable return on its investment. Identify other initiatives already under way, then show how your project fits with and reinforces those programs.

- **Show the link between sound HR programs and business performance.** For example, one Watson Wyatt study revealed that companies with superior HR initiatives can provide three times as much shareholder return as those without such initiatives and help companies recover from an economic downturn. Thus it may be even *more* important to commit to HR projects during tough times.

- **Learn the language of business.** Master business terminology, and make sure you understand notions such as revenue, operating margin, fixed assets, and shareholder value. Provide the numbers to back up your project's potential, including important benchmark data such as HR cost per employee.

- **Present a compelling case.** Explain how your project will reduce the company's current budget, help the company avoid higher costs or lower revenues, and make life easier for managers and the workforce (for example, managers will spend less time preparing reports, and employees will spend less time traveling).

Participating in Defining Your Firm's Strategy

For many HR professionals, opportunities to contribute to strategic planning have not come automatically. Indeed, as William Kent, vice president of human resources for PK USA, contends, in the past too many executive committees have viewed HR as solely "an administrative function with little or no voice in determining how the business operates. . . ."[8] When attitudes like this prevail, companies, HR staff members, and employees suffer, as HR fails to fulfill its true potential. (See *The Essentials of Managing Change and Transition* in the Business Literacy for HR Professionals series for more information on how you can be an effective strategic partner in your organization.)

To build and keep the opportunity to provide input on how your company can reach its strategic aims—you need to "demonstrate initiative, commitment and an understanding of the organizational needs and issues that impact [your firm's] success."[9] And as with other negotiations involving your boss, peer managers, and other company executives, you'll strengthen your bargaining position by taking a broad view of your firm's business and familiarizing yourself with key business concepts. Here are some suggestions:[10]

- **Recognize your true purpose.** Your purpose is to help your organization manage its human resources well, thereby serving your company's needs—not the needs of your department, your position, or even the firm's employees. This means that every time you present a proposal related to corporate strategy, you need to show how the organization *overall* will benefit from it—in terms of bottom-line profitability.

- **Know your organization and its industry.** Network with coworkers in other departments and get involved in committees and task forces outside the scope of HR duties. Learn as much as you can about the issues facing your firm and its various departments. Look for opportunities to quickly make a contribution to each business area's needs, then plan ways to support their strategy-related goals over the long term. Also, know your company's and its departments' budgets and forecasts, so you can translate them into human capital terms.

- **Know your company's competitors.** Through current staff referrals, solicited and unsolicited résumés, and business newspaper or journal articles, get as full a sense as possible of what your firm's rivals have in the way of human capital. Ask yourself how your company's human capital compares, and use your knowledge to devise strategies for attracting needed talent at the right time.

- **View yourself as a consultant, not a decision maker.** Provide advice to other management based on your expertise and experience, then let the entire executive committee make decisions based on all of the input. But don't accept decisions that violate the law.

- **Back up proposals with objective data.** For example, use numbers and statistics to show how a training or staffing initiative will give your company the headcount and skills to support new growth generated by implementation of the firm's competitive strategy. Provide regular reports on how HR activities are adding value for the organization. Express that value in objective terms— such as "Labor expense as a percentage of revenue decreased 15 percent over the past year, boosting profitability 70 percent."

- **Support the executive committee's decisions.** As other members of the executive committee weigh various strategy-related decisions, consider whether you agree or disagree with a decision. If you disagree, present your opposing views respectfully during the decision-making process, and back your views with objective data. But once the entire committee has made a decision and communicated it throughout the company, support the decision publicly.

See assessment tool 13-1 for a checklist that can help you gauge where you need to strengthen your strategy-shaping skills.

Assessment Tool 13-1
Gain and Strengthen Strategic Input

Use this tool to identify where you need to strengthen your skills so as to gain or strengthen your role in strategic management of your organization. For each statement below, circle "Yes" or "No." "No" responses indicate areas where you might improve your skills.

1. Do you view your purpose at your company as serving the firm's needs, not those of your department or your position?

    Yes   No

2. Every time you present a proposal related to corporate strategy, do you show how the organization overall will benefit from it in terms of bottom-line profitability?

    Yes   No

3. Have you thoroughly familiarized yourself with your company's business and its industry, including the most pressing issues facing your organization and its various departments?

    Yes   No

4. Do you seek opportunities to address each of your firm's business area's needs and support their strategy-related goals over the long term?

    Yes   No

5. Do you know your company's and its departments' budgets and forecasts, and do you translate them into human capital terms?

    Yes   No

6. Do you provide advice to management based on your expertise, then let executive team members make decisions based on your and other managers' input?

Yes   No

7. Do you back up HR proposals with objective data showing how your proposals will help your company achieve its strategic goals?

Yes   No

8. Do you provide other executives with ongoing information about how HR activities are adding value for your organization?

Yes   No

9. Once your executive team has made a decision and communicated it throughout the company, do you support the decision publicly?

Yes   No

Jim Jose, principal of Tucson, Arizona–based HR consulting firm Jim Jose Associates LLC, adds to these recommendations. "HR professionals need to talk the language of strategy," Jose explains, "and that means metrics, metrics, metrics. Know how your company measures strategic performance—is it market share? Bottom-line profits? And master HR metrics, such as retention's impact on the bottom line, the costs of turnover and recruiting."[11] To master the concepts and language of strategy, Jose recommends spending as much time as possible with strategy-involved thinkers in your firm—and absorbing as much information from them as you can. For example, dedicate several hours a week to networking with individuals. Commit to having lunch with six strategy-involved people every month. And ask to be invited to strategy-related meetings. Even better, create such meetings yourself; for instance, by sponsoring forums on specific business topics and scheduling one-on-one discussions with other executives to find out what their biggest challenges and most effective solutions are. As Jose maintains, your goal is to build relationships and to demonstrate the behavior and knowledge of a strategic thinker. By being proactive and behaving like a strategic partner, you'll encourage others to view you as one.

"Boss, Peer, and Executive Negotiation Do's and Don'ts" pulls together key points for negotiating with your company's decision makers.

Boss, Peer, and Executive Negotiation Do's and Don'ts

- *Do* strengthen and demonstrate your understanding of the "big picture"—your company's strategy and its place in the industry.

- *Don't* impose your ideas for projects and initiatives on others without inviting their input and listening for their concerns.

- *Do* build a network of relationships with diverse people throughout your firm to develop a strong awareness of how the various departments in your company work—and what their problems, concerns, and needs are.

- *Don't* assume that your boss, peer managers, and other members of the executive committee will view HR as a strategic partner unless you speak their "language" and view issues in strategic terms.

- *Do* make sure you understand basic strategic and financial terminology and concepts.

Summing Up

This chapter explored four kinds of situations in which you need to use negotiation skills to influence others over whom you have no formal authority:

- **Getting your boss's support.** This is crucial when you launch an HR initiative or take on more challenging duties. To effectively negotiate these situations, you need to cultivate a strong relationship with your boss and understand the "big picture" of your company's business.

- **Negotiating HR policies with peer managers.** In these situations, helpful negotiation skills include ensuring that HR policies are sound, involving peer managers early in shaping policies, and keeping managers informed of the status of policy changes.

- **Obtaining executive approval for HR projects or expenditures.** Negotiation skills include demonstrating your knowledge of the forces that influence your firm's performance, HR trends, and HR projects' strategic impact; using the language of business; and presenting a compelling case for how an HR project will help address your company's most pressing problems.

- **Building and increasing input into strategic decisions.** Negotiation skills for participating in strategic planning include demonstrating your understanding of your company's business and industry, backing up your proposals with objective data, and supporting your executive team's decisions.

Leveraging Chapter Insights: Critical Questions

- How do you typically go about getting your boss's support for an HR initiative or other idea? What is the usual outcome of these efforts? What might you do differently to boost your chances of gaining your boss's support for your ideas?

- How do other managers in your firm usually respond to new or changed HR policies? What steps could you take to get a more positive, cooperative response from them?

- How successful are you at obtaining executive approval for HR projects and expenditures? What changes in your approach might help you be even more successful?

- How involved are you in your company's strategic planning and direction-setting? What skills do you need to build or increase your role in strategic planning? How will you go about strengthening those skills?

CHAPTER FOURTEEN

Negotiations with Vendors and Consultants

Forging the Best Agreements
for Your Company

Key Topics Covered in This Chapter

- *Clarifying your needs*

- *Interviewing and evaluating candidates*

- *Checking references and evaluating written proposals*

- *Negotiating fees and contract terms*

Y OUR WORK as an HR professional likely includes negotiating with vendors and consultants to perform a variety
of services for your company. For example, perhaps your
firm outsources several HR processes such as payroll or benefits administration, and you must find and manage providers of these services. Or perhaps you hire consultants to do special projects such as
designing and delivering training curricula, recruiting new hires, or
developing and implementing workforce surveys.

Whatever the situation, the negotiation process begins long before you talk price with providers and continues long after the ink on
the contract has dried. You need to know how to evaluate and select
providers before you negotiate the terms of the contracts you arrange
with them, and handle problems and surprises that may come up
once providers have begun delivering on the contract. In this chapter,
you'll discover tips and guidelines for dealing with these various
aspects of negotiations with vendors and consultants.

Determining Your Needs

According to Les Rosen, owner of national pre-employment screening firm ESRcheck, "more and more companies are outsourcing
repetitive HR processes."[1] One of the biggest challenges facing HR
professionals who are selecting service vendors and negotiating contract terms is what Rosen calls "vendor overwhelm." "It's a real buyer's
market," he says, "and vendors are calling companies all day looking

for business." That's good news for you. The hungrier a vendor is for business, the better your bargaining position.

But first you have to sift through all the available service providers and decide which is the best one for your company's needs—and what constitutes an appropriate fee. How do you begin? Rosen recommends clarifying in your own mind exactly what services—and what quality of service—you need from a potential vendor or consultant. Moreover, find out what each provider can really give you in terms of services. "Don't discuss price until you've got three or so finalists," Rosen advises. "In the earlier stages of evaluating proposals from providers, you want to find out whether a company or consultant can give you the service you need."

Rosen cites an example from the pre-employment screening industry. "With companies that conduct pre-employment background screening," he says, "one such service can look a lot like another. But there are worlds of differences in what these vendors provide. A company that sells criminal records for $12 each may seem like a good deal compared to one that charges $18 per record. But perhaps the first company is only checking for felonies and reporting court research results without reviewing legal compliance."

Rather than viewing services as commodities, Rosen recommends issuing requests for proposals (RFPs) asking prospective providers to clarify what makes their methodology different from other firms offering similar services. "Use the same common sense you'd use when choosing a law firm or a physician," he says. In other words, look into the potential vendor's credentials. Is the company reputable? Does it have the knowledge and skills you need? "After discussing a potential agreement with a vendor or consultant," Rosen suggests, "ask them 'What else do *you* think I need? How can you give us an advantage?'"

During the proposal evaluation stage, keep negotiations centered on terms of the potential agreement, not on price. Once you've clarified your needs, you can put a valuation on those needs by shifting to price issues. "Your negotiation position is strongest *before* you've signed a contract with a vendor," Rosen continues. "Once the contract is implemented, it's going to be very difficult switching to a new vendor if problems arise. Few people want to start the search all over again. So make sure you carefully evaluate everything before signing on the dotted line."

You've clarified your needs. Now what? Thomas Ucko, author of *Selecting and Working with Consultants: A Guide for Clients*, outlines a structured approach to interviewing, evaluating, and selecting finalists, and then negotiating fees and contracts.[2]

Interviewing Candidates

Once you've clarified your needs, prepare a checklist of questions you want to ask during candidate interviews, including:

- "What is your understanding of our needs?"

- "How would you approach this project?"

- "How does your approach differ from that of other consultants?"

- "Tell me about your successful and less successful projects. What went well? What went wrong?"

- "What will your role in the project be, and who else will be involved?"

- "How much time can you devote to our project?"

To get the most valuable information from the interview, be sure you spend more time listening than talking. Create a relaxed, informal climate, and ask open-ended questions starting with "how," "what," "when," and "tell me about . . . ."

Evaluating Candidates

After each interview, decide how good a match the candidate would be for your project. Based on what came up during the interview, how well do you think each vendor or consultant could meet the needs you've defined?

The quality of the relationship with a provider is just as important as his or her expertise. After all, you'll be working together on important efforts for your company, so you want to be sure that you can trust the provider and collaborate in a positive, effective way. Therefore, take time to assess the quality of the interpersonal chemistry and level of trust between you and the candidate. Ask yourself:

- "Does the person seem interested in the project?"

- "Is he the individual who will lead the work?"

- "Does she seem to have integrity? Do I believe that she will maintain confidentiality?"

- "Does he seem direct and straightforward?"

- "What are her critical strengths and limitations?"

Checking References

After you've conducted interviews with provider candidates, call the clients listed in the candidates' reference lists. Track down additional references on your own—such as former clients of the vendor or consultant you're considering. And ask consultants whom you've worked with before, even in other disciplines, to provide their insights. When talking with former clients of a candidate, ask questions such as:

- "How did you like working with this consultant?"

- "What kind of project did he do for you?"

- "What methods or solutions did she offer?"

- "Did you get the results you wanted, on time and within budget?"

- "Did you feel that this consultant understood your business?"

- "What are this provider's strengths and weaknesses?"

- "How does she compare with other consultants you've used?"

- "Would you use him again?"

Requesting Written Proposals

After you've used interviewing and reference checking to narrow your choices down to two or three candidates, ask the candidates for written proposals. Consider proposals as the consultant's calling card. Never pay for a proposal or agree to a "handshake deal" for consulting services. And although there is no set formula for preparing a written proposal, a well-crafted document will enable you to clearly and concisely answer the following questions:

- Does the consultant understand what you're trying to accomplish?

- Are the consultant's approach and methodology clearly and succinctly presented?

- Are the benefits quantifiable?

- What are the consulting team's qualifications and experience?

- What are the fees?

- What schedule for deliverables is the consultant proposing?

- Does the proposal inspire your confidence in the quality of this provider's work?

Review the proposals carefully. Also invite others who will be affected by the project to review and comment. Studying the proposal will give you a good feel for the consulting firm's fit with your company. Jargon-filled proposals that don't define the end product are useless; you need to clearly understand what results the firm plans to deliver and by when.

Selecting the Vendor or Consultant

Now pull all your impressions together from the interviews, reference checks, and written proposals, and see if one candidate clearly has the edge over the others. If the decision doesn't present itself so neatly, consider these approaches:

- Ask the candidates to show you reports from similar projects, with client names deleted.

- Try out top candidates with a small test project.

- Ask the candidates to come in for another interview, this time with additional people in your company who haven't met with them before and thus can evaluate them from a fresh perspective.

Whatever your decision turns out to be, treat all candidates with decency and respect. Notify them as promptly as possible of your decision, and return phone calls within a reasonable amount of time.

Negotiating Fees and Contract Terms

Consultants and vendors may use different fee structures that have advantages and disadvantages to you, the client. For example, with consultants who charge an hourly fee, you pay only for actual time worked on the project. However, there's no incentive for the consultant to work efficiently, and you may not be able to estimate the project's ultimate cost. With consultants who charge a project fee, you know the total costs in advance, though conflict may arise if you find that you need services beyond the original agreement's scope. Consider these advantages and disadvantages while working toward an agreed-upon fee.

In negotiating fees, keep in mind that pricing for vendors' or consultants' services can vary considerably, depending on a provider's reputation, firm size, and area of expertise. And as Les Rosen recommended, don't assume that the least expensive provider is your best choice.

Also, fees are often highly negotiable. Don't be afraid to ask for discounts and to inform the consultant if you have a fixed budget for the project. Moreover, as you would in any negotiation, seek to forge agreements that meet needs beyond just price for both parties. For example, perhaps a vendor who is just starting out would be willing to charge a somewhat lower fee if you give him permission to include your company on his client list—especially if your firm is highly prestigious. The promise of additional business can also strengthen your bargaining position. For instance, if you're considering initiating a series of projects on which you'll need outside help, let the vendor know that: He might be willing to "cut you a good deal" if he senses that repeat business may be coming his way. Likewise, you can negotiate over terms such as delivery dates to get the best possible agreement. To illustrate, if the vendor is insisting on a fee that you consider uncomfortably high, and doesn't seem to want to budge, try bargaining for a faster delivery of the final product—if that's something that holds value for you.

As with any negotiation, arriving at a final agreement with vendors and consultants involves much more than price. The contract you ultimately agree to should specify the following:

- **Terms:** when the agreement will take effect and end

- **Objectives:** what results you desire

- **Definition of success:** what constitutes success, and how it will be measured

- **Project scope and schedule:** which tasks and activities the consultant will perform and when they will be finished

- **Deliverable:** what form the "final product" will take; e.g., a written report, a working system, an oral report

- **Product ownership:** who will own the copyright for the final product if it is a written or digital document

- **Fees and payments:** when payments will be made and what fee structure the consultant will work from

- **Confidentiality:** whether you will want the consultant to be able to disclose proprietary or other sensitive information encountered during the project

Negotiating the "Spirit of the Deal"

You've hammered out pricing and other contractual terms with your selected vendor or consultant. But don't assume that your negotiating is finished simply because the ink on the contract has dried. Ucko and other experts also recommend specifying terms related to what's often referred to as the "spirit of the deal," as opposed to the "letter of the deal."

According to Ron Fortgang, David Lax, and James Sebenius, the *spirit of the deal* includes considerations such as:[3]

- How the two parties will communicate, resolve disputes, and handle surprises

- Who will make which decisions

- Whether the agreement represents a one-time transaction or a longer-term partnership

Many agreements that may have looked fine on paper sour once the contract is implemented because the parties never shared their assumptions about such matters. Parties are at greatest risk for misunderstandings related to the spirit of deal when they come from markedly different cultures or when third parties drive the negotiation process. So if these circumstances characterize your current negotiation with a vendor or consultant, take care to attend as much to the spirit of the deal as you do to the letter of the deal.

See assessment tool 14-1 for a checklist that can help you effectively handle an upcoming negotiation with a vendor or consultant.

When you are negotiating with a vendor or consultant offerings, bear in mind the guidelines offered in "Vendor and Consultant Negotiation Do's and Don'ts."

Assessment Tool 14-1
Choose and Negotiate with a Vendor
or Consultant

Use this worksheet to effectively plan for and handle an upcoming negotiation with a vendor or consultant. For each statement below, circle "Yes" or "No." Any "No" responses indicate possible areas where you need to strengthen your skills.

In clarifying your needs, have you . . .

1. Clearly defined the kind of services you want the vendor or consultant to provide and specified the needs you want addressed?

   Yes   No

In interviewing candidates, have you . . .

2. Gauged candidates' understanding of your needs?

   Yes   No

3. Discerned how their approach differs from other consultants'?

   Yes   No

4. Learned about candidates' successful and unsuccessful projects, including the reasons behind effective and not-so-effective work?

   Yes   No

5. Found out what the candidates' role in your project would be and who else would be involved in the work?

   Yes   No

6. Clarified how much time candidates could devote to your project?

Yes No

7. Spent more time listening than talking?

Yes No

8. Asked open-ended questions?

Yes No

In evaluating candidates, have you . . .

9. Assessed how good a match each candidate would be for your project?

Yes No

10. Gauged candidates' level of interest in the project?

Yes No

11. Assessed candidates' integrity?

Yes No

12. Determined how much trust you have in the candidates?

Yes No

13. Summed up candidates' critical strengths and limitations?

Yes No

In checking candidates' references, have you asked references . . .

14. How they liked working with the consultant in question?

Yes No

15. What solutions the consultant offered?

Yes   No

16. What methods the consultant used?

Yes   No

17. Whether they got the results they wanted, on time and within budget?

Yes   No

18. Whether they felt that the consultant understood their business and their needs?

Yes   No

19. What they considered the consultant's major strengths and weaknesses?

Yes   No

20. How the consultant compared with other consultants they've used?

Yes   No

21. Whether they would use the consultant again?

Yes   No

In evaluating written proposals, have you assessed whether . . .

22. The consultant understands what you're trying to accomplish?

Yes   No

23. The proposal clearly and succinctly presents the consultant's approach and methodology?

Yes   No

24. The benefits the consultant is offering are quantifiable?

Yes   No

25. The proposal communicates the consultant's qualifications and experience?

Yes   No

26. The fees are clearly specified?

Yes   No

27. The schedule for deliverables is clearly specified?

Yes   No

In negotiating fees and contract terms, have you . . .

28. Decided on the appropriate fee structure (hourly versus flat fee) for you?

Yes   No

29. Resisted any urge to automatically go with the lowest bidder, and instead compared the quality of what the candidates are offering?

Yes   No

30. Brought other interests besides price into the conversation, such as possible repeat business or flexibility on schedule?

Yes   No

31. Ensured that the contract you agreed on specifies terms, objectives, definition of success, project scope and schedule, deliverable, product ownership, fees and payments, and confidentiality?

Yes   No

32. Negotiated terms related to the "spirit of the deal," such as how disputes or surprises will be handled?

Yes   No

Vendor and Consultant Negotiation Do's and Don'ts

- *Do* define in crystal-clear terms what services—and what quality of service—you need from a vendor or consultant.

- *Don't* assume that vendors charging the lowest fees are going to be your best choices.

- *Do* include terms related to the "spirit of the deal," not just the "letter of the deal," in the final written contract.

- *Don't* discuss price until you're satisfied that you have a handful of candidates who can provide the services you need, at the level of quality you require.

- *Do* use a structured, disciplined approach to interviewing, evaluating, and selecting vendor and consultant candidates, and to negotiating fees and contractual terms.

Summing Up

This chapter described how negotiating with vendors and consultants starts long before you talk about price, and ends long after the ink has dried on the contract. The negotiation process consists of several steps:

- Clarifying the needs you want a vendor or consultant to fulfill

- Evaluating candidates through interviewing, checking references, and assessing written proposals

- Selecting the right vendor or consultant for the job

- Negotiating fees, other contract terms such as project scope and schedule and desired results, and terms related to the "spirit of the deal" (such as how surprises or disputes will be handled once the work begins)

Leveraging Chapter Insights: Critical Questions

- What has worked well in past negotiations you've handled with vendors and consultants? What hasn't worked as well? What steps might you take to improve the outcomes of these negotiations?

- While arriving at agreements with vendors and consultants, which part of the process do you tend to find most difficult? How might you strengthen your skills in those areas?

- How might you help other managers in your company to forge better agreements with vendors and consultants?

CHAPTER FIFTEEN

Negotiations with Labor Unions

Handling the Complexities Successfully

Key Topics Covered in This Chapter

- *Understanding new developments in organized labor*
- *Building positive relationships between management and union leaders*
- *Navigating the process of negotiating with labor unions*
- *Understanding methods and benefits of facilitating the negotiation process*

AMONG ALL the negotiations you and other HR professionals may find yourself participating in, those with labor union representatives might at times seem the most demanding. Such negotiations frequently involve numerous individuals on both sides of a conflict, as well as complex laws. Moreover, recent developments in union membership and concerns have changed certain aspects of the negotiating process. In this chapter, we'll explore some of these changes and examine strategies for successfully handling the complexities of negotiations with labor unions.

New Developments in Organized Labor

Like many other aspects of business, organized labor is experiencing change. As just one example, in a recent *HR News* article, Stephanie Overman noted that in the airline industry, managers "are confronting new faces across the bargaining table."[1] Apparently, many members of long-standing, international unions in this industry are voting to switch to new, independent, and more specialized unions that they believe will better understand the issues specific to their industry or local. Negotiating with these grassroots unions can be difficult if the organization doesn't yet have rules and bylaws in place and hasn't yet established a relationship with management. Cultural differences may arise, too. For instance, if the new union places a high emphasis on consensus building, it may take longer to reach agreement on an issue.

Also, according to HR consultant and attorney John Gaffin, "union representation is decreasing in the private sector while growing in the public sector."[2] Negotiations unfold differently, Gaffin points out, in these two realms. Specifically, in the public sector, where state jurisdictions have stringent public-employee relations laws, negotiations can prove quite challenging. Complex rules govern the issues over which employees can strike, and bargainers must negotiate terms other than wages, which are set by city councils. And of course, public employers can't lock out firefighters and other employees, and those same employees can't easily go on strike. That means negotiations center on issues such as staffing and promotions rather than pay.

Meanwhile, Gaffin continues, union negotiations play out quite differently in the private sector. In that realm, "a union's ultimate power is to strike, while a company's ultimate power is to have a lockout or permanent replacement of striking workers." But Gaffin sees interesting changes happening in private-sector union negotiations. In particular, union representatives are jockeying less for higher pay and better work schedules than they have in the past—and putting more emphasis on the need for better benefits, particularly health care. And as the ranks of retirees swell, more unions are fighting for these and other nonworkers' interests. Finally, though only about 8–9 percent of the private-sector workforce is unionized, some unions are stronger in particular industries, such as health care and janitorial and other services. In each of these industries, union members' interests will differ. For example, many nurses tend to consider staffing a far more vital issue than pay, while janitors tend to focus more on pay.

Laying the Groundwork for Positive Relationships

If you're on your company's negotiating team during a series of bargaining sessions with union representatives, you can take several steps to ensure that the negotiations lead to outcomes that will satisfy both parties and lead to enduring solutions and improved relationships. But first lay the groundwork for positive relationships between management and unionized labor by ensuring that everyone in your firm understands—and avoids—the specific actions that violate the *National Labor Relations Act* (NLRA) or other federal or state legislation governing relationships between companies and unionized employees. In the United States, such actions include the following— all of which can lead to the imposition of cease-and-desist orders and other penalties by the National Labor Relations Board:[3]

- Interfering with, coercing, or restraining any employee's right to organize a union or bargain collectively

- Dominating or controlling a union

- Discriminating in the hiring or tenure of an employee because of union membership or the lack thereof

- Terminating an employee based on his or her union activity

- Failing to bargain in good faith (e.g., not supplying required information, not evaluating alternative options, and not explaining the reasons behind a decision) with an employee's chosen union representative

In addition to complying with NLRA provisions, also take time to build positive relationships with union members in your firm. Gaffin recommends serving on committees and using face-to-face, daily informal encounters to get to know unionized employees and their representatives. Your goal? To learn as much as you can about employees' issues and concerns and their perceptions of management's and the union's proposals. And if your firm has a formal grievance procedure, Gaffin adds, look for patterns in the grievances filed. Do complaints seem to center on perceived unfair overtime assignments? Workplace safety? Other concerns? What seems to have the most value for workers?

Navigating the Bargaining Process

Building on a foundation of NLRA compliance and deep knowledge of your firm's unionized labor force, you and other negotiation team members can use additional techniques to successfully navigate the bargaining process. Gaffin offers several recommendations:

- **Don't fall into win/lose, short-term thinking.** "If your company has an advantage such as an industrywide shortage of jobs," Gaffin says, "don't abuse that advantage just to 'win' the negotiation." This is short-term thinking. Union members have long memories, and when the job market picks up and your company needs employees, your short-term thinking may make it difficult for you to attract the talent the organization needs.

- **Avoid getting caught up in emotions.** Letting emotions dominate the negotiation process puts both parties at risk for making unwise decisions. Gaffin cites an example of an airlines union whose members so resented the company's owner that they went on strike when the company was teetering on bankruptcy. The strike put the organization out of business, taking union members' jobs with it—but the employees rejoiced that they had "taken down" the hated owner. "They missed the big picture," Gaffin says. An intense desire to achieve "victory" can put negotiators on either side of a dispute in peril.

Other experts suggest getting help with facilitating the negotiation process.[4] Especially during negotiations that risk being derailed by high emotion, participants may find it helpful to have an outside expert guide the two sides through the negotiation process. Skillful facilitation can be powerful because it enables both parties to see the possibility of pursuing a shared goal and contributing to what's in the company's best interest. Tensions ease, leading to a desire to address specifics. Often, negotiating teams who use able facilitators find that agreement is possible in areas where they'd long been deadlocked. For instance, at one company, union members acknowledged that many of the grievances they had filed had only "annoyance value." Managers responded by admitting that they had deliberately avoided answering those grievances whenever possible. The union agreed to drop these grievances and focus on the "real issues" instead. See "Facilitating the Negotiation Process" for an example of one model that some companies use.

Facilitating the Negotiation Process

In their *Harvard Business Review* article "Overcoming Group Warfare," Robert S. Blake and Jane S. Mouton describe a facilitated negotiation process that they call the "interface approach":

1. **Visualize a sound relationship.** The process facilitator invites each negotiating team to meet separately and prepare descriptions of what a sound union-management relationship would look like at the company. The teams record these descriptions on large sheets so as to compare them at a joint session. Each team selects a spokesperson to present its conclusions at the joint session. Often, it can be helpful to choose someone other than the designated team leader to serve as spokesperson.

2. **Compare the sound-relationship visions.** At a joint session, the two sides display their sheets and examine the visions described on them, looking for similarities and differences.

3. **Rate agreement on the other side's vision.** The groups separate again and assess the degree of their agreement with each statement in the other party's vision. They rate each statement as "1" ("We agree with the statement as is"), "2" ("We agree with the statement as revised in the following way"), "3" ("We wish to ask the following questions for further clarification"), or "4" ("We disagree with the statement for the following reasons").

4. **Develop a consolidated ideal model.** The parties come together again and share their ratings, explaining the reasons behind the numbers. They make changes to convert statements rated "4," "3," and "2" into "1," reflecting mutual agreement and building a shared ideal model.

5. **Describe the current actual relationship.** Still in the joint session, each group describes as objectively as possible the

present reality of their relationship. They explore specific factors that have shaped the relationship, as well as barriers that have prevented progress. Often, the parties will be surprised by one another's insights.

6. **Rate agreement on the other side's perceptions of current reality.** The groups return to their separate team rooms and assess the degree of their agreement with the other party's perception of current reality. They use the same 4-point rating system that they employed to develop a consolidated ideal model.

7. **Develop a consolidated perception of current reality.** The parties come together again and share their ratings, once more making changes to convert statements rated as "4," "3," and "2" into "1" to build a shared perception of current reality. For example, at one company, management perceived an adversarial, "we versus they" relationship, while union members saw hopelessness and an assumption that only a shutdown would "bring management to its senses." The consolidated view of reality became "Our adversarial relationship promotes readiness for win-lose clashes; a strike is preferable to perpetual humiliation."

8. **Identify contributions to relationship problems and current thoughts and feelings.** Through frank discussion and introspection, the teams separately brainstorm ways in which they might have contributed to the current, negative reality. They write down five statements describing their thoughts and feelings at the time.

9. **Devise a plan for moving from current reality to desired vision.** The groups reunite and share their five statements, then explore ways to build the kind of relationship expressed in the consolidated vision.

SOURCE: Robert R. Blake and Jane S. Mouton, "Overcoming Group Warfare," in *Harvard Business Review on Negotiation and Conflict Resolution* (Boston: Harvard Business School Press, 2000), 68–86.

Harrison Darby, a partner at Los Angeles, California–based law firm Jackson Lewis LLP, provides additional guidance for HR professionals who participate in negotiations with labor unions:[5]

- **Understand the power of language.** "The wording in a collective-bargaining agreement stays with that agreement unless it's changed in a later negotiation," Darby explains. "So if you're negotiating such a contract, know how one clause may affect subsequent clauses and contracts. That means having a good understanding of and familiarity with the language used in these agreements."

- **Address compliance issues.** In addition, pull together your company's policies and programs and see whether they're in compliance with the current union contract. If you're involved in negotiations over the first union contract at your firm, takes steps to ensure that the terms of that agreement comply with your organization's existing policies and programs. Or plan to change them.

- **Get help if you're a novice.** If you're unfamiliar with collective bargaining negotiations, consider sitting in or participating at a lower level until you gain experience. If that isn't an option, "get good guidance or assistance," Darby advises. "Have experts sit at the table with you or at least be in the background or help you with the language. Evaluate who's currently on the negotiating team and whether you need to add others, such as an outside lawyer, plant manager, and so forth."

- **Consider an agreement's impact on nonunionized employees.** Darby points out that agreements resulting in higher pay or other advantages for unionized over nonunionized employees may result in dissatisfaction among nonunion staff. You and the other members of the negotiating team need to think through how the final agreement with the union will affect employees not covered by the contract—*before* anyone signs on the dotted line.

- **Don't give away your "last penny."** As in any negotiation, take care that you don't make your best offer too early during collective bargaining discussions. Darby cites this example: "Suppose your company can afford to go as high as a forty-five-cents-an-hour pay raise for unionized workers, and the union wants fifty cents. If you begin the negotiations by offering forty-five cents, and it's rejected, you have nowhere to go from there. But if you start by offering forty-three cents and it's rejected, you've still got some room to go higher—and end up at a point that's acceptable to you."

Guidelines for handling labor negotiations are shown in "Labor Negotiation Do's and Don'ts."

Labor Negotiation Do's and Don'ts

- *Do* suggest that your company hire an outside facilitator to guide the negotiation process, including setting ground rules, monitoring communications for candor, and curbing the open expression of hostile attitudes.

- *Don't* take any actions that risk violating sections of the National Labor Relations Act (NLRA).

- *Do* familiarize yourself as much as possible with the NLRA and with public- and private-employee relations laws.

- *Don't* assume that union representatives are concerned only about pay and work schedules.

- *Do* take pains to exchange and test assumptions with union representatives about how each side sees the other and what each wants for the future.

Summing Up

This chapter covered several aspects of negotiations with labor unions:

- Changes unfolding in the world of organized labor, such as the rise of smaller, grassroots unions in specific industries and the new emphasis on interests beyond pay among unionized workers

- Strategies for building positive relationships between management and organized labor, including establishing ongoing dialogue with union leaders and ensuring that everyone in your firm understands—and avoids—the actions that violate the National Labor Relations Act (NLRA) or other federal or state legislation governing relationships between companies and unionized employees

- Ideas for navigating negotiations with labor unions; for example, avoiding high emotion; using skilled facilitators; avoiding win-lose, short-term thinking; and considering the impact on nonunionized workers of any agreement forged between management and unionized workers

Leveraging Chapter Insights: Critical Questions

- How would you describe the quality of the relationship between management and organized labor at your company? What steps might you and other HR professionals in your organization take to improve that relationship?

- What changes, if any, have you seen in organized labor in your company's industry? What do those changes imply for how you and other HR professionals approach and participate in negotiations with labor unions?

- Among the various negotiation techniques described in this chapter, which ones do you think would yield the most benefits if you applied them during union negotiations at your company? What steps might you take to begin putting those techniques into practice?

CHAPTER SIXTEEN

Negotiations over Legal Disputes

Protecting Your Organization

Key Topics Covered in This Chapter

- *Understanding changes in the realm of legal disputes*

- *Establishing a dispute-prevention program*

- *Leveraging your emotional intelligence to negotiate legal disputes*

- *Exploring alternatives to litigation*

COMPANIES TODAY can find themselves embroiled in a wide variety of legal disputes. Some of these may be initiated by current or former employees, as workers file claims with federal or state enforcement agencies. Others occur when employees file lawsuits over issues such as discharge, demotion, pay cuts, sexual harassment, or discrimination based on race, age, gender, or sexual orientation.

Such disputes can have numerous undesirable consequences for employers—including damaging publicity, steep jury verdicts, and lost time and money. As an HR professional, you can help protect your organization from these scenarios by using your negotiation skills to prevent legal disputes from even arising, or to increase the chances that such disputes will end in outcomes that favor your company.

Understanding Trends in the Realm of Legal Disputes

Several trends are complicating the legal-dispute picture, and the more you understand them, the better you'll be able to negotiate skillfully for your company. For example, as Michael Karpeles, an attorney with law firm Goldberg Kohn, explains, "There's been a rise in retaliation claims."[1] In such claims, employees argue that their company treated them adversely in order to discriminate against them or to punish them for engaging in protected conduct, such as whistle-blowing. Anyone can bring retaliation claims, regardless of age, race, and other characteristics, Karpeles adds, and companies are now facing wider restrictions on what may be defined as retaliatory actions against employees.

Equally disturbing for companies, certain types of complaints—particularly sexual harassment and discrimination—are mounting, along with the damages awarded to successful plaintiffs.

In addition to the increase in such claims, plaintiffs' attorneys are formulating more creative strategies for winning lawsuits for their clients. Some attorneys and clients, Karpeles says, even fabricate claims. For instance, an employee who receives a negative performance review might set up a whistle-blowing incident and then accuse the employer of retaliation after the company disciplines him or her for poor performance, not the whistle-blowing.

The Importance of Prevention

Clearly, you and other managers can best help your company avoid the consequences of legal disputes by knowing where the line is drawn between "legal" and "not legal" in these types of matters. You also need to know what's negotiable—and what isn't. Behavior that's outright illegal—whether on the part of an employee or the company—simply isn't open to negotiation.

It's also crucial to know how to apply your negotiation skills *before* an employee files a claim or hires an attorney with an eye toward filing a lawsuit. The adage "An ounce of prevention is worth a pound of cure" applies particularly accurately to negotiations over legal matters. And HR professionals play a key role in prevention. To be sure, legal disputes can be settled at any point in the process—for example, before or after a charge is filed and before or after a case goes to court. But once a lawsuit or claim is filed, Karpeles says, the participants cross a psychological threshold and become less willing to drop the case. And the further the process advances, the greater the risks and expenses for employers.

Craig Pratt—HR investigator, expert witness, and author of *Investigating Workplace Harassment*—maintains that HR professionals bring unique advantages to the dispute-resolution process, especially early in that process. "Once a claim or lawsuit is filed," he says, "attorneys handle settlement discussions." Moreover, Pratt continues, claims and lawsuits involve intense emotions and all-too-common human reactions to difficult events. HR professionals, with their deep understanding of human beings' experiences in and contributions to the workplace, can help negotiate resolutions to disputes before they escalate into court cases.[2]

Experts offer numerous suggestions for settling charges, claims, and lawsuits for your company—which you'll learn more about below. But before implementing any of these suggestions, heed the advice of employment and business litigation attorney Gene Thornton: "Be careful about fulfilling your agency duties to your principal. You work for the company, not the employees. Don't . . . lose your job by trying to help employees gain an advantage against your employer." But do tell your employer what you think is the right thing to do, Thornton adds, and remind executives that doing the right thing has sound business benefits as well as moral implications.[3]

With this caveat in mind, consider the following strategies for preventing or settling legal disputes in your company:

Establish a Prevention Program

You can take several steps to stave off charges or other claims brought by current or former employees to government enforcement agencies. In the United States, such agencies include the Equal Employment Opportunity Commission (EEOC), the U.S. Department of Labor (DOL), and the Occupational Safety and Health Administration (OSHA). Effective prevention programs have the following characteristics:[4]

- They are documented in writing.

- They clearly define the prohibited behavior (such as sexual harassment and discrimination) and declare that the company will not tolerate it.

- They lay out a step-by-step procedure for filing a complaint.

- They include training and education programs aimed at sensitizing supervisors and employees to the issues.

- They stipulate a prompt and thorough investigation of every complaint, characterized by confidentiality, comprehensive gathering of information from all the relevant sources, thorough documentation, and prompt corrective action if appropriate.

Leverage Your Emotional Intelligence

When someone feels angry or hurt, merely acknowledging that person's emotions can often reduce his or her desire to take legal action and help bring resolution to the situation. According to Craig Pratt, employees who are threatening to file a claim or lawsuit are experiencing intense emotions resulting from perceived injustice, inequality or unfairness, or interpersonal conflict. They also feel powerless to challenge what has happened to them. The combination of intense emotions with feelings of powerlessness leads to a desire to take legal action.

HR professionals can reduce this desire to sue or file a claim by detecting this emotional powder keg and reaching out to affected employees *before* they light the fuse. Whether someone comes to you with a complaint or you sense that an employee has a problem, Pratt recommends using perceptive, assertive listening to identify the issues at hand and acknowledge the person's feelings. For example, if an employee claims that a manager has made disparaging remarks about her appearance, you might say something like "If I were in your spot, I'd be hurting too." But don't declare any agreement on the issue or say something like, "Yes, this has come up before in this company." Instead, stay focused on the person's emotions. Ask what would have to happen for the situation to improve—without appearing to promise changes that you may not be able to provide.

Be just as empathetic and careful when you speak with the accused manager. Say something like, "There may be a problem. Tell me how things are going in your unit. Has anyone indicated that they're hurting because of conditions at work? Are you aware of any anger?" Don't name the accuser, and prepare yourself for some defensiveness.

Again, reflect the emotions you're hearing; for example, "I can see how you're upset. But let me get your perspective."

After gathering information, see if any obvious solutions come to mind—such as explaining the realities of sexual harassment and obtaining the manager's agreement to stop making disparaging comments about employees' appearance. Document the information you've collected and the solutions you've proposed and implemented. Then monitor the aftermath of these steps to ensure that everyone involved has complied with the terms of the solution.

Attorney Jathan Janove, author of *Managing to Stay Out of Court: How to Avoid the Eight Deadly Sins of Mismanagement*, offers additional recommendations for how you and other managers can exercise your emotional intelligence to discourage the filing of lawsuits and claims:[5]

- A manager who has to discipline, fire, or lay off an employee should deliver the hard news personally rather than having someone else do it. This communicates responsibility and respect to affected employees, which reduces their sense of feeling insulted.

- Don't withhold information from employees regarding legal matters or behaviors and situations that have caused them complaint.

- Give angry or upset employees opportunities to express their point of view.

- Explain the reasons behind a difficult decision.

In short, treat employees with respect and dignity—and encourage other managers to do the same. As Janove explains, one study showed that employees who are made to feel insulted and disrespected are thirty-five times more likely to file claims than those who aren't treated badly. Indeed, Gene Thornton structures complaint-settlement negotiations in such a way that the employee makes the final offer, while the company (Thornton's client) makes the final concession. For example, if the company is willing to pay $25,000 to settle a claim and the employee last demanded $30,000,

Thornton offers $20,000, in the hope that the employee will respond with an offer for $25,000, which Thornton then accepts. This approach helps the employee to feel that he or she has "won"—even if the final number was also what the company was aiming for.

Alternatives to Litigation

Litigation of legal disputes in a court of law is expensive and time-consuming. Moreover, litigation may result in court decisions that establish legal precedents that will be unfavorable to employers in future dealings with their employees. For these reasons, many organizations are exploring alternatives dispute resolution (ADR) as they seek to negotiate resolution of employee-related disputes. ADR has two forms—mediation and arbitration. Let's take a closer look at these forms below.

Mediation

The *mediation* process is offered as *voluntary and confidential*. Through mediation, two or more disputing parties resolve their conflict through the aid of a neutral third party from outside the company—a mediator. The mediator facilitates a process that leads to a resolution that all parties support. The solution is documented in a "memorandum of understanding" that both parties sign. This document is the only item from the mediation that goes into participants' personnel files.

Mediation offers several advantages over litigation—including lower costs, quicker resolution of the issue, protection of participants from recriminations and the accused from public embarrassment, and protection of the company from liability. And successful mediation often results in valued employees' and managers' deciding to remain at the company.

Consider these guidelines for effective use of mediation:[6]

- **Know when to mediate.** Mediation is ideal in situations where questionable behavior, such as sexual harassment, has occurred but the "target" doesn't necessarily wish to see the accused lose his or her job and probably wishes to keep his or her own job as well. The target simply wants the behavior to stop. Mediation is *not* appropriate when behavior is so outrageous that immediate disciplinary action is required or the activity has taken place over a long period of time involving numerous targets. To make this determination, familiarize yourself with the mediation process and promptly investigate accusations of wrongdoing.

- **Select the right mediator.** The best mediators are good listeners and communicators, and have a genuine interest in serving. As with any consultant you're considering hiring, look for mediators who have adequate training and expertise as well as good referrals from former clients. Candidates should be cooperative during the evaluation process and have a record of resolving cases promptly and successfully.

- **Support the mediation process.** Offer mediation as an *option*, first to the "target" and then to the accused employee. Provide background information to the mediator, and make arrangements (e.g., meeting times and places). Consider institutionalizing the mediation process, articulating its advantages to upper management, and communicating the program to employees through small-group meetings and printed literature. Cover mediation during employee orientation as well.

Arbitration

Arbitration is more adversarial in nature than mediation and produces a legally binding decision made by a third party (one or more arbitrators) based on evidence provided by disputants' attorneys.[7] Thus many experts consider this form of ADR similar to litigation. Still, arbitration is much less formal than litigation and requires significantly less time and money. (See "Resolving Disputes at NCR" for more on this alternative form of dispute resolution.)

Resolving Disputes at NCR

By developing a systematized approach to negotiating conflict resolution, NCR (now AT&T Global Information Solutions) saw its number of filed lawsuits drop from 263 in March 1984 to 28 in November 1993. Legal fees during that same time period decreased to less than half of what they had been before the company instituted the arbitration process.

What does NCR's process look like? In brief, it consists of these steps:

1. When a dispute arises—whether initiated by NCR or another party—an ombudsman reviews it.

2. The dispute is entered into a database within twenty-four hours of its inception, and everyone at NCR who needs to know about it is informed.

3. Within three days, the company notifies opposing counsel that it is addressing the complaint with the goal of peaceful resolution.

4. NCR's legal department monitors the process and measures the ombudsman's performance based on number of issues resolved, number resolved without litigation, quality and permanence of solutions, efforts made to identify ways of preventing similar disputes in the future, and amount of time and money saved through use of arbitration.

SOURCE: Todd B. Carver and Albert A. Vondra, "Alternative Dispute Resolution: Why It Doesn't Work and Why It Does," in *Harvard Business Review on Negotiation and Conflict Resolution* (Boston: Harvard Business School Press, 2000), 192.

In America, many states and some federal district courts have stipulated compulsory but nonbonding arbitration as a prerequisite to litigation. Often, the parties involved in arbitration have a clause in their contract committing them to arbitration of disputes arising from their business together. For example, in labor relations, many collective bargaining contracts stipulate arbitration as a capstone of the grievance process.

To initiate and conduct arbitration, many disputants adopt the arbitration procedures recommended by the American Arbitration Association (AAA). They select a single arbitrator or panel of arbitrators (often three), who hear evidence and arguments from the disputants' attorneys and then render a legally binding decision. Arbitrators aren't required to have a legal background or follow the formal rules of law or evidence unless the disputants so stipulate. Moreover, many arbitrators aren't compensated unless the process becomes unusually lengthy, or unless they participate in labor-relations disputes.

Though arbitration offers advantages over litigation, some critics claim that this form of ADR has become more expensive than it should be. If your company uses arbitration, here are some guidelines for ensuring that it fulfills its promise:[8]

- **Streamline the proceedings.** Encourage the arbitrator to rule on disputed matters of law in summary form before hearing evidence, to specify which issues will most likely generate disputes, and to avoid asking the disputants to submit pre-hearing briefs on other issues.

- **Participate in pre-hearing exchanges.** Suggest that disputants trade exhibits and witness lists before the hearing and that they determine which items have relevance for the case and which do not. The goal is to reduce the number of documents used in the hearing.

- **Agree to limit damages.** Ask arbitrators to rule on the reasonableness of damage limitations before hearing evidence. Or have each party pick a damage figure and then ask the arbitrator to choose one or the other.

- **Use experts selectively.** Suggest that the two parties agree on a single, neutral expert. The parties and arbitrator submit key questions for that expert to examine. Often, such experts can suggest solutions to problems—a much more productive activity than when disputants try to "out-expert" each other.

See "Legal Disputes Do's and Don'ts" for points to remember when involved in legal negotiations.

Legal Disputes Do's and Don'ts

- *Do* remember that your best chance of resolving a legal dispute is to negotiate resolution *before* an employee has filed a claim or obtained an attorney.

- *Don't* neglect your agency duties: You're negotiating on behalf of your company, not the employees.

- *Do* know as much as you can about employment law.

- *Don't* assume that legal action and monetary settlements are the only ways to resolve employee-employer disputes. Consider mediation and arbitration as well.

- *Do* make sure that managers and employees throughout your company know the laws regarding sexual harassment, discrimination, and other actions that lead employees to file lawsuits and claims.

Summing Up

This chapter explored several aspects of negotiations involving legal disputes:

- The importance of *understanding trends in legal disputes*, such as the increase in sexual harassment and discrimination complaints filed by current and former employees

- The importance of *negotiating early solutions to disputes* before they escalate to expensive lawsuits. Strategies for avoiding lawsuits include establishing a prevention program characterized by a clear process for filing complaints and training programs aimed at sensitizing managers and employees to legal issues. Use of emotional intelligence to ameliorate the intense emotions and sense of powerless that can lead people to want to sue constitutes another valuable negotiation skill.

- *Alternatives to litigation,* including mediation (whereby disputants resolve their conflict through the aid of a neutral third party from outside the company, who helps them devise a solution that all parties support). Alternatives also include arbitration, which is more similar to litigation and produces a legally decision made by one or more arbitrators based on evidence provided by the disputants' attorneys. Both mediation and arbitration can save companies considerable time and money.

Leveraging Chapter Insights: Critical Questions

- What systems and procedures does your company have in place for preventing workplace conflicts from escalating into lawsuits? How might those systems and procedures be improved?

- Does your company use mediation or arbitration? If so, what are the typical outcomes of using these forms of ADR? How might the mediation and arbitration processes in your firm be improved?

- How much do you and other managers throughout your firm know about employment law? What steps might you and they take to expand that knowledge?

CHAPTER SEVENTEEN

Negotiations Related to Mergers and Acquisitions

Navigating Complex New Terrain

Key Topics Covered in This Chapter

- *General strategies for ensuring a successful merger or acquisition*

- *Restructuring HR after a merger or acquisition*

- *Integrating rewards systems in the new corporate entity*

- *Integrating HR technology in merged or acquired companies*

W E S E E M to be living in an age of business *mergers* and *acquisitions* (M&As), as companies increasingly seek economies of scale, market penetration, and new processes or capacities by integrating with other firms or acquiring the assets of "target" organizations. According to Dennis Roberts, "In 1998 in the United States alone, the value of mergers and acquisitions exceeded $1.6 trillion with 11,400 transactions. These numbers exceed the totals for the combined years of 1990–1995. The recent annual global value of mergers and acquisitions is said to top $3.5 trillion." [1]

But despite the energy devoted to M&A, Roberts notes that about half of such efforts don't achieve the intended benefits. Indeed, some merged companies end up having less value six months after the deal than they had on the day of closing. Roberts suggests that such failure rates stem from companies' decision not to include HR professionals in the pre-deal planning activities. As he explains, of the five biggest obstacles to M&A success—inability to sustain financial performance, loss of productivity, incompatible cultures, loss of key talent, and clash of management styles—three fall directly within HR's sphere of competency.

HR can thus play a central role in boosting a merger or acquisition's chances of success—by contributing its skills both before and after an M&A deal. Moreover, in a merger, the HR professionals in *both* affected companies play equally important roles in influencing the success of the deal. And in an acquisition, your HR capabilities are essential whether your company is the "buyer" (acquirer) or the "seller" (the "target" firm).

General Strategies for Ensuring a Successful Merger or Acquisition

Roberts maintains that HR can contribute five essential capabilities during the M&A process:[2]

1. **Evaluating another company quickly.** Prepare to be a part of the M&A process, including researching due-diligence models relevant to your industry. (During due diligence, companies evaluate whether the proposed merger or acquisition will achieve the intended long-term goals.) Prepare a plan for conducting the due-diligence stage. Understand your company's key HR metrics and how they relate to business success. Have as detailed picture as possible of the envisioned strategic advantages of the newly combined company. Ensure that the right resources are available to support due diligence.

2. **Provide integration know-how.** Know the basics of your company's finance, accounting, and treasury functions; the economics of the business; and the connections among the various functions. Identify potential risks related to combining workforces, organizational structures, and cultures—and educate the M&A team about these risks.

3. **Provide advice about employee sensitivities and attitudes.** Review the employee communications vehicles in your company, and share your insights into when and how best to communicate about the upcoming merger or acquisition. Consider establishing an employee hot line. Decide how best to communicate the newly combined firm's strategy and integration philosophy in ways that build broad-based employee support for the move.

4. **Motivate and retain key employees.** In many M&A situations, rival companies will try to snap up the affected companies' best employees, knowing that some people will want to change employers owing to the uncertainties associated with a merger or acquisition. To prevent such "poaching," know who your

company's most valuable people are in each function and division and, if your firm is acquiring another company, find out who the key players are in the target organization. Then reach out to them early with communications that motivate them to stay.

5. **Plan and lead integration projects.** After a merger or acquisition, many HR departments must be restructured. In addition, reward systems and technologies need to be integrated. Prepare yourself to lead such integration projects while simultaneously supporting the integrations of administration functions and business units after an M&A.

Different HR capabilities become more or less crucial at different stages of the M&A process. For example, during the due-diligence stage, HR professionals must assist in gathering the required documents and alerting the M&A team to any potential problems or liabilities that might cause the team to want to negotiate a lower purchase price of the target company or that might cause significant problems in merging.[3]

Areas to look at in the target company include:

- Severance practices, retirement plans, "golden parachutes," obligations to disabled employees, and other benefits

- Pay levels and performance goals

- Whether the target company has filed appropriate tax returns, made all contributions to retirement plans, or engaged in prohibited transactions or fiduciary violations

- Questionable employment practices relating to federal and state laws (such as the Fair Labor Standards Act and Equal Pay Act, the Family and Medical Leave Act, and employment discrimination laws)[4]

To guard against any liabilities that may be associated with these scenarios, HR professionals must be able to pull together the right documentation, understand the implications of the information in those documents, and ensure that their company's legal counsel has thoroughly reviewed all information.

Dean Black, the managing consultant for Indianapolis, Indiana–based HR consulting firm Just Ask HR, offers several additional guidelines for contributing your HR skills to a successful merger or acquisition. "Organizations have very different personalities," Black explains, "and when one acquires another, a mesh of two forms. It's incumbent on the acquiring organization to ensure that the staff of the acquired company be treated with respect and understanding."[5] That may mean briefing members of the acquired organization on sensitive issues before notifying the general public of the M&A.

Black also recommends that HR professionals get involved in the development and implementation of the purchase agreement in an M&A. Because that agreement is legally binding, HR needs to ensure that everyone involved in its implementation is thoroughly familiar with the contract's contents. Also be careful about confidentiality; in many cases, Black points out, personnel-related information about the acquired company's employees is legally protected as confidential. HR professionals can help maintain that confidentiality. Finally, because M&A activities can prove extremely time-consuming, Black advises outsourcing activities such as employee benefits review, integration planning, and workforce and training needs assessment if possible.

After an M&A deal has been implemented, HR professionals' project-management skills need to kick in. These capabilities are especially important for restructuring HR in the newly combined entity to boost the chances of achieving the intended goals, integrating reward systems, and integrating technology. Below are some guidelines to successfully handling these post-M&A projects:

Restructuring HR

All new companies formed through a merger or acquisition define a competitive strategy—whether it's "win through innovation," "know our customers," "contain costs," or some other plan.[6] To support successful implementation of that strategy, the new company's HR department must structure itself in ways that support the competitive strategy. For example, if you work for a newly combined company that has defined the strategy "win through innovation," you may want to propose that the HR group structure itself in ways that support creation of a work environment in which people rotate through successive product development teams. To persuasively negotiate your proposed changes to HR, you need to clarify the following:

- **People.** How will the HR function's job structure work? Which competencies are needed to match that structure? Who are the candidates for the jobs that need filling?

- **Culture.** What is the desired work environment for the company's HR function? What is your strategy for cultivating that environment? How will you measure progress toward that goal?

- **Process.** What core HR processes will the new company's HR function need to be involved in? What roles and responsibilities do you associate with those processes?

- **Technology.** What technologies will enable you to support administration of the core HR processes you've identified? What technologies will enable you to deliver HR services to managers and employees?

Once you've clarified these parameters of the restructured HR function, compare your team's ability to support the company's competitive strategy against that of rival companies who are competing in the same realm. For instance, is your firm equal to competitors in managing product costs, employee performance, customer service, and other key processes? Is it better than competitors at these activities? Worse than competitors? Identify causes of any gaps in terms of *people* ("Our HR group lacks the skills to develop strategic staffing models"), *culture* ("We tend to react to short-term needs instead of planning for the future"), *process* ("We have no way of conducting effective workforce planning"), *structure* ("No one has been assigned the responsibility for strategic staffing"), and *technology* ("We have no systems in place to enable efficient workforce planning"). Use the resulting insights to negotiate resources for closing the gaps.

Integrating Rewards

The way you integrate rewards programs in the newly formed company can help revitalize the new entity—or produce cultural tensions, raise costs, or impede productivity.[7] Don't assume that the newly combined company will either keep the two component companies' rewards systems as they were or that the acquiring company will impose its rewards programs on the acquired firm. Instead, use the M&A opportunity to make major changes and to get rid of outdated or expensive rewards programs and practices. And if you haven't done so already, think of rewards in the broadest sense possible—in terms of not only pay and benefits but also learning and development opportunities (such as performance and career management) and work environment factors (e.g., culture, work/life balance, and diversity) that will align employees behind the corporate strategy. In other words, think "total rewards."

Decide what *total* rewards will most enable your firm to achieve its competitive strategy. Your firm may or may not already be using some of these. In proposing continued use of existing policies or new or changed reward systems for the organization, be ready to show executives exactly how your ideas will help the firm achieve its strategy. For instance, if your company's strategy involves a sharper focus on customers, demonstrate how pay vehicles you've designed will encourage employees to anticipate and respond to customer needs. Do the same for supporting plans, such as proposed training, recognition programs, job-performance metrics, and so forth. If the company's strategy hinges on building an engaged workforce, explain how flexible benefits, profit sharing, financial-planning education, and other rewards will support that strategy.

As with other processes, designing and negotiating for the right total rewards system in your newly combined company requires several steps:

- **Set objectives.** Establish a clear, complete, and shared statement of the company's competitive strategy—including reward objectives and outcome measures.

Revising Rewards in the Energy Industry

When two regional energy companies in the United States merged in 1999, the two senior management teams decided to conduct a thorough review of the firms' total rewards program during integration planning. Members of the two teams began by clarifying requirements for the success of the newly formed company, including the key organizational capabilities needed in each major business segment. They also defined key reward elements that they believed would foster a high-performance culture in the new company—such as opportunities for learning and development and a high-quality work environment.

A total rewards design team used this input, along with employee opinions expressed during focus groups, to draft a proposed total rewards program. When the team submitted the proposal design to the compensation committee for approval, it was able to demonstrate how the design reflected the data gathered from employees and senior management—boosting the likelihood that the resulting program would meet the new organization's needs.

SOURCE: Adapted from Kenneth T. Ransby and John M. Burns, "Planning the Integration of Rewards." In Jeffrey A. Schmidt, ed. *Making Mergers Work: The Strategic Importance of People* (Alexandria, VA: Towers Perrin/Society for Human Resource Management, 2002), 179.

- **Assess current rewards.** Evaluate the usefulness of existing rewards programs. How well have they worked? How strongly do you think they will support the new organization's strategy?

- **Develop a total rewards blueprint.** Confirm existing rewards programs or develop new ones, including assessments of costs and funding, communication strategy and requirements, and plans for initial implementation.

- **Implement and measure.** Develop plans for introducing changed or new rewards programs, and for assessing their impact once you've implemented them.

If you can clearly and compellingly show how existing, changed, or new rewards of all kinds will support your organization's competitive strategy, you can most successfully negotiate for the approval and resources needed to roll your ideas into action. See "Revising Rewards in the Energy Industry" for an example of how integrating a rewards program unfolded for two merging companies.

Integrating HR Technology

When two companies combine through a merger or acquisition, numerous questions crop up about how the organizations' HR technologies will be integrated and how they'll function.[8] These technologies usually include base record-keeping systems (such as SAP, PeopleSoft, and others), service-center technologies (e.g., call tracking), Web-based systems that enable employee self-service (for instance, the ability to check on retirement account balances), single-purpose applications such as recruiting, and external vendors' technologies (e.g., payroll suppliers and firms handling 401(k) plans).

The questions the come up during an M&A include:

- What HR programs do we need to deliver in the new company? When will each need to be delivered?

- Will we use either company's HR technologies? An entirely new strategy? A hybrid solution?

- How can we meet the immediate needs of employees, dependents, and retirees while overhauling HR technologies?

- What overall technologies solution will best help us increase the effectiveness of the new company's HR programs?

- What solutions will best help us meet the new company's business objectives?

- What solutions are realistic, given the rapid pace of technology development?

- How should we prioritize systems projects?

- How will we choose technology vendors?

- How will we meet federal, state, and local regulatory and compliance requirements?

- Who will manage the content of the HR services delivered through the integrated technology?

- How will HR services be charged?

To negotiate successfully for the approval and support you need to implement the best possible HR technology integration plan, be able to show that you've taken a systematic approach to the planning process:

1. **Create a vision of the future HR services–delivery model.** In a perfect world, what would the integrated HR technology solution deliver? How much would it cost? How would it help the company achieve its goals? Develop a preliminary picture, then ask employees and managers to react to it through focus groups or interviews.

2. **Select HR technology components.** These might include interactive voice response, intranet/Web applications, fax-back capabilities, Lotus Notes databases, and other components that increase employees' self-sufficiency, streamline processes, and capture the organization's intellectual capital. Multimedia solutions; résumé-reading and -handling methodologies; and optical scanning, imaging, and voice-recognition systems may also be desirable components.

3. **Clarify the assumptions on which you're building your proposals.** For example, are you assuming that there are sufficient funds available for carrying out at least the major near-term priorities of the merger or acquisition at an acceptable level of quality? That management and IT staff at all levels will support the proposed HR technology integration plan? That

Merger and Acquisition Negotiation Do's and Don'ts

- *Do* know as much as you can about the M&A process, including the purpose of due diligence and your role in supporting it.

- *Don't* analyze due diligence documents without getting help from legal counsel.

- *Do* get managers' and employees' input on new or changed HR programs and technology solutions you're considering for the newly combined organization.

- *Don't* assume that the dominant company in a merger or acquisition should impose its HR programs and practices and technology systems on the less dominant or acquired company. Sometimes a hybrid or entirely new approach is best.

- *Do* demonstrate how every new or changed HR program or technology system you propose will support the new company's ability to achieve its competitive strategy.

the priorities you're laying out will need to be reexamined and possibly altered in a year or two after the M&A? That existing HR technology systems will continue operating in both companies until your longer-term plan is implemented? In presenting your proposals to management, be ready to explain these assumptions—and the reasoning behind them.

4. **Propose the architectural framework.** What framework will the HR service delivery architecture use? For example, what will the user interface look like, and how will it work? (Will it consist of telephones, computer terminals, and handheld personal computers?) What will the server-side tier consist of?

(Directory services? Search and report engines? Usage metrics? Content management?) Finally, what will the enterprise-information tier consist of? (An ERP system? An HR management system? Legacy data? Specific applications?)

5. **Involve users in converting and testing new HR systems.** Unforeseen business needs, regulatory requirements, and workforce demands can arise at any time during the HR technology integration process. Thus you need to manage users' expectations throughout the process. That means involving them at every stage—including conversion and testing when implementation of new HR systems begins.

See "Merger and Acquisition Negotiation Do's and Don'ts" for points you'll need to consider when negotiating M&A issues.

Summing Up

In this chapter, you discovered five basic capabilities that HR professionals can contribute to help ensure that their companies negotiate a successful merger or acquisition:

- Evaluating another company quickly

- Providing integration know-how

- Providing advice about employee sensitivities and attitudes

- Motivating and retaining key employees

- Planning and leading integration projects

You also learned techniques for handling negotiations during three major phases of mergers and acquisitions:

- Restructuring HR to support successful implementation of the new company's strategy—including clarifying needed people, cultural characteristics, processes, and technologies

- Integrating rewards in the newly formed company so that the resulting rewards program enables the company to achieve its strategy

- Integrating HR technology so that you can deliver the needed HR programs in the new company

Leveraging Chapter Insights: Critical Questions

- If your company is considering merging with or acquiring another firm, or may be acquired by another business, what structural changes to HR do you think would most help the newly formed entity achieve its strategic goals? How would you negotiate these changes with others in the newly formed organization?

- If an M&A is on the horizon for your firm, what changes in the new entity's rewards program would you suggest? How might you negotiate with other players to ensure that the needed changes are implemented?

- If your company is experiencing a merger or acquisition, what changes would you recommend to integrate the HR technology systems of both participating firms? How would you negotiate these changes with others involved in the integration process?

CHAPTER EIGHTEEN

Making Negotiation a Core Capability

Building Organizational Competence

Key Topics Covered in This Chapter

- *Continuous improvement—learning from every experience*

- *Building organizational capabilities for negotiating*

- *HR's role in building negotiation competence in organizations*

MOST MANAGERS now understand the importance of building core competencies in areas essential to their organization's strategies. For some companies, new-product development is an essential core competence; for others, it's marketing or engineering. Many organizations require competence in several fields. We can think of these competencies as the mechanisms that make the execution of high-level strategy possible. As such, they underpin current and future success.

Negotiating is one field in which all organizations need substantial competence. Yet few managers view it as such. As we've pointed out throughout this book, businesspeople need negotiating skills for effective interactions with supervisors and subordinates; with colleagues in different departments; with suppliers, customers, and unions; and in many other situations. As an HR professional, every time you handle a negotiation competently, you contribute to the overall success of your organization. You are also uniquely positioned to further the development of negotiation skills throughout your company's workforce.

Continuous Improvement

In the past two decades, many executives and managers have embraced the notion of continuous improvement in organizational processes. This "process thinking" rests on two assumptions. The first is that almost everything done within an organization—from handling expense reports to fulfilling orders to developing new products—

results from processes. *Processes* are activities that turn inputs into outputs of higher total value. The second assumption is that processes can be improved. They can be made faster, cheaper, or more effective through analysis, redesign, and the application of learning. Together, these two fundamental tenets form the pillars of continuous improvement, one of the most powerful business ideas to emerge in recent times.

Continuous improvement can be applied to just about any process in any industry. Motorola pursued continuous improvement when it adopted Six Sigma Quality as the long-term goal of its manufacturing program, eventually reducing product defects to just a few in every million. Improved product quality added billions of dollars to Motorola's bottom line over the years.

The concept of continuous improvement has spread to other sectors of the economy and to other activities. For example, banks have used continuous process improvement to reduce the time needed to approve or reject a loan application from several days to just hours, with no reduction in decision-making quality. Insurance companies have done the same with claim processing.

As you might expect, we can also apply continuous improvement practices to our companies' negotiation process—and get better bottom-line results for our organizations. Imagine how much better off your own organization would be if its negotiations with suppliers, customers, alliance partners, and employees were just 10 percent more effective than they are today. Material costs would be lower. Relationships with customers and partners would be stronger and more profitable. Collaboration among individual employees and departments would reach higher levels, producing major benefits for the organization as a whole. Each of these improvements would certainly find its respective path to a stronger bottom line.

As the first step toward encouraging continuous improvement in negotiations at your firm, you need to remind yourself and other managers to treat negotiation as a process consisting of a fairly universal set of steps, like those shown in figure 18-1. Whether a negotiation involves two individuals or multiple participants, and whether it aims to settle a damage dispute or a labor contract, these steps generally apply. Each step in this process represents an opportunity for improvement, and you can analyze each with that goal in mind.

As your second step, you need to devise ways for managers throughout your company to learn from the negotiation process as it takes place, and learn from the outcome of each negotiation itself. For example, bargainers should continually evaluate progress during negotiations and revise their approaches as necessary. They should also use what they've learned in one phase of a negotiation to prepare for the next phase. The feedback loop labeled "ongoing evaluation and learning" in figure 18-1 represents this activity. And, of course, participants should conduct a "postmortem" at the conclusion of every negotiation to determine what worked, what didn't work, and how they and others can use their experiences to improve future negotiating outcomes.

Finally, you can help managers at your company to capture postmortem learning in forms that they can easily disseminate and future negotiators can readily use. These forms include training courses, checklists, and databases. Learning capture and reuse is reflected in figure 18-1 through a feedback loop.

FIGURE 18-1

The Negotiation Process: Learning Capture and Reuse

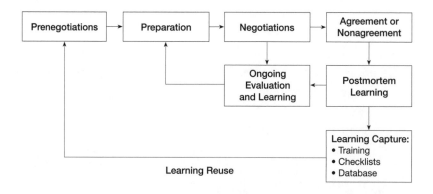

Source: *Harvard Business Essentials: Negotiation* (Boston: Harvard Business School Press, 2003), 132.

As you take steps to improve your company's negotiating processes and capabilities, you'll likely encounter four key barriers:

- **The outcomes of a negotiation are not always clear.** For example, the HR manager who negotiates a rock-bottom price with a key outsourcing vendor may not realize that he or she has soured an important relationship.

- **You may not be able to measure the true consequences of a negotiation for many years.** For instance, suppose you and other top managers at your company have participated in a series of overly aggressive negotiations with your firm's unionized workforce during an economic downturn. The dealings have left a bad taste in union leaders' mouths, though that's not apparent in the next few years. But suddenly the economy picks up, and workers have more job opportunities open to them. You start noticing that it's become difficult to attract new hires to your firm—a long-delayed reaction to your company's reputation for aggressive bargaining with labor.

- **In learning from the negotiating experience, you can't always say, "*This* action produced *those* results."** The presence of many uncontrolled variables makes such certainty impossible. Consider this situation: You've just completed a series of negotiations with Harry, a representative from an HR information services vendor. Several days later, Harry calls you and says, "You know, I've been thinking about the terms we settled on the other day, and I'd like to revisit the fees we agreed on." You mutter to yourself, "Where's *that* coming from? I thought we had an agreement."

  In thinking back to your conversations with Harry, you'd be hard-pressed to determine what exactly caused his about-face. Was it too hard a push on your part for the lowest possible fee? Was it something else over which you had no control? For example, perhaps Harry had family problems on his mind during his last meeting with you, and was too distracted to negotiate more skillfully. In any experience where it's difficult to discern cause and effect links, it's also hard to learn from that experience.

- **Some people may not want to impart their negotiating know-how to others—especially if they believe that sharing information makes them more disposable in the mind of the company.** Certain individuals believe (wrongly) that hoarding knowledge affords them power in their company. But as you've probably seen during your tenure as an HR professional, people acquire much more influence (the ability to use power to change others' behavior) when they share knowledge and help others around them strengthen their skills. Of course, the desire to make oneself indispensable to a company can increase particularly during tough economic times—when more people begin worrying about job security.

These barriers can be tough to surmount. But by developing ways by which you and other managers in your company systematically learn from your own and one anothers' negotiating experiences, you can help your company vastly improve its performance and sharpen its competitive edge in the marketplace.

Negotiating as an Organizational Capability

Despite all the benefits described above, few companies apply continuous improvement to their negotiations. Nor do they think systematically about their negotiating activities as a whole or of negotiating as a key organizational capability. Instead, they take a situational view—perceiving each negotiation as a separate event with its own goals, tactics, participants, and measures of success. As a consequence, they fail to capture learning for future use. By treating negotiating as an ad hoc activity instead of an organizational capability, they never get better at it—and they often pay a high price when they engage in bargaining.

Yet in any organization, executives and managers—HR included—can improve the company's overall negotiating skill and turn that skill into an important capability. How? Start by heeding the following guidelines:

- Provide training and preparation resources for negotiators.

- Clarify organizational goals and expectations regarding any agreement, including when negotiators should walk away.

- Insist that every negotiating individual and team develop a best alternative to a negotiated agreement (BATNA) and work to improve it.

- Develop mechanisms for capturing and reusing lessons learned from previous negotiations.

- Develop negotiating performance measures and link them to rewards.

Let's consider each of these measures in greater detail.

Provide Training and Resources

In his article "Turning Negotiation into a Corporate Capability," Danny Ertel described how a Mexican bank, Serfin, had to renegotiate many loans in the wake of that country's 1994 currency devaluation. "Desperate to improve its negotiation process, the bank decided to take a new tack. It looked for opportunities to standardize and codify its negotiation processes, to impose some management controls, and to change the negotiator's concession-oriented cultures. In short, it set about building a corporate infrastructure for negotiations." [1]

Serfin began with a training curriculum that put its negotiators in real-world positions. It followed up with the technical resources that its "work out" negotiators would need in the field. These steps helped with pre-negotiating preparation. Finally, the bank linked its negotiators with its analysts. For each case, the analysts were charged with defining the bank's and the debtor's interests, defining the bank's BATNA, and developing a set of creative options for resolution.

If you work in a company that's aiming to increase its negotiating capabilities, as Serfin did, you can likewise provide preparation checklists and access to lessons learned from earlier negotiating experience. You can also help novice negotiators gain experience through apprenticeship programs. Apprentices assigned to more experienced negotiators can participate in actual bargaining and develop a sense of how the process works. This "sense" is part of the art of negotiating. Good negotiators learn to recognize threats *and* opportunities in a background of unimportant clutter. They develop this pattern recognition through frequent, firsthand experience. Apprenticeships give novice negotiators opportunities to develop this same ability—while freeing them from the risk of making mistakes. Case studies and simulations can provide the same advantages.

Clarify Goals and Expectations

When negotiators in your company begin bargaining with an outside party, they shouldn't have to guess at the organization's goals and expectations. They should have clear direction on these matters from senior management. For example, suppose executives at your firm are most eager to improve operations by using the best new technology, but they don't communicate that goal effectively. In this case, you and others in HR may drive hard bargains with IT vendors in order to get the least costly technology possible—which isn't what management wants.

The antidote? Executives must clearly define their expectations, and tell the company's negotiators when they expect them to walk away from an agreement-in-the-making. In short, executives need to align negotiating goals with organizational goals and support negotiators throughout the firm with the right incentives. You can help ensure that they do by suggesting strongly that executives communicate these expectations in precise terms to negotiators, by designing incentive systems to reward skillful negotiation, and by devising ways to assess negotiators' understanding of top management's expectations.

Insist That Every Negotiator Knows His or Her BATNA

You've encountered the concept of BATNA, or best alternative to a negotiated agreement, many times throughout these pages. A strong BATNA relative to the other party's BATNA gives negotiators bargaining power. And knowledge of their own BATNA tells negotiators when it's smart to walk away from a possible deal.

You can contribute powerfully to your company's negotiating prowess by firmly suggesting that your organization's representatives—

whether individuals or teams—define a BATNA *before* a negotiation and look for opportunities to continually strengthen it as the bargaining unfolds. And of course, you should practice these techniques in your own negotiations as well.

Capture and Reuse Lessons Learned

The idea of capturing experience and reusing it in future analogous situations is an essential part of the now-popular field of knowledge management. Consulting firms, tax accounting firms, and other knowledge-based enterprises have pioneered knowledge management—and for very practical reasons. Learning how to solve a knotty business problem or how to apply an ambiguous provision of the tax code is often time-consuming, costly, and subject to error. Through knowledge capture and reuse, these firms avoid "reinventing the wheel."

Companies can obtain similar benefits by systematically recording the outcomes of all their negotiations. As reported by Danny Ertel, one major professional services firm is developing a centralized database to help its project managers negotiate scope-and-fee agreements with clients. "Every time a manager negotiates with a client," Ertel writes, "he or she will now be expected to fill out a brief questionnaire that captures the approaches taken, the results achieved, and the lessons learned."[2] These reports are entered into a database and made available to other project managers as they prepare for upcoming negotiations with clients.

Develop Performance Measures and Link Them to Rewards

You've heard the old saying "Companies get what they measure and reward." Thus, when companies base sales bonuses on revenue instead of operating profits from sales, the sales force has every motive to use costly service perks and other inducements to bring in as many new customers as possible—lots of whom won't necessarily be profitable to serve. The same applies to negotiators. When companies reward their negotiators for squeezing the lowest possible price out of vendors, they enjoy short-term gains at the expense of relationship quality. Their negotiators ignore win-win opportunities in favor of the zero-sum game. And vendors have every reason to leave them in the lurch as soon as they find better clients. But change the measurement and rewards system, and companies can get far different—and better—outcomes.

To that end, HR professionals can help encourage alignment between the company's goals and the ways in which it measures and rewards negotiators. Danny Ertel provided *Harvard Business Review* readers with the example of a set of measures used by an engineering and architectural services firm (see table 18-1). As you can probably tell from these measures, executives at this firm were less interested in simply booking more business at higher rates—and more interested in a broader spectrum of financial and relationship values. They used those measures to evaluate negotiation results and negotiators' performance; employees used the same measures to prepare for impending negotiations.

TABLE 18-1

Evaluate the Success of Negotiations

Relationship	Has the negotiation helped build the kind of relationship that will enable us and our clients to work effectively together over the project's life cycle?
Communication	Do these negotiations help create an environment in which both parties can engage in constructive, problem-solving conversations?
Interests	Does the deal satisfy our interests well at the same time that it satisfies our client's interests to an acceptable level and the interests of relevant third parties to at least a tolerable level?
Options	Have we searched for innovative and efficient solutions with the potential for joint gain?
Legitimacy	Have we used objective criteria to evaluate and select an option that can be justified by both sides?
BATNA	Have we measured the proposed deal against our best alternative to a negotiated agreement? Are we confident that the deal satisfies our interests better than does our best alternative?
Commitment	Have we generated well-planned, realistic, and workable commitments that both sides understand and are prepared to implement?

Source: Adapted from Danny Ertel, "Turning Negotiation into a Corporate Capability," *Harvard Business Review*, May–June 1999, 55.

Which measures does *your* organization use to evaluate and prepare for negotiations? Consider these questions:

- Can you and other negotiators in your organization identify your company's measures?

- If so, are those measures broad enough?

- Are the measures used to align negotiators' behavior with organizational goals?

- Does the company use those measures to determine rewards?

If you answered "no" to any of these questions, start thinking of ways you can help your company create new measures or refine its existing measures.

HR's Role in Building Negotiation Competence

As you may have gathered, HR executives, managers, and staff members can play a crucial role in developing negotiation as a core competence throughout their organizations. For example, as Kathryn Tyler explains in her article "Extending the Olive Branch," your HR department can develop and deliver training programs that teach negotiation techniques such as:[3]

- How to bargain with a superior, a direct report, and a peer

- How to actively listen and communicate your needs and interests

- How to separate emotions from the situation during a negotiation that takes an inflammatory turn

Workshops can also show participants how to formulate agreements or contracts that spell out each person's responsibilities and list the consequences of breaking the accord. Role playing, book learning, and talks given by experienced negotiators can all provide additional powerful insights to workshop attendees.

As with all such efforts, you'll of course want to take steps to evaluate the effectiveness of training programs. As people begin putting their new knowledge into action, evaluate the quality of negotiation outcomes. See whether you can detect major changes that stem directly from the training.

You may also remember from chapter 1 that HR professionals can further encourage organizationwide competence in negotiation by serving as *advocates* (constantly spreading the word about the importance of this process to the company's bottom line); as *builders* (helping others build their skills); and as *practitioners* (modeling skill development and effective negotiation skills themselves).[4] As an HR professional, you occupy a unique position in your company to help yourself and others sharpen their skills through every stage of a negotiation. Table 18-2 lists tools and procedures you can develop and/or maintain for each negotiation step.

TABLE 18-2

Make Negotiation an Organizational Capability

Step in the Negotiation Process	Tools and Procedures HR Professionals Can Develop
Determining the objectives of a negotiation	• Deal and relationship "scorecards" • Negotiation instructions template
Preparing for a negotiation	• Database of past negotiations • Worksheet for understanding negotiation counterpart's choices • Checklist for BATNA review and refining
Conducting the negotiation	• Negotiation "playbook" linking strategies to categories of negotiations • Training programs for negotiators and their managers • "Yellow Pages" enabling efficient consultation with experienced colleagues
Reviewing the negotiation	• Structured review questions focusing on the quality of both negotiation outcomes and process • Debriefing forms feeding into best-practices database • Training in constructive debriefing

Source: Adapted from Danny Ertel, "Turning Negotiation into a Corporate Capability," *Harvard Business Review*, May–June 1999, 55.

Summing Up

It's one thing to develop your own negotiating skills. Developing the negotiating skills of an *organization* at many levels poses a very different challenge—but one with great potential rewards. This chapter explored that challenge from several perspectives.

- The discipline of continuous improvement can help managers improve their organization's internal capabilities and, over time, enhance bottom-line results. This same discipline can be applied to the negotiation process.

- The first step toward continuous improvement in negotiations is to treat negotiation as a process with a fairly universal set of process steps: pre-negotiations, preparation, negotiations, agreement or nonagreement, postmortem learning, and learning capture. Learning capture feeds back to the next negotiating experience. The second step is to organize to learn from the negotiation process as it takes place, and from the outcome of each negotiation.

- HR professionals can improve individuals' overall negotiating skill and turn that skill into an important organizationwide capability by providing training and preparation for negotiators, clarifying organizational goals and expectations for any agreement and explaining when negotiators should walk away, insisting that every negotiating individual or team develop a BATNA and work to improve it, developing mechanisms for capturing and reusing lessons learned from previous negotiations, and developing negotiating performance measures and linking them to rewards.

The chapter concluded with a section describing how HR professionals can help build negotiation as a core competence in their organizations, including the kinds of tools and procedures they can develop and/or maintain for each stage of the negotiation process.

Leveraging Chapter Insights: Critical Questions

- Does your company currently consider negotiation a core competence that must be strengthened throughout the organization? If not, what steps can you take to send a message about the importance of negotiation as an organizational capacity?

- What steps are you currently taking to serve as a negotiation advocate, builder, and practitioner? Of these three roles, which are you strongest in? weakest? How might you strengthen your abilities in the roles where you're weakest?

- Look again at table 18-2. Which of the tools and procedures shown in the table do you currently develop or maintain in your organization? What steps might you take to create or support more of these resources for all four stages of the negotiating process described in the table?

CHAPTER NINETEEN

Sharpening Your Skills, Benefiting Your Company

HR Professionals as Seasoned Negotiators

Key Topics Covered in This Chapter

- *A review of key principles and techniques*

- *Strategies for enhancing your skills*

- *Benefits for your company, your department, and yourself*

CONGRATULATIONS! You've worked your way through a lot of information in this book. In this chapter, we step back and look at the big picture of HR negotiations, summing up key principles and techniques you encountered in previous chapters. We then examine ways in which you can further enhance the knowledge and skills you've developed by reading this book—as you begin applying your negotiation talents on the job. We wrap up the chapter by assessing the benefits that accrue to your company, your department, and yourself when you enhance your negotiation skills and help make negotiation a core capability in your organization.

Key Principles and Techniques

The negotiation situations you've read about in this book vary widely, in terms of who participates, what's at stake, and which obstacles and opportunities for agreement might arise. But despite these differences, there *are* some common threads that wind through all of these differences—some key principles and techniques that will help you handle any negotiation situation more effectively. If we were to boil these down from the more detailed information presented earlier in the book, we might phrase these core principles and techniques as follows:

- **Serving as a negotiation agent presents special challenges.** In many of the negotiations you participate in as an HR professional, you'll likely serve as an agent for your company. As you saw in chapter 2, the role of agent involves complex legal considerations. HR executives or managers must strike a delicate balance between serving their principal (the company) and serving their internal customers (peer managers and employees). The key technique for achieving this balance? Ensure that you understand, in crystal-clear terms, your legal duties as a negotiation agent. And know when *not* to embrace the role of agent.

- **Integrative negotiations create more new value than distributive negotiations.** In chapter 3, you discovered there are many paths to agreement during any negotiation. The parties can use the distributive approach, each claiming as much of the available "pie" as possible—which means that the more value one party claims, the less remains for his or her counterpart. On the other hand, the negotiators can use the integrative approach—creating unexpected new value by exploring their different interests beyond just price. Often, this approach leads to more mutually beneficial outcomes in which both participants feel that they've "won."

- **Relationships have value.** When negotiators build positive relationships during the bargaining process, they set a virtuous cycle in motion: The trust and credibility that come with strong relationships fuel more open and creative negotiating in future bargaining sessions—which in turn further strengthen the relationship between the parties. As you learned in chapter 4, when you add the quality of your relationship with another negotiator to the "pie," you create new forms of value for yourself and your negotiation counterpart. But make sure the other party also values the relationship: If not, that party may "hold you hostage" to the relationship while grabbing all he or she can from the bargaining process.

- **Preparation is vital.** The negotiating process actually begins long before the parties sit down together and start talking. Chapters 5 and 6 showed you that the best bargainers clarify their BATNA (their best alternative to a negotiated agreement) and reservation price (or walk-away terms), as well as define a desirable outcome and identify potential value-creation opportunities while preparing for a negotiation. They also estimate the other party's BATNA and reservation price, and use those estimates to estimate a ZOPA, or zone of possible agreement. In addition, they constantly look for ways to strengthen their BATNA, anticipate any authority issues, and learn as much as possible about the other party.

- **You have numerous opportunities to shape the negotiation process.** Chapters 7–10 revealed that negotiators have many means at their disposal for influencing the negotiation process—and directing it in a more positive direction. For example, starting a bargaining session on a promising note can pay big dividends later in the process. And knowing how to recognize—and deal with—a manipulative negotiation ploy (such as lying, refusal to share information, or attempts to intimidate you) can help you put the process on more productive footing. Finally, anticipating and addressing barriers to agreement (for example, lack of information or trust, or communication difficulties) can help you further shape the negotiation process in positive ways.

- **All negotiators can be prone to mental errors.** As chapter 11 made clear, we human beings tend to fall victim to common mental errors—such as overestimating our own abilities, giving in to unchecked emotions, and forming expectations of one another that have little to do with reality. To negotiate skillfully, hone your awareness of these errors. Familiarize yourself with them, and watch for signs that you may be committing one or more of them. Develop routines for counteracting them; for example, checking the reasonableness of your expectations with an outside party during a negotiation.

- **The world of HR negotiations is rich and complex.** In chapters 12–17, you gained a glimpse into a wide variety of negotiations that HR professionals often participate in—from negotiating salaries, benefits packages, and raises with job seekers and employees and persuading peer managers to adopt HR policies, to gaining a seat at the "strategy table" and winning support for your proposed changes during a merger or acquisition. Other situations involve negotiating contracts and fees with vendors and consultants, participating in bargaining sessions between management and unionized labor, and negotiating legal disputes involving employees.

Though the players and contexts may differ widely across each of these situations, certain techniques and strategies crop up again and again in these different settings. For instance, the adage "know your business" applies to most if not all of these negotiation situations. Educate yourself on your company's competitive strategy and needs—so you can select the right vendors, help get a newly merged or acquired organization started on the right foot, participate in your firm's strategic planning and implementation, attract the right talent, and protect your company from legal reprisals.

Moreover, know how things work within your organization, by networking with peer managers and strategic thinkers. Build relationships, and find out what each of these individual's key concerns are. That way, you can develop and gain buy-in for the changed or new HR policies you're proposing. Also learn as much as you can about employment law while also consulting your firm's legal counsel about such laws—so you can help your company navigate negotiations with labor union representatives and with employees who have filed (or who are considering filing) lawsuits against your firm or claims with federal or state agencies.

And finally, with all of these situations, view negotiation as a process rather than a series of one-time, disparate events. Through your everyday encounters and responsibilities, keep accumulating "negotiation capital" in the form of trust, credibility, and positive working relationships. That means taking a disciplined approach to educating yourself, networking with people inside and outside your company, and demonstrating your knowledge and skills. Then, whenever you engage in a negotiation, you can draw from that "account"—to arrive at agreements that benefit you, the other party, and your company.

- **You can help make negotiation a core capability in your firm.** As you saw in chapter 18, HR professionals can play a major role in enabling their organizations to develop negotiation skill as a core, company-wide competency. How? Practice effective negotiation yourself. Deliver a consistent, ongoing message about the importance of effective negotiation to the company's bottom line. Develop programs that help managers in your firm master the art and science of negotiation. And suggest ways of capturing lessons learned from negotiations handled by numerous people within your firm—and making the resulting insights available to others.

Enhancing Your Negotiation Skills

As you put into practice the knowledge and techniques you've gained from reading this book, you'll want to continually sharpen your negotiation skills. Like many abilities, negotiation skills will likely atrophy if you don't keep using and improving them. Table 19-1 lists five core negotiation skills and provides space for you to document strategies for enhancing each skill. To help you get started, we've also offered a few examples of how to strengthen each skill.

In addition to developing an action plan for sustaining and enhancing your negotiation skills, consider these guidelines:

- **Read all about it.** Consult your local library or bookstore for additional written resources on the art and science of negotiation. The "For Further Reading" list at the end of this book contains valuable, recommended selections. Professional associations, such as SHRM and other organizations, can provide or recommend additional resources.

- **Talk with talented negotiators.** Find other HR professionals who are skilled at negotiating. Take them to lunch or dinner, and ask them how they approach negotiating situations and how they keep their skills sharp.

- **Role play.** With a trusted friend, colleague, or family member, use role play to practice dealing with various real and fictional negotiation challenges. Work on your demeanor, your body language, and your statements and questions. Invite your role-

TABLE 19-1

Strengthen Your Negotiating Skills

Skill	Ideas for Enhancing
Maintaining your composure: Keeping your cool during stressful or heated negotiations, and enabling yourself and the other person to stay focused on the objective	*Examples:* Take a moment of silence or count to 10.
Developing data: Gathering facts relevant to the situation, impressions from the other person's body language, and other information that can help you respond to the other person's arguments and claims	*Examples:* Document your bottom line on important issues and know your BATNA and reservation price.
Refocusing the negotiation: Putting the conversation back on track after an intentional or unintentional diversion or an emotional eruption	*Examples:* Ask problem-solving questions and request clarification on comments that seem unclear or antagonistic.
Generating creative ideas: Looking at situations from several angles and gaining the other person's support for creative solutions	*Examples:* Think up forms of value beyond price and look for ways to concede your low-priority items in return for concessions on your high-priority items.
Handling information strategically: Releasing and asking for information in ways that lead to long-lasting, mutually beneficial agreements	*Examples:* Reveal some information and give the other person ample time to digest what you're saying.

Source: Adapted from Rollin Glaser and Eileen Russo, *Dealing with Tough Negotiators Workbook* (King of Prussia, PA: HRDQ, 1998), 9–18.

play partner to comment honestly on how you came across during the exercise. Consider video- and audiotaping the exercise so you can analyze your behavior and approach and identify opportunities for improvement.

- **Compile your "negotiation history."** After every negotiation, write down what went well and what didn't go well. Document any missteps you made and brainstorm ideas for handling problem situations differently the next time around.

- **Attend workshops.** Participate in negotiation skills-building workshops offered by local adult-education institutions or by your own company. If you arrange to provide negotiation training as part of your role in building this core capability in your firm, attend the training sessions yourself!

- **Ratchet up your learning.** If you're focusing on strengthening particular negotiation skills and don't want to risk making a misstep during an important business-related negotiation, try out your abilities in less-risky, non-business situations first. Then work your way up to the more challenging, higher-stakes situations.

Benefits to Your Company, Your Department, and You

When you continually improve your negotiation talents and help your firm make negotiation a core capability, you generate important benefits for your company, your HR department, and yourself. The savvier you are at negotiating, the better your on-the-job performance—which yields value for your organization. You also gain more satisfaction from your work, which in turn further improves your performance.

And you benefit your HR department as well: When you demonstrate that you and other HR staff members know how to negotiate, you further enhance the HR function's reputation among peer managers and executive leaders. Equally important, you gain additional credibility for the department—and thus the entire company—in the eyes of employees and vendors. In these ways, you send the message that HR truly is a strategic partner that can offer far more than administrative services.

When you enable your company to make negotiation a core capability, you help the organization gain a competitive advantage, streamline costs, boost profits, and enhance relationships with parties inside and outside the firm. As people in the organization engage in the multitude of negotiations that characterize daily business life, the *collective* impact of those bargaining situations helps the company achieve its strategic objectives. Moreover, managers and employees from every organizational function avoid the typical mistakes that

occur when companies *don't* treat negotiation as a core competency—for example, taking a negotiation in a direction that contra-
dicts the goals of another agreement made by a different set of parties, or missing opportunities to create new value because a bargainer
lacked important information about his or her counterpart.

When your firm, your department, and you score greater successes through savvy negotiating, you've clearly generated the ultimate in win–win scenarios!

Summing Up

In this chapter, you reviewed key principles and techniques that are
crucial to know for any negotiation situation:

- Serving as a negotiation agent presents special challenges.

- Integrative negotiations generate more new value than distributive negotiations.

- Relationships have value.

- Preparation is vital.

- You have numerous opportunities to shape the negotiation
  process.

- All negotiators are prone to mental errors.

- The world of HR negotiations is rich and complex.

- You can help make negotiation a core capability in your firm.

You also had the opportunity to develop an action plan for continually enhancing five important negotiation skills:

- Maintaining your composure

- Developing data

- Refocusing the negotiation

- Generating creative ideas

- Handling information strategically

Finally, you saw how enhancing your own and your company's negotiation abilities can benefit your firm, your HR department, and yourself.

Leveraging Chapter Insights: Critical Questions

- As you begin applying the knowledge you gained from reading this book, which negotiation skills will you focus on most? Which do you consider already strong?

- What techniques and strategies will you use to enhance your negotiation skills?

- Which *new* types of negotiation situations do you anticipate contributing to in the near future? How will you prepare yourself to handle these situations successfully?

Notes

Chapter 1

1. Danny Ertel, "Turning Negotiation into a Corporate Capability." In *Harvard Business Review on Negotiation and Conflict Resolution* (Boston: Harvard Business School Press, 2000), 102–103.

2. Kathryn Tyler, "Extending the Olive Branch," *HR Magazine*, November 2002.

3. Marick F. Masters, Robert R. Albright, and Frank Irr, "Another Hat for HR: Negotiator-in-Chief," *HR Magazine*, June 2003.

4. James H. Hopkins, "Negotiations and the Human Resource Professional," white paper, Society for Human Resource Management, Alexandria, VA, February 2000.

Chapter 2

1. Michael Watkins and Joel Cutcher-Gershenfeld, "Representing Others in Negotiations," paper presented to the Academy of Management, August 1997, and reprinted in *Negotiating on Behalf of Others: Advice to Lawyers, Business Executives, Sports Agents, Diplomats, Politicians, and Everybody Else*, eds. Robert H. Mnookin, Lawrence E. Susskind, and Pacey C. Foster (New York: Sage Publications, 1999).

2. Ibid.

3. Carolyn Hirschman, "Fiduciary Fitness," *HR Magazine*, September 2003.

4. Ibid.

5. This section draws extensively from a report by Edward Lee Isler, Steven W. Ray, and Michelle L. Bodley, "Personal Liability and Employee Discipline," legal report, Society for Human Resource Management, Alexandria, VA, September–October 2000.

6. Society for Human Resource Management Code of Ethical and Professional Standards in Human Resource Management, Society for Human Resource Management, Code Provisions, Alexandria, VA.

7. Howard M. Pardue, "Ethics: A Human Resource Perspective," white paper, Society for Human Resource Management, Alexandria, VA, December 1998.

8. Ibid.

9. Frank Z. Ashen, "Corporate Ethics—Who Is Minding the Store?," white paper, Society for Human Resource Management, Alexandria, VA, July 2002.

Chapter 3

1. "Win-Win with Mark Gordon," *Harvard Management Communication Letter*, March 1999, 1–3.

2. Ibid.

3. This section is adapted from the Negotiating module of Harvard ManageMentor, an online service of Harvard Business School Publishing.

Chapter 4

1. John Kotter, *Power and Influence* (New York: Free Press, 1985), 40.

2. Danny Ertel, "Turning Negotiation into a Corporate Capability," *Harvard Business Review*, May–June 1999, 55.

3. Ibid., 62.

4. Ibid., 64.

Chapter 6

1. The nine steps are adapted from the Negotiating module of Harvard ManageMentor, an online service of Harvard Business School Publishing.

2. Deborah M. Kolb and Judith Williams, "Breakthrough Bargaining," *Harvard Business Review*, February 2001, 93.

3. Ibid.

Chapter 7

1. Adapted from the Negotiating module of Harvard ManageMentor, an online service of Harvard Business School Publishing.

2. Deborah M. Kolb and Judith Williams, "Breakthrough Bargaining," *Harvard Business Review*, February 2001, 90.

3. Max H. Bazerman and Margaret A. Neale, *Negotiating Rationally* (New York: Free Press, 1992), 23.

4. Ibid., 31.

5. Marjorie Corman Aaron, "The Right Frame: Managing Meaning and Making Proposals," *Harvard Management Communication Letter*, September 1999, 1–4.

6. Michael Watkins, "Rethinking 'Preparation' in Negotiations," Class Note 9-801-286 (Boston: Harvard Business School, revised 9 October 2001), 11.

Chapter 8

1. Adapted from the Negotiating module of Harvard ManageMentor, an online service of Harvard Business School Publishing.

Chapter 9

1. Roger Fisher, William Ury, and Bruce Patton, *Getting to Yes: Negotiating Agreement Without Giving In*, 2d ed., (New York: Penguin Books, 1991), chapter 8.

2. Rollin Glaser and Eileen Russo, *Dealing with Tough Negotiators Workbook* (King of Prussia, PA: HRDQ, 1998).

Chapter 10

1. Diane Coutu, "Negotiating Without a Net: A Conversation with the NYPD's Dominick J. Misino," *Harvard Business Review*, October 2002, 50.

2. Michael D. Watkins, "Diagnosing and Overcoming Barriers to Agreement," Class Note 9-800-333 (Boston: Harvard Business School, revised 8 May 2000), 15.

3. Gary Hamel and Yves Doz, *Alliance Advantage: The Art of Creating Value through Partnering* (Boston: Harvard Business School Press, 1998), 14.

Chapter 11

1. Max H. Bazerman and Margaret A. Neale, *Negotiating Rationally* (New York: Free Press, 1992), 10.

2. David Bunnell with Richard Luecke, *The eBay Phenomenon* (New York: John Wiley & Sons, 2000), 48.

3. Irving Janus, *Groupthink: Psychological Studies of Policy Decisions and Fiascos* (Boston: Houghton Mifflin, 1982), 9.

Chapter 12

1. *Negotiating Rewards Poll*, Society for Human Resource Management Research and CareerJournal.com, July 2001.

2. Paul Falcone, *The Hiring and Firing Question and Answer Book* (New York: AMACOM, 2002), 129–133.

3. Paul Falcone, "How to Make a Counteroffer," *HR Magazine*, November 2003.

4. Chris Velissaris, "Combating the Counteroffer," *Employment Management Today* 5, no. 1 (winter 2000).

5. Falcone, "How to Make a Counteroffer."

6. Debbie Rodman Sandler, "Noncompete Agreements: Considering Ties That Bind," legal report, Society for Human Resource Management, Alexandria, VA, November 1997.

7. Louis K. Obdyke, "Written Employment Contracts: When? Why? How?" legal report, Society for Human Resource Management, Alexandria, VA, May 1998.

8. Sandler, "Noncompete Agreements."

9. Attison L. Barnes III and Tara M. Vold, "When Trade Secrets Take Flight: Protecting Valuable Assets from Your Competitors," legal report, Society for Human Resource Management, Alexandria, VA, September–October 1999.

10. Stephen Roush, "Managing Risk During Employee Separations," white paper, Society for Human Resource Management, Alexandria, VA, December 1999.

11. Francis T. Coleman, *Ending the Employment Relationship Without Ending Up in Court* (Alexandria, VA: Society for Human Resource Management, 2001), 98.

12. Ibid., 99–112.

13. Ibid., 111.

14. Obdyke, "Written Employment Contracts: When? Why? How?"

Chapter 13

1. This section draws extensively from Lin Grensing-Pophal, "Are You Promotable? What Does It Take to Succeed in HR?," white paper, Society for Human Resource Management, Alexandria, VA, July 2001; and Gene C. Mage, "Stuck with an Unsupportive Boss? Learn How to Rise Above," *Managing Smart* (fall 2003).

2. Stephen Rubenfeld and James Laumeyer, "Human Resource Policies: Are They 'Anchors' or 'Oars'?," white paper, Society for Human Resource Management, Alexandria, VA, February 2000.

3. Mary Jo Case, telephone conversation with author, 27 January 2004.

4. Nancy J. Campbell, *Writing Effective Policies and Procedures: A Step-by-Step Resource for Clear Communication* (New York: AMACOM, 1998), 318.

5. Adapted by permission of the publisher from chapter 10 of *Writing Effective Policies and Procedures* by Nancy Campbell © 1998 AMACOM. Published by AMACOM, a division of American Management Association, New York, New York. All rights reserved. <http://amacombooks.org.>

6. Julie Britt, "How to Get Executive Approval for Projects," *HR News*, 9 October 2003.

7. Ibid.

8. William Kent, "Human Resources: A Strategic Partner," white paper, Society for Human Resource Management, Alexandria, VA, July 2002.

9. Lin Grensing-Pophal, "Getting a 'Seat at the Table': What Does It Really Take?," white paper, Society for Human Resource Management, Alexandria, VA, August 2000.

10. This section draws extensively from Grensing-Pophal, "Getting a 'Seat at the Table'"; and from Douglas Wiley, "Human Resources Capital Management: Marking the Way for Executive Involvement," white paper, Society for Human Resource Management, Alexandria, VA, August 2001.

11. Jim Jose, telephone conversation with author, 28 January 2004.

Chapter 14

1. Les Rosen, telephone conversation with author, 22 January 2004.

2. Thomas J. Ucko, *Selecting and Working with Consultants: A Guide for Clients* (Los Altos, CA: Crisp Publications, Inc., 1990), sections V and VI.

3. Ron S. Fortgang, David A. Lax, and James K. Sebenius, "Negotiating the Spirit of the Deal," in *The Nuts and Bolts of Negotiation*, a *Harvard Business Review* OnPoint Enhanced Collection (Boston: Harvard Business School Publishing, 2003), 19–34.

Chapter 15

1. Stephanie Overman, "Confronting New Faces Across the Bargaining Table," *HR News*, 26 August 2003.

2. John Gaffin, telephone conversation with author, 22 January 2004.

3. James H. Hopkins, "The Penalties Employers Face for Violating the National Labor Relations Act (NLRA)," white paper, Society for Human Resource Management, Alexandria, VA, January 2002.

4. Robert R. Blake and Jane S. Mouton, "Overcoming Group Warfare," in *Harvard Business Review on Negotiation and Conflict Resolution* (Boston: Harvard Business School Press, 2000), 68–86.

5. Harrison Darby, telephone conversation with author, 28 January 2004.

Chapter 16

1. Michael Karpeles, telephone conversation with author, 23 January 2004.

2. Craig Pratt, telephone conversation with author, 27 January 2004.

3. Gene Thornton, e-mail to author, 27 January 2004.

4. Gilbert F. Casellas and Irene L. Hill, "Sexual Harassment: Prevention and Avoiding Liability," Society for Human Resource Management Legal Report, November 1998.

5. Jathan W. Janove, "Don't Add Insult to Injury," *HR Magazine*, May 2002.

6. John Smoyer, "Resolving Sexual Harassment Disputes Through Mediation," white paper, Society for Human Resource Management, Alexandria, VA, October 1994.

7. John R. Allison, "Five Ways to Keep Disputes Out of Court," in *Harvard Business Review on Negotiation and Conflict Resolution* (Boston: Harvard Business School Press, 1999), 169–170.

8. Todd B. Carver and Albert A. Vondra, "Alternative Dispute Resolution: Why It Doesn't Work and Why It Does," in *Harvard Business Review on Negotiation and Conflict Resolution* (Boston: Harvard Business School Press, 1999), 201–203.

Chapter 17

1. Dennis L. Roberts, "The Role of Human Resources in Mergers and Acquisitions," white paper, Society for Human Resource Management, Alexandria, VA, January 2002.

2. Ibid.

3. Linda S. Johnson and John E. Rich, Jr., "Dealing with Employee Benefit Issues in Mergers and Acquisitions," legal report, Society for Human Resource Management, Alexandria, VA, March–April 2000.

4. Linda S. Johnson, "The Human Resource Perspective in Mergers and Acquisitions: Non-Benefits Issues," legal report, Society for Human Resource Management, Alexandria, VA, July 2000.

5. Dean A. Black, e-mail to author, 27 January 2004.

6. Information about HR restructuring is drawn extensively from Mary Cianni, "Transforming the HR Organization," in Jeffrey A. Schmidt, ed., *Making Mergers Work: The Strategic Importance of People* (Alexandria, VA: Towers Perrin/Society for Human Resource Management, 2002), chapter 7.

7. Information about integrating reward systems is drawn from Kenneth T. Ransby and John M. Burns, "Planning the Integration of Rewards," in Jeffrey A. Schmidt, ed., *Making Mergers Work: The Strategic Importance of People* (Alexandria, VA: Towers Perrin/Society for Human Resource Management, 2002), chapter 8.

8. Information about integrating technology is drawn from Alfred J. Walker, "HR Technology Integration Strategy," in Jeffrey A. Schmidt, ed., *Making Mergers Work: The Strategic Importance of People* (Alexandria, VA: Towers Perrin/Society for Human Resource Management, 2002), chapter 9.

Chapter 18

1. Danny Ertel, "Turning Negotiation into a Corporate Capability," *Harvard Business Review*, May–June 1999, 55.

2. Ibid., 57.

3. Kathryn Tyler, "Extending the Olive Branch," *HR Magazine*, November 2002.

4. Marick F. Masters, Robert R. Albright, and Frank Irr, "Another Hat for HR: Negotiator-in-Chief," *HR Magazine*, June 2003.

Glossary

ACQUISITION   One company's taking over controlling interest in another company.

AGENT   A person charged with representing the interests of another in negotiations with a third party. Agents can be independent (such as outside lawyers) or non-independent (such as a manager negotiating a contract with a vendor for the manager's company).

ANCHORING   An attempt to establish an initial position around which negotiations will make adjustments.

ARBITRATION   A process that produces a legally binding decision made by a third party (one or more arbitrators) based on evidence provided by disputants' attorneys.

BATNA   Acronym for "best alternative to a negotiated agreement." Knowing your BATNA means knowing the options of what you will do or what will happen if you do not reach agreement in the negotiation at hand.

BLUFFING   A tactic in which one party in a negotiation indicates that it may be willing to do or accept something that it actually has no intention of following through on. For example, a union representative may bluff that he will urge his constituency to go on strike unless certain improvements are made to union members' working conditions.

COMPLIANCE TRANSPARENCY   The ability to monitor compliance with the terms of an agreement from the outside.

CONFIDENTIALITY AGREEMENT   See *nondisclosure agreement.*

COUNTEROFFER   An offer that an employer makes to a valued employee who has received a job offer from another company.

DIE-HARD BARGAINERS   People for whom every negotiation is a battle.

DISTRIBUTIVE NEGOTIATION   A type of negotiation in which the parties compete over the distribution of a fixed pool of value. Here, any gain by one party represents a loss to the other. Popularly referred to as a *zero-sum negotiation* or *win-lose* negotiation.

EMPLOYEE RETIREMENT INCOME SECURITY ACT OF 1974 (ERISA)   A U.S. federal law governing employee benefit plans, including 401(k) plans, savings plans, annuity plans, defined benefit plans, pension plans, profit-sharing plans, money purchase plans, and employee stock ownership plans. ERISA also governs health, accident, disability, death, unemployment, vacation, day care, and severance benefits.

EMPLOYMENT CONTRACT   An agreement in which an employer lays out the term of employment, any noncompete or nondisclosure provisions, compensation, and other terms for a new hire; often used when a company wants to ensure the services of a particularly desirable employee for a specified period of time.

EXPLODING OFFER   An offer with an expiration date.

FAIR LABOR STANDARDS ACT (FLSA)   A U.S. federal statute setting minimum wage, overtime pay, equal pay, record keeping, and child-labor standards for employees covered by the act.

FAMILY AND MEDICAL LEAVE ACT (FMLA)   A U.S. federal statute requiring employers with at least fifty employees to provide eligible employees with up to twelve weeks of leave for the birth or adoption of a child, to care for a family member with a serious health condition, or for the employee's own serious health condition.

FIDUCIARY   A person who stands in a special position of trust, confidence, or responsibility in his or her obligations to others, as an agent of a principal.

GROUPTHINK   A mode of thinking that engages members of a cohesive "in" group. Groupthink is driven by consensus and tends to override the motivation to realistically appraise alternative courses of action.

INFORMATION ASYMMETRY   A situation in which one party has more information than another.

INSECURE AGREEMENT   An agreement that is hedged or more narrow or limited than it would otherwise be because of lack of trust between the negotiating parties.

INTEGRATIVE NEGOTIATION   A type of negotiation in which the parties cooperate to achieve maximum mutual benefit in an agreement. Long-term partnerships and collaborations between colleagues are often characterized by integrative negotiation. More popularly known as a *win-win* negotiation.

IRRATIONAL ESCALATION   Continuing a previously selected course of action beyond what rational analysis would recommend.

MEDIATION   An alternative to arbitration as a means of resolving workplace disputes. In this voluntary, confidential process, two or more disputing parties resolve their conflict with the aid of a neutral third party, or mediator. The mediator facilitates the formation of a resolution that all parties support and agree to.

MERGER   The combining of two companies through a pooling of their accounts and interests, a purchase (where the amount paid over and above the purchased company's book value is carried on the purchaser's books as goodwill), or a consolidation (where a new company is formed to acquire the net assets of the combining companies).

MULTIPARTY NEGOTIATIONS   Negotiations that involve more than two parties. Such negotiations can differ significantly from two-party negotiations, especially when coalitions—alliances among parties that wield less power separately than they do together—form among the parties.

MULTIPHASE NEGOTIATIONS   Negotiations that will be implemented in phases, or that have the prospect of subsequent involvement in the future. The context of the negotiations allows parties to negotiate based on follow-through and continuing communication.

NATIONAL LABOR RELATIONS ACT (NLRA)   A U.S. federal statute prescribing acceptable treatment of unions and union members by employers.

NATURAL COALITION   A group of allies who share a broad range of common interests.

NEGOTIATOR'S DILEMMA   The tension caused by the negotiator's attempt to balance competitive strategies—trying to discern when to compete where interests conflict, and when to create value by exchanging the information that leads to mutually advantageous options.

NONCOMPETE AGREEMENT   An agreement by which an employee promises not to work for a competing company for a specified period after he or she leaves the current employer.

NONDISCLOSURE AGREEMENT   An agreement by which an employee promises not to share sensitive information about his or her employer (such as trade secrets, proprietary knowledge, client lists, and so forth) during the term of employment and during a specified time period after the term of employment ends; also called a *confidentiality agreement.*

PARTISAN PERCEPTION   The psychological phenomenon that causes people to perceive truth with a built-in bias in their own favor or toward their own point of view. For example, an HR manager who is negotiating a contract with a consultant mistakenly interprets the consultant's pleasant demeanor as willingness to accept the proposed terms.

POSITION   What the parties in a negotiation are asking for—in other words, their demands.

PRINCIPAL   The person or organization whom a negotiation agent represents.

PROCESSES   Activities that turn inputs into outputs of higher total value.

RESERVATION PRICE   The least favorable point at which a party would accept a negotiated deal. The reservation price is derived from, but is not usually the same thing as, the BATNA. Also known as *walk-away.*

SINGLE-ISSUE COALITION   A group whose members may differ on other issues, but who nevertheless unite (though often for different reasons) to support or block a certain particular issue.

SPIRIT OF THE DEAL   Assumptions about how the two parties in a negotiation will work together once the agreement is put into practice—including who will make what decisions, how conflicts and surprises will be handled, and whether the agreement represents a one-time transaction or a long-term relationship.

STRATEGY   A planned sequence of how one is going to approach a negotiation, including what the negotiator will offer and ask for (give and get).

TRADE OFF   To substitute or bargain one issue for another; this tactic is often used in sales negotiations.

VALUE CREATION THROUGH TRADES   A concept that holds that negotiating parties can improve their positions by trading the values at their disposal. Value creation through trades occurs in integrative negotiations. It usually takes the form of each party *getting* something it wants by *giving* something else it values much less.

WALK-AWAY See *reservation price*.

WIGGLE ROOM The flexibility that may exist in a particular offer, whether it has to do with money or time frame. If you have no wiggle room, you should strongly convey the message that this is your best offer.

WIN-LOSE See *distributive negotiation*.

WIN-WIN See *integrative negotiation*.

WINNER'S CURSE After a deal has been reached, the nagging conviction that one could have negotiated a more favorable deal.

ZERO-SUM NEGOTIATION See *distributive negotiation*.

ZOPA Acronym for "zone of possible agreement." This is the area in which a potential deal can take place. Each party's reservation price defines one of the boundaries of the ZOPA. The ZOPA itself exists, if at all, in the overlap between the parties' reservation prices.

For Further Reading

Articles and Papers

Conger, Jay. "The Necessary Art of Persuasion." *Harvard Business Review* OnPoint Enhanced Edition. Boston: Harvard Business School Publishing, 2000. Persuasion is a major part of any negotiation. This article explains the four essential elements of persuasion: (1) establishing credibility, (2) finding common ground, (3) providing vivid evidence for your position, and (4) connecting emotionally with your audience.

Ertel, Danny. "Turning Negotiation into a Corporate Capability." *Harvard Business Review* OnPoint Enhanced Edition. Boston: Harvard Business School Publishing, 2000. Every company today exists in a complex web of relationships formed, one at a time, through negotiation. Purchasing and outsourcing contracts are negotiated with vendors. Marketing arrangements are negotiated with distributors. Product development agreements are negotiated with joint venture partners. Taken together, the thousands of negotiations a typical company engages in have an enormous effect on both its strategy and its bottom line. But few companies think systematically about their negotiating activities as a whole. Instead they take a situational view, perceiving each negotiation to be a separate event with its own goals, tactics, and measures of success. Coordinating them all seems an overwhelming and impracticable job. In reality, the author argues, it is neither. He presents four broad changes in practice and perspective that, taken together, will let companies establish closer, more creative relationships with suppliers, customers, and other partners.

Falcone, Paul. "How to Make a Counteroffer." *HR Magazine*, November 2003. Falcone explains when it makes sense to make a counteroffer to an employee who has received a job offer from another company—and when it's better to let the person depart. He also shows how to present a counteroffer in ways that meet the employee's needs, so that he or she won't feel compelled to search for another job six months down the road. Your negotiating strategy? Don't just throw money at the person.

Instead, ask what would have to change in order for him or her to remain with your company. Then see if you can reshape conditions to meet those needs.

Fortgang, Ron S., David A. Lax, and James K. Sebenius. "Negotiating the Spirit of the Deal." In *The Nuts and Bolts of Negotiation*, a *Harvard Business Review* OnPoint Enhanced Collection. Boston: Harvard Business School Publishing, 2003. Even though the ink has dried on your contract, that doesn't mean your negotiating is over. As these authors explain, too many deals sour once they're implemented because the negotiators neglected the *spirit* of the deal—assumptions about who will participate in which decisions, how the parties will communicate, how they'll resolve disputes, and what they'll do if surprises come up. Cultural differences, the use of third parties to drive the bargaining process, and an insufficient number of parties involved in the negotiating can increase the risk of misunderstandings about the spirit of the deal. The authors provide strategies for ensuring that you and your negotiation counterpart clarify not only the letter of the deal, but also the spirit—and that both aspects of your agreement reinforce one another.

Harvard Business School Publishing. "How to Get What You Want." *Harvard Management Communication Letter*, March 2000. How do you improve your chances while negotiating? Start by understanding how you can help or hurt your competition, and how your competition can help or hurt you. Answer these three questions: (1) What do you want? (2) Why should your competition negotiate with you? and (3) What are your alternatives? Includes dos and don'ts for navigating negotiation sessions.

Kolb, Deborah M., and Judith Williams. "Breakthrough Bargaining." *Harvard Business Review* OnPoint Enhanced Edition. Boston: Harvard Business School Publishing, 2001. Unspoken, subtle elements in the bargaining process—the "shadow negotiation"—can set the tone for any negotiation. The authors provide three kinds of strategies for successful bargaining: (1) Power moves show the other side that it's in their interest to negotiate with you, (2) process moves influence how others view the negotiation, and (3) appreciative moves alter the tone of the interaction so that the parties can have a more collaborative exchange.

Masters, Marick F., Robert R. Albright, and Frank Irr. "Another Hat for HR: Negotiator-in-Chief." *HR Magazine*, June 2003. The authors describe the benefits that accrue when HR professionals hone their negotiating skills and help make negotiation a core competency throughout their organization. They outline three roles you can play as "chief negotiator" in your firm: advocate (spreading the word about negotiation as a preferred method of reaching agreement), builder (helping managers and employees throughout the company strengthen their negotiation skills), and practitioner (setting an example by enhancing and demonstrating your own negotiation abilities). The article concludes with a list of principles of effective negotiation, such as focusing on problems rather than personalities, emphasizing interests instead of positions, and being willing to walk way from a negotiaton.

Obdyke, Louis K. "Written Employment Contracts: When? Why? How?" Legal report, Society for Human Resource Management, Alexandria, VA, May 1998. More and more companies are negotiating written employment contracts with new hires—primarily to ensure the services of a particularly desirable employee for a specific period of time. Obdyke discusses the typical content of such agreements and explains how to develop them. The report concludes with a sample employment contract.

Roberts, Dennis L. "The Role of Human Resources in Mergers and Acquisitions." white paper, Society for Human Resource Management, Alexandria, VA, January 2002. As the number of mergers and acquisitions (M&As) skyrockets, HR professionals need to deepen their knowledge of the M&A process and contribute their skills to help ensure a successful blending of companies. Roberts outlines five critical capabilities you must leverage to your fullest ability so that you can contribute to M&A success. These capabilities include evaluating another company quickly, demonstrating your integration know-how, providing advice about employee and cultural issues, retaining valued talent, and planning and leading complex integration projects.

Sandler, Debbie Rodman. "Noncompete Agreements: Considering Ties That Bind." Legal report, Society for Human Resource Management, Alexandria, VA, November 1997. This report explains the practical considerations related to noncompete, nondisclosure, nonsolicitation, and no-raid agreements companies make with their current and former employees. Sandler also provides advice for handling situations in which you're considering hiring someone who is subject to such an agreement with his or her current or former employer.

Sebenius, James K. "Six Habits of Merely Effective Negotiators." *Harvard Business Review* OnPoint Enhanced Edition. Boston: Harvard Business School Publishing, 2002. Even seasoned negotiators fall prey at times to six all-too-common mistakes that keep them from solving the right negotiation problem: neglecting the other party's problem, letting price eclipse other interests, letting positions eclipse interests, searching too hard for common ground, neglecting no-deal alternatives, and failing to correct for skewed vision. The author contrasts good and bad negotiating practice, drawing from fifty years of research and analysis.

Shell, G. Richard. "When Is It Legal to Lie in Negotiations?" *MIT Sloan Management Review* 32, no. 3 (spring 1991): 93–101. This short and clearly written article sets forth the legal framework for understanding when and why lying will get you into trouble in negotiation. Using case examples, it provides guidance for those uncomfortable with the sometimes fuzzy distinctions between lying and bluffing, puffing, or not telling.

"The SHRM Ethics Toolkit." This toolkit is available on the Society for Human Resource Management (SHRM) Web site at <http://www.shrm.org/hrtools/toolkits/Ethicsresources.asp>. It includes "A Guide to Developing Your Organization's Code of Ethics," the SHRM Code of Ethics, and links to numerous valuable resources relating to corporate ethics, ethical issues for HR professionals, and the SHRM/ERC 2003 Business Ethics Survey.

Wiley, Douglas G. "Human Resources Capital Management: Marking the Way for Executive Involvement." white paper, Society for Human Resource Management, Alexandria, VA, August 2001. Wiley explains how HR professionals can negotiate for greater involvement in strategic planning and implementation in their firms. He provides tips for understanding the needs and wants of your company's various functions and using metrics to demonstrate your knowledge of HR programs' impact on the bottom line.

Williams, Monci J. "Don't Avoid Conflicts—Manage Them." *Harvard Management Update*, July 1997. Regardless of our hierarchical position in an organization, most of us believe it is expedient, and therefore preferable, to avoid conflict. Research indicates, however, that avoiding conflict may hinder managers in achieving their goals. To manage conflict successfully you need to understand the difference between positions and underlying needs. You should also understand the other party's position before asserting your own. By concentrating on common interests and knowing your own "hot buttons," you and your partners in conflict can arrive at an optimal solution rather than a simple compromise.

Books

Bazerman, Max, and Margaret Neale. *Negotiating Rationally*. New York: Free Press, 1992. Professors Bazerman and Neale bring their psychologists' lens to this work on negotiation theory and practice. Their bottom-line advice is much like that in *Getting to Yes* and *The Manager as Negotiator* (see entries below), but they also weave in explanations and insights from psychological research and literature.

Camp, Jim. *Start with No*. New York: Crown, 2002. A contrarian approach to personal and business negotiation problems. Of particular interest is the author's critique of the conventional win-win mentality advocated by many other authors and consultants. Camp believes that this mentality results in win-lose outcomes.

Fisher, Roger, William Ury, and Bruce Patton. *Getting to Yes: Negotiating Agreement Without Giving In.* 2d ed. New York: Penguin, 1991. The original 1981 edition had a tremendous impact on everything from international politics to professional schools and executive education courses in negotiation. *Getting to Yes* sets up a polemic between "positional bargaining" and "principled negotiation." The heart of the book articulates a basic prescriptive framework for "principled negotiation" or "negotiation on the merits": Separate the people from the problem; focus on interests, not positions; invent options for mutual gain; and insist on objective criteria.

Glaser, Rollin, and Eileen Russo. *Dealing with Tough Negotiators Workbook.* King of Prussia, PA: HRDQ, 1998. The authors describe fifteen particularly difficult negotiation styles and explain how to respond to them. They describe five core negotiating skills that can help you handle any or all of the fifteen types: maintaining your composure, developing information, refocusing the discussion, generating creative ideas and solutions, and handling information strategically. A facilitator's guide and self-assessment can be purchased along with the workbook.

Harvard Business School Publishing. *Harvard Business Review on Negotiation and Conflict Resolution.* Boston: Harvard Business School Press, 1999. This collection of *Harvard Business Review* articles offers the best thinking on negotiation practice and conflict management.

Harvard Business School Publishing. *The Manager's Guide to Negotiation and Conflict Resolution. Harvard Management Update* Collection. Boston: Harvard Business School Publishing, 2000. One of the most difficult issues managers must deal with every day is negotiation in the broadest sense. Whether it's negotiating for a raise, or with your colleagues to promote a project, or more formally with other companies to find ways to work together, this essential interpersonal task produces anxiety and stress in most of us. This set of articles hits many of the key issues you confront as a negotiator.

Harvard Business School Publishing. *Winning Negotiations That Maintain Relationships.* Boston: Harvard Business School Press, 2004. Packed with articles from *Harvard Management Update* and the *Harvard Management Communication Letter*, this volume in the Results-Driven Manager Series shows you how to negotiate collaboratively, not competitively; forge and sustain strategic partnerships through your negotiations; bargain in high-pressure situations; and handle cultural differences during negotiations.

Janove, Jathan. *Managing to Stay Out of Court: How to Avoid the Eight Deadly Sins of Mismanagement.* Alexandria, VA and San Francisco: Society for Human Resource Management and Berrett-Koehler, 2005. This volume contains a wide range of valuable information, including advice for using emotional intelligence to discourage the filing of lawsuits and claims. Tips include delivering hard news personally to the employees affected, rather than having someone else do it; giving angry or upset employees opportunities to express their point of view; and explaining the reasons behind a difficult decision.

Lax, David A., and James K. Sebenius. *The Manager as Negotiator.* New York: Free Press, 1986. This book brings together scholarship and experience in a useful way. It covers not only the basics that any manager, attorney, or diplomat would need to know, but also discusses negotiations in situations of special interest to managers, including negotiating in hierarchies and in networks and with internal and external entities.

Mnookin, Robert H., Lawrence E. Susskind, and Pacey C. Foster, eds. *Negotiating on Behalf of Others: Advice to Lawyers, Business Executives, Sports Agents, Diplomats, Politicians, and Everybody Else.* New York: Sage Publications, 1999. This specialized and somewhat academic book offers a framework for understanding the complexity and outcomes of negotiations by agents, including legislators, diplomats, salespersons, sports agents, attorneys, and committee chairs. A book of chapters contributed by leading scholars and practitioners, it examines five arenas in detail: labor-management relations, international diplomacy, sports agents, legislative process, and agency law.

Schmidt, Jeffrey A., ed. *Making Mergers Work: The Strategic Importance of People.* Alexandria, VA: Towers Perrin/Society for Human Resource Management, 2002. This is the first comprehensive business book to examine the role that people play in a successful merger or acquisition, and to offer solutions to many of the people-related issues that arise. The book also provides detailed results of a survey of more than 450 HR executives on the challenges that must be overcome during the M&A process.

Ucko, Thomas J. *Selecting and Working with Consultants: A Guide for Clients.* Los Altos, CA: Crisp Publications, Inc., 1990. This concise guide takes you through the process of deciding when it's time to hire a consultant, clarifying your goals for the project, finding and evaluating qualified candidates, selecting the right consultant, and negotiating fees and contracts. A wealth of checklists and worksheets helps you take a systematic approach to this common HR negotiation situation.

Watkins, Michael. *Breakthrough Negotiations.* New York: John Wiley & Sons, 2002. This excellent book presents principles that apply to business negotiations, and tools for achieving good results. Of particular interest are the author's approaches to diagnosing a situation, building coalitions, and creating strategic alliances.

Zeckhauser, Richard J., Ralph L. Keeney, and James K. Sebenius, eds. *Wise Choices: Decisions, Games, and Negotiations.* Boston: Harvard Business

School Press, 1996. Leading scholars in economics, psychology, statistics, and decision theory grapple with strategic uncertainty and the question of how to make good decisions. The papers in this collection address topics such as individual decision making under uncertainty, games of strategy in which one player's actions directly influence another's welfare, and the process of forging negotiated agreements.

Other Information Sources

Fisher, Roger, William Ury, and Bruce Patton. *Getting to Yes! Video Workshop on Negotiation*. Boston: Harvard Business School Publishing, 1991. Videocassette. This video workshop is the next best thing to having Roger Fisher as your personal negotiation trainer and coach. It brings Fisher's work to life and makes it easy to apply to your own situations. You'll see more than a dozen vignettes that vividly illustrate how to turn adversarial negotiations into mutual problem solving. The workshop gives you everything you need to help you and your managers become more powerful negotiators. Seven video segments take you step-by-step through the key elements of successful negotiation and act as a springboard for role play.

eLearning Programs

Harvard Business School Publishing. *Influencing and Motivating Others*. Boston: Harvard Business School Publishing, 2001. Online program. Have you ever noticed how some people seem to have a natural ability to stir people to action? *Influencing and Motivating Others* provides actionable lessons on getting better results from direct reports (influencing performance), greater cooperation from your peers (lateral leadership), and stronger support from your own boss and senior management (persuasion). Managers will learn the secrets of "lateral leadership" (leading peers), negotiation and persuasion skills, and how to distinguish between effective and ineffective motivation methods. Through interactive cases, expert guidance, and activities for immediate application at work, this program helps managers assess their ability to effectively persuade others, measure motivation skills, and enhance employee performance.

Harvard Business School Publishing. *Persuading Others*. Boston: Harvard Business School Publishing, 2004. Harvard ManageMentor Plus online program. This program covers many of the principles and techniques that effective negotiators use—such as building credibility, understanding the other party, and overcoming resistance to your proposals. You'll find steps to reading your negotiation counterpart quickly, tips for using statistics and body language effectively, an interactive practice scenario, and tools for assessing and improving your skills.

Harvard Business School Publishing. *Yes! The Online Negotiator.* Boston: Harvard Business School Publishing, 2000. Online program. Based on the techniques developed by world-renowned negotiation expert Roger Fisher and the Harvard Negotiation Project and detailed in the best-seller *Getting to Yes*, this program helps you build strategies for effective negotiation and conflict resolution. You'll negotiate in realistic scenarios, see the consequences of your choices play out, and receive coaching, feedback, and expert advice from Roger Fisher and other experts. *Yes! The Online Negotiator* includes three interactive scenarios: buying a house, acquiring a company, and making a sale.

Index

About the Series Adviser

WENDY BLISS, J.D., SPHR, has experience as a human resource executive, attorney, senior editor, and professional speaker. Since 1994, she has provided human resource consulting, corporate training, and coaching services nationally through her Colorado Springs–based consulting firm, Bliss & Associates.

Ms. Bliss is the author of *Legal, Effective References: How to Give and Get Them* (Society for Human Resource Management, 2001) and was a contributor to *Human Resource Essentials* (Society for Human Resource Management, 2002). She has published numerous articles in magazines and periodicals, including *HR Magazine, Employment Management Today, HR Matters*, and the *Denver University Law Review*.

Ms. Bliss has a Juris Doctor degree from the University of Denver College of Law and has been certified as a Senior Professional in Human Resources (SPHR) by the Human Resource Certification Institute. Since 1999, she has conducted human resource certificate programs for the Society for Human Resource Management. Previously, she was an adjunct faculty member at the University of Colorado at Colorado Springs and at the University of Phoenix, where she taught graduate and undergraduate courses in human resource management, employment law, organizational behavior, and business communications. Additionally, Ms. Bliss has served on the board of directors for several professional associations and nonprofit organizations and was a President of the National Board of Governors for the Society for Human Resource Management's Consultants Forum.

National media including *ABC News, Time* magazine, the *New York Times*, the *Associated Press*, the *Washington Post, USAToday.com*, and *HR Magazine* have used Ms. Bliss as an expert source on workplace issues.

About the Subject Adviser

MICHAEL WATKINS is the founder of Genesis Advisers LLC, a leadership strategy consultancy, and Professor of Practice at INSEAD in Fontainebleau, France. Professor Watkins is the author of *The First 90 Days: Critical Success Strategies for New Leaders at all Levels* (Harvard Business School Press, 2003) and *Breakthrough Business Negotiation: A Toolbox for Managers* (Jossey-Bass, 2002), winner of the CPR Institute's prize for best book in negotiation and conflict management. He is also the coauthor of *Winning the Influence Game: What Every Business Leader Should Know About Government* (Wiley, 2001), which provides tools and techniques for influencing government, and *Breakthrough International Negotiation: How Great Negotiators Transformed the World's Toughest Post-Cold War Conflicts* (Jossey-Bass, 2001), which describes the techniques of great diplomatic negotiators.

A native of Canada, he received a undergraduate degree in Electrical Engineering from the University of Waterloo, did graduate work in law and business at the University of Western Ontario, and completed his Ph.D. in Decision Sciences at Harvard University. Between 1991 and 1996 he was a professor at Harvard's Kennedy School of Government, where he taught negotiation and did research on international diplomacy and organizational change. Between 1996 and 2003 he was an Associate Professor of Business Administration at the Harvard Business School. In this role he did research on leadership and coalition building. He also was a faculty member of the Program on Negotiation at Harvard Law School.

Professor Watkins' most recent book, *Predictable Surprises: The Disasters You Should Have Seen Coming and How to Prevent Them*, co-authored with Max H. Bazerman, was published by the Harvard Business School Press in October 2004.

About the Writers

LAUREN KELLER JOHNSON has contributed to several volumes in the Business Literacy for HR Professionals series. Based in Harvard, Massachusetts, Ms. Keller Johnson writes for numerous business publications, including the *Harvard Business Review* OnPoint series, *Harvard Management Update, Balanced Scorecard Report*, and *MIT Sloan Management Review*. She has ghostwritten several books and online training modules for managers. She has a master's degree in technical and professional writing from Northeastern University.

RICHARD LUECKE is the writer of several books in the Harvard Business Essentials series. Based in Salem, Massachusetts, Mr. Luecke has authored or developed more than thirty books and dozens of articles on a wide range of business subjects. He has an M.B.A. from the University of St. Thomas.

About the Society for Human Resource Management

THE SOCIETY FOR HUMAN RESOURCE MANAGEMENT (SHRM) is the world's largest association devoted to human resource management. Representing more than 170,000 individual members, the Society's mission is to serve the needs of HR professionals by providing the most essential and comprehensive resources available. As an influential voice, the Society's mission is also to advance the human resource profession to ensure that HR is recognized as an essential partner in developing and executing organizational strategy. Visit SHRM Online at www.shrm.org.

Acknowledgments

The writers and advisers would like to thank the talented HR professionals and experts in a wide range of fields who agreed to share their expertise and offer insights and recommendations from their experiences. They are:

- Dean Black
- Mary Jo Case
- Harrison Darby
- John Gaffin
- Jim Jose
- Michael Karpeles
- Craig Pratt
- Les Rosen
- Gene Thornton

These individuals' contributions greatly strengthened the book and enabled us to provide valuable guidance to our readers.

The Results-Driven Manager

The Results-Driven Manager series collects timely articles from *Harvard Management Update* and *Harvard Management Communication Letter* to help senior to middle managers sharpen their skills, increase their effectiveness, and gain a competitive edge. Presented in a concise, accessible format to save managers valuable time, these books offer authoritative insights and techniques for improving job performance and achieving immediate results.

These books are priced at US$14.95
Price subject to change.

Title	Product #
The Results-Driven Manager **Face-to-Face Communications for Clarity and Impact**	3477
The Results-Driven Manager **Managing Yourself for the Career You Want**	3469
The Results-Driven Manager **Presentations That Persuade and Motivate**	3493
The Results-Driven Manager **Teams That Click**	3507
The Results-Driven Manager **Winning Negotiations That Preserve Relationships**	3485
The Results-Driven Manager **Dealing with Difficult People**	6344
The Results-Driven Manager **Taking Control of Your Time**	6352
The Results-Driven Manager **Getting People on Board**	6360
The Results-Driven Manager **Becoming an Effective Leader**	7804
The Results-Driven Manager **Managing Change to Reduce Resistance**	7812
The Results-Driven Manager **Motivating People for Improved Performance**	7790

How to Order

Harvard Business School Press publications are available worldwide
from your local bookseller or online retailer.
You can also call

1-800-668-6780

Our product consultants are available to help you
8:00 a.m.–6:00 p.m., Monday–Friday, Eastern Time.
Outside the U.S. and Canada, call: 617-783-7450
Please call about special discounts for quantities greater than ten.

You can order online at

www.HBSPress.org